Also by Rachel Corrie
_____

My Name Is Rachel Corrie
edited by Alan Rickman and Katharine Viner
(a play)

LET ME STAND ALONE

The Journals of Rachel Corrie

EDITED AND WITH AN INTRODUCTION

BY THE CORRIE FAMILY

Granta Books
London

Granta Publications, 12 Addison Avenue, London W11 4QR

First published in Great Britain by Granta Books, 2008
Published by arrangement with W.W.Norton & Company, Inc.

Corrie, Rachel

A CIP catalogue record for this book
is available from the British Library.

Let me stand
alone : the
journals of

1 3 5 7 9 10 8 6 4 2

818.
54

ISBN 978 1 84708 050 9

1808825

Printed and bound in Great Britain by MPG Books Ltd, Bodmin, Cornwall.

To those lost
loved
and remembered

And to Butch
who brought the sushi

Introduction from the Corrie Family

I was across the parking lot doing the laundry, and Cindy was cleaning our apartment late on a Sunday morning in March, when the phone rang. It was our son-in-law, Kelly, and he asked Cindy if he could speak to me. Detecting something ominous in Kelly's voice, she asked, "Is something wrong?"

Kelly hesitated . . . "I'm afraid we've had some very sad news." Only then could Cindy hear our daughter Sarah sobbing in the background. She and Kelly had seen scrolling at the bottom of their television screen, "Olympia woman killed in Rafah, Gaza."

Cindy appeared in the apartment's laundry room doorway, cordless phone still at her ear. There was no graceful way to break it to me. "It's Sarah and Kelly. They say that Rachel's dead." That is how the nightmare unfolded. That is how we learned our lives had been ripped apart—the same way we learn of other people's tragedies: from words scrolling at the bottom of the TV.

Rachel was killed on March 16, 2003, in Rafah in the Gaza Strip, when she was crushed to death under an armored Caterpillar D-9R bulldozer operated by members of the Israel Defense Forces.

This book is about Rachel's life. It is about Rachel as a creator. It is her journey, told in her own words and illustrated with her own drawings. It is about Rachel the writer and artist, and also the daughter, sister, granddaughter, student, coworker, and friend. It is told through her writing: the letters, e-mails, journal entries, school papers, and sometimes paper napkins saved by Rachel or collected by her mother, stashed in tubs that sat for years in our attic. This book is not our daughter's complete story. It is an attempt to show

the development of Rachel's writing and the concurrent development of her sense of self, her sense of community, and her belief that
people from a community of privilege have particular responsibility
for how they relate to and impact others.

Rachel was born on April 10, 1979, in Olympia, Washington. She
was five years younger than her sister, Sarah, seven years younger
than her brother, Chris, and a full ten years younger than the family
cat. She grew up in a small house wedged between Puget Sound and
the Black Hills of Washington State. We had two acres, mostly gone to
blackberries, but enough room for chickens, fruit trees, and—some
summers—a vegetable garden.

From earliest childhood, Rachel was immersed in words: rhymes,
stories, songs—in thought. I remember listening each night as Cindy
cradled her in arms, singing a stream of lullabies as she rocked her
to sleep. Rachel was our third child, our baby; and by the time she
entered our lives, we understood the need to cherish every moment.
Wintry days would find Rachel and her mother cuddled together
under a blanket before the fire, reading for hours. Some weekend
mornings, the whole family piled into our double bed and Cindy read
chapters from *Pinocchio, The Lord of the Rings,* or *Where the Red Fern
Grows*. In December I laid claim to Richard Scarry's *The Animals'
Merry Christmas,* my holiday favorite from childhood.

Rachel was the observer in the family, the child on the floor in the
evening—sometimes with toys, but as often with paper and crayons—
always joining in the family conversation, but also chronicling it in a
drawing or poem. Her more formal education began at Westside
Cooperative Preschool, a cottage on the beach where Cooper Point
juts north into Puget Sound. It was an idyllic place to be a child, with
swings and climbers among the rhododendrons, a short trail to the
beach, and the Olympic Mountains in the distance to the north.
Rachel loved the book room where, with clusters of young friends,
she pored over stories read by parent-helpers. She would pull on a
billowy pink dress-up outfit, don a floppy blue hat, and dramatize
the tales she had just heard or the original ones already swirling in
her head.

At fifteen, Rachel pondered this early history:

I have been writing for as long as I can remember. Fed by the books my parents read aloud to me, when I was little I would wander around my yard imagining I was a bird, or a runaway princess, or a fairy; and I would make up narratives about what I did. That pastime blossomed into dictating stories to my family and teachers until I learned to write well myself. I have always loved to draw. I have never been sure which hobby I am more passionate about. Now, as I write this, I realize that I would not love drawing if I didn't make up stories in my mind about the things I draw. Both of these passions come from my need to capture what I see without destroying it, to clarify images and make them mine, and to express to the world the love I have for the things I perceive. When I wake up just before dawn and hear the throbbing voices of birds as they echo against the silence, I am overpowered by yearning. When I ride in the dark on stark roads through dry, bald hills, I ache with desperate longing. I don't know what I am longing for, maybe for some place of my own within these images, some place where I fit, instead of being the one human being still awake, the only thing moving across the hills in the arid darkness. Maybe that ache is loneliness. I haven't found a name for the feeling yet, nor do I know exactly what awakes it in me. But instinct warns me that it is too potent for me, that my soul is on the verge of cracking when I feel it that way. I cannot handle the sheer power of those wild emotions by myself. I have to find some way to share them. That is why I write. It's instinctive. I just have to— because it is awake like lava in my blood, and sustains me.

Rachel explored the natural and political worlds of the Pacific Northwest, and these experiences are reflected in her art and writing. She and her fifth-grade classmates in the Olympia School District Options Program took a weeklong field trip around the Olympic Peninsula. In those five days, Rachel slept on a gymnasium floor in Neah Bay (home to the Makah Nation), learned about Olympic National forest clear-cuts from a Department of Natural Resources employee, walked among towering trees in the Hoh Rain Forest, and investigated her own four-by-four-inch square of earth to discover all the life within it. In college, writing of her forays into local history, she recalled Perry Creek, the stream that empties out of the hills onto the mudflats near our home, and where Rachel learned the Squiaitl Indians had lived before her. She wrote,

> *In the summer the rushes grow so tall you can hide in them and be completely invisible. This is where I came from: tunnels through rushes . . . This is where I came from and this is where I would have liked to stay: sunburned and hidden and close to water, making up whole pretend histories about shipwrecks and Swiss Family Robinson.*

Of course, Rachel would grow out of the rushes of her childhood. In middle school she wrote of her first impressions of war and death. Operation Desert Storm, which began in 1991, introduced her to a country at war and a citizenry trying to understand it. In earlier years, summer trips with family to the Midwest had been a time to explore her Iowa farming roots and to cement relationships with cousins. But now, these visits were also to care for ailing grandparents. Rachel was pushed from the nurturing cocoon of childhood, and her writing from that time reflects a struggle with the complexities and losses of adult life.

Rachel shared our home with exchange students, each of whom we welcomed with anticipation. The first was Kazuyo, who traveled from Japan to spend three weeks with us the summer Rachel was seven. Gustavo, Anyuta, and Saiko lived with us during Rachel's high school years, after both her siblings had moved away to college, creating room in the house. Rachel learned to make origami and to play Ohajiki and was introduced to Carnival, feijoada, samba, and Lula. Her international siblings opened her eyes and mind to life beyond our borders. In 1995, after Anyuta spent three months with us, Rachel returned with her to the eastern Russian city of Yuzhno-Sakhalinsk on Sakhalin Island and lived six weeks with Anyuta's family, part of an exchange coordinated by the Washington Secretary of State's Office. This was a seminal experience in Rachel's life. Russia was emerging from the dissolution of the Soviet Union. Its economy was in shambles, the ecology in near ruin, and the society in upheaval— yet there Rachel met people full of generosity eager to share their lives. The contrast between the historical U.S. view of our Cold War enemy and the reality of her experience with Russian people was jarring. She processed that trip over and over through later writing. Her view of the world and her life were never the same.

In the spring of 1997, Rachel graduated early from high school and matriculated to The Evergreen State College, a small liberal arts school in Olympia where her classes ranged from writing and art to local history, labor and environmental studies, and political science. Although she was close to home, she lived independently and chose to mostly support herself in her later college years. Many of her longer pieces in this book, even some of her most deeply personal, were originally submitted as Evergreen class writing. It was during this time that Rachel met Colin, establishing a love that did not end, even when the relationship did.

Rachel was never comfortable residing only in the student world. Her need to connect with things "real" and an ongoing search for grounding and meaning in her life prompted diversions. She spent a year in the Washington Conservation Corps, much of it at Mount Rainier and in Olympic National Park. During high school and college, Rachel spent hours each week taking calls for the Crisis Clinic's teen and adult crisis lines. This led to her work as a mental health care provider for Behavioral Health Resources (BHR), our community's oldest mental health and chemical dependency services agency.

We did not always think of Rachel as an activist, but looking back, I recall that her fifth-grade class studied world hunger and organized a press conference at the state capitol in support of UNICEF's State of the World's Children 1989 Report. In middle school, she led a lunchtime student walkout in sympathy with teachers lobbying for smaller classes and contacted the local newspaper, attempting to get coverage. As a young high school student, Rachel sat at Safeway on dark, cold, rainy evenings and collected food for the Olympia Food Bank. "Don't forget a can for the needy!" she called out as shoppers entered the store—then, as they came back out, "Did you remember a can for the needy?" One man walked past, silently ignoring Rachel's query, but then turned and acknowledged her with a smile and a dollar after she called out to his back, "Well, you're in luck, because the needy take cash too!" During her college years, Rachel advocated for the Labor Center at Evergreen when it was threatened with budget cuts and spent a night sleeping at Olympia's tent city in response to concerns for the homeless.

After the September 11, 2001, attack on the United States, Rachel began to focus on what she viewed as the ill effects of the U.S. war on terrorism: the rise of U.S. militarism, the war in Afghanistan, the impending war in Iraq, and repression at home through the U.S. Patriot Act. She worked with several local peace groups, including the Olympia Movement for Justice & Peace (OMJP), Olympians for Peace in the Middle East (OPME), Students Educating Students About the Middle East (SESAME), and the Olympia Fellowship of Reconciliation (FOR). She was drawn to Palestine and Israel by people in Olympia—by an Israeli woman whose family members survived the Holocaust, and who had become a powerful voice against the Israeli occupation of Palestinian lands; by activists who had spent years in the West Bank and continue their work on the issue; and by local International Solidarity Movement (ISM) volunteers who traveled to the West Bank and Gaza in the summer of 2002 to join Palestinians in nonviolent, direct-action resistance to the Occupation.

Rachel studied the Israeli-Palestinian conflict and began to learn Arabic. She rearranged her life to finance her own trip to Palestine. As she packed her bags, I called her on the phone. "Rachel, you know you don't have to go. No one will blame you if you don't."

"I know, and I'm really scared," she replied, "but I think I can do this, and I know I have to try." As much as I wished for her to stay in Olympia, I could not ask my daughter to be something less than she could be.

In January 2003, Rachel made her way to Israel and, then, to the West Bank for training with the International Solidarity Movement, a Palestinian-led human rights and nonviolent resistance group with international participants of all ages. ISM was formed after the U.S. and Israeli governments rejected a proposal by Mary Robinson, the United Nations High Commissioner for Human Rights, to send international human rights monitors to the region. The movement has only two requirements for participation: one must believe that the Palestinian people have a right to freedom based on international law and UN resolutions, and one must agree to use only nonviolent methods in pursuit of that freedom.

When Rachel arrived in Rafah, she entered a world of tanks, bulldozers, sniper towers, and checkpoints—a world of smashed greenhouses, crumbled homes, and a giant steel wall being constructed on the rubble near the border with Egypt. But she also entered a world of families—people resisting oppression by simply maintaining their own humanity as they struggled through the day-to-day activity of their lives under occupation. And as she entered this world, Rachel brought us with her through her phone calls and e-mail.

Rachel recognized that there was danger. When she first called us from a Palestinian home where she was staying, there was fear in her voice as she asked, "Can you hear that? Can you hear that?" Over the phone we could hear the shelling outside this home, thousands of miles away. While in Rafah, Rachel and other activists stood between Palestinian municipal water workers trying to repair wells and Israeli military towers from which shots rang out harassing the workers and the internationals. They spent nights sleeping at wells to protect them from demolition. Rachel documented the destruction of Palestinian olive orchards, gardens, and greenhouses and the harassment of Palestinians at checkpoints. She worked with youths at the Children's Parliament who democratically debated issues impacting their lives. She learned Arabic from Palestinian children and helped them with their English homework. She participated in demonstrations in Rafah opposing the Iraq war—part of the worldwide protests on February 15, 2003, that were the largest in history. Always, she planned for a long-term commitment to the people of Rafah and connections between this Palestinian city and her hometown of Olympia—through women's and children's groups, fair trade, and an Olympia-Rafah sister-city project. Finally, Rachel lived with Palestinian families whose homes were threatened with demolition and stood with other internationals to oppose this destruction—illegal under international law and carried out against thousands in Rafah because their homes were near the border with Egypt where the IDF was expanding a buffer zone along the Philadelphi Corridor.

On March 16, 2003, there were two Israeli bulldozers and an

armored personnel carrier operating in the area of Hi Salaam in Rafah along the Egyptian border. Each bulldozer had two occupants: an operator and, sitting next to him, a vehicle commander. The on-site commander of the operation watched from the armored personnel carrier nearby. Late in the afternoon, one of the bulldozers headed toward the home of the Nasrallah brothers (a pharmacist and an accountant), their wives, and five young children. The older brother's family lived on the first floor, the younger brother's family on the second. Rachel knew the Nasrallahs, had often spent time with them, and sometimes had slept in their home. She wrote,

> *The two front rooms of their house are unusable because gunshots have been fired through the walls, so the whole family—three kids and two parents—sleep in the parents' bedroom. I sleep on the floor next to the youngest daughter, Iman, and we all share blankets.*

Rachel knew the Nasrallah family was inside their home as the bulldozer approached it. At approximately 5 p.m., she positioned herself between the home and the D-9. From eyewitness accounts, we know that her actions were the same as those taken by other ISM activists in the preceding hours. Bulldozers had often come so close that the dirt they were pushing touched the activists' feet. On one occasion, a U.S. activist was rolled over into barbed wire; on another, a British activist was pinned against a wall. In both instances, the bulldozer stopped in time. But on this run, with Rachel in its path, the bulldozer did not stop. The ISM activists screamed and waved frantically, but the machine continued ahead. Witnesses state that as the D-9 pushed earth forward, Rachel managed to climb up the mound to avoid being engulfed by it. They report that she was up high enough to see directly into the cab; but as it continued to advance, she lost her footing and was pulled under the blade. The bulldozer continued forward until its cab was over Rachel, then backed up, revealing her crushed body. Rachel was alive when her friends rushed to her. She told them, "I think my back is broken." But the Palestinian ambulance driver later told us there was no sign of life when he arrived. She was pronounced dead a short while later in the local hospital.

On March 17, 2003, according to U.S. Department of State press briefings, Israeli Prime Minister Ariel Sharon promised President Bush a "thorough, credible, and transparent" investigation into Rachel's killing. Months later, the Israeli military stated in conclusions to their investigative report that the Israel Defense Forces (IDF) did not see her, that no charges would be brought, and that the case was closed. The official position of the U.S. Department of State is that the Israeli report does not reflect an investigation that was "thorough, credible, and transparent." This was declared without equivocation in the department's letter to our family and in testimony before a subcommittee of the U.S. House International Relations Committee.

In her work, Rachel joined Palestinians, Israelis, and internationals from many countries—Jews, Muslims, Christians, and others—who seek to end the Israeli Occupation by nonviolent means. She consulted with both Palestinian municipal water employees and Israeli peace activists to better understand the destruction of the Palestinian water supply. Danny, a reservist in the Israeli military, taught her Hebrew phrases to shout through her megaphone when she encountered bulldozer and tank operators, while Palestinians helped her to safely negotiate the streets of Rafah. When she caught a flu bug, Rachel was cared for by Muslim mothers; and as she died, she was held by Alice, a Jewish ISM activist from the UK.

On March 16, 2003, Rachel stood with seven other internationals from the United States and the United Kingdom nonviolently resisting the demolition of Palestinian homes—mass clearing demolitions that the Israeli human rights organization B'tselem said were in most cases a flagrant breach of international humanitarian law and that Human Rights Watch reported were generally carried out in the absence of military necessity. Rachel and other ISM activists stood in their belief that both Palestinian and Israeli families have the right to be secure in their homes, in their restaurants, and on their buses—and with the conviction that an end to an oppressive, decades-old Israeli Occupation is the best way to achieve that. They stood in their belief that the nonviolent direct action they were supporting, if effective, could make Palestinians, as well as Israelis, Americans, and the entire world, more secure.

This book is a milestone for Rachel and for our family. It started, in a sense, with Rachel's e-mail correspondence from Rafah to her mother. She hoped her writing from there would be published, at least in her local newspaper, maybe as a human interest story. She did not live to see her e-mails from Gaza picked up by *The Olympian* or any other newspaper. Knowing how important it was to Rachel that people in the United States be aware of what she was witnessing, and having felt the impact of her writing on our own family's understanding of the situation in Israel-Palestine, we made her e-mail letters from Gaza available within hours after her death. Three days later, *The Guardian*, a British newspaper of international reputation, ran them nearly in their entirety in a section they titled "Rachel's War." Alan Rickman, the stage and screen actor, read the article and took it to friends at London's Royal Court Theatre, who eventually contacted our family. There began the several-year collaboration resulting in the play *My Name is Rachel Corrie* and its performance in London, New York, and eventually other cities in the United States and the world. Alan Rickman and Katharine Viner, coeditors of the play, were the first to suggest that Rachel's writing should become a book. When that possibility became a reality, we began the search for more of her work. The material from which this book was created was nearly twice that given to the Royal Court. Aside from the letter from Danny that she passes along in her e-mail from Rafah, the writing and artwork included are all Rachel's. With few exceptions, the writing is presented chronologically. The date ascribed to each piece is sometimes approximate and was determined by the content, the relation to the material found around it, and what we knew to be happening in Rachel's life at the time. Rachel's sketches are important to this book, but they, too, posed challenges. In one case, we took an unidentified drawing of someone who seemed to resemble my maternal relatives and circulated it among our extended family to see if Rachel had drawn from a photograph in one of their homes. No one recognized the picture or even the subject. Perhaps, in this case, Rachel was just sharpening her eye by sketching a picture from a magazine. To solve all these little mysteries, the one thing we could not do was ask the author.

The pieces included in this book were chosen for their literary merit, as well as for how they enhance the narrative. There is no way of knowing which selections Rachel would have considered finished, which she would have reworked, which she would have wanted published, and which she would now judge unfit to share. Acting as her editors, we anguished over each minor change in punctuation, formatting, or preposition. We have made minimal edits and done so with great care—trying to determine what Rachel might have done had she been preparing the material for publication and always, always remaining true to her words.

Much of the book is an internal conversation from Rachel's journals. Reading these entries, it is clear that there were some ideas and subject matter that she mulled for long periods of time. These may appear first in a list or initial observation and later resurface in a story, essay, or perhaps in a poem or drawing. This aspect of Rachel's creative process is reflected throughout the book. There is no attempt in this text to record what was not written—the asides to friends and family, the jokes, the secrets shared late at night. These have been left to the private memories of Rachel's confidants.

Two of Rachel's early utterances have become enshrined in family lore. At a playground in Olympia when she was just over two, Rachel wandered with her grandmother away from the wooden climbers toward Capitol Lake. As she walked, she opened her arms and announced, "This is the wide world, and I'm coming to it!" Rachel's grandmother found this pronouncement extraordinary. I didn't have the heart to tell her that Rachel was making a literary allusion to the children's book *Grover and the Everything in the Whole Wide World Museum*. A few months later, Rachel asked her mother, "Is *brave* part of growing up?" We don't remember the context of the question; but in hindsight, it serves as a sort of measuring stick—a metaphorical stand-in for the marks we would make on the door at our extended family's Minnesota lake cabin every year to record each child's growth. When I read Rachel's writing now, I am struck by her determination to hang on to the wonderment of her early childhood as she reached for the "brave" of becoming an adult.

Rachel wrote, "Writing is brave. It is maybe the only brave thing about me." Rachel was brave enough to write from the soul, powerfully and personally articulating the human condition. She understood that moral beliefs require more from us than dinner-table banter. Her words as a ten-year-old, "They are us. We are them," resonated even more for me when I read her journals. In offering Rachel's writing to the public, our family helps her complete the journey to become a published author. But we also put her very human soul on display. In so doing, we share her trepidation, and we envy her courage. In offering Rachel's writing, our family hopes that you will find reflected in it a bit of your own insight, ethic, and humor—a bit of your own soul.

The world knows of Rachel from how she died, but we know her from how she lived. She was, first and last, a writer and artist. Compelled to create, she was left only with the choice to become good at it. Rachel worked hard at her craft from an early age. When she was ten, a friend of mine asked her what she wanted to be when she grew up. "I *am* a poet!" she declared. Words were sacred to Rachel, and her words have become treasures to us. They are what we have left and are an immense gift to our family. With this book, we offer that gift to you.

Craig Corrie
for the Corrie family

LET ME STAND ALONE

1995–1997

If the words I use buzz away from my lips meaninglessly, then we'll let them hang in the air for a while. We'll let those silly words sit and make fools of themselves until other words come and crowd around them.

I need to flutter and hover and look at the diamond ripples through six swirled insect eyes. Just don't touch me for a moment. Let me sit and stare at everything through my own eyes for a while. Let me dance in the lily petals and skim the trembling water and buzz like useless words in the air.

Do you understand? Let me lie alone on my back in tall grass and see the sun and the water droplets on the branches and the red tree trunks through my own eyes. Let me color them and build them with my own words. Lonely, strong words. Let me stand alone at the edge of the earth and look at it honestly, alone.

1989–1990

I must walk with care
as I wander in the wood
that I may crush no flower below my shoes.

1989–1990

leaves

lie down on your back
gaze up to the sky
ignore prickly grass
the ant passing by
look up to the branches
with sun glinting through
see the sparkle of leaves
they are whispering to you

1989–1990

There are few things which have
the pride and the shyness of a soft, wet trillium.

4

Summer 1998

The question is always where to start the story. That's the first question. This is why writers are destined to be crazy people. This is why Sylvia Plath offed herself quietly beneath her suction cup Bell Jar and why Hemingway wrote every morning until 11:00 and took his first drink at 11:05. Trying to find a beginning is the first pitiful backward step at trying to impose order on the great psychotic fast-forward merry-go-round, and trying to impose order is the first step toward ending up in a park somewhere, painted blue, singing "Row, row, row your boat" to an audience of saggy-lipped junkies and businesspeople munching oat bran muffins.

And that's how this story ends, good buddy, so if you are concerned with the logic and sequence of things and the crescendo of suspense up to a good shocker of an ending, you best be getting back to your video game and your amassing wealth. Leave the meaningless details to the poets and the photographers.

And they're all meaningless details, my friend.

April 14, 1991

My name is Rachel Corrie. I was born on April 10th, 1979, in Olympia, Washington, to my mother and father, Craig and Cindy Corrie, a brother, Chris, who was about seven, a sister, Sarah, who was two years younger, and a really old cat named Phoebe.

I went to preschool. It was a little house down the hill from a swing set and up the hill from the beach, with multicolored bells on the windowsill, eagles, a green carpet in the library, and what seemed like millions of windows with leafy light falling through them.

I grew. I learned to spell cat, to read little books. I continued to draw and I started to watercolor. When I was five I discovered boys, which made my life a little more difficult. Just a little. And a lot more interesting. In first grade I started my five years in the Options Program. Options was a place to truly learn, to learn how to feel, how to be, and how to be the kind of person I want to be.

I remember waiting for the carpool. I would wait for whoever was driving that day on the bridge down the hill from my house with my mom. She would read to me from different books or just stand and talk to me while I gazed through the concrete posts of the bridge at the mouth of the creek. My dad also read to me. We read things like *The Mowgli Stories*, *The Chronicles of Narnia*, and around Christmastime I would crawl into his lap to listen to him reading stories from a big red Christmas book.

I graduated from Options last summer, and there followed an episode of "This huge part of my life just fell away. What do I do now?" and "I have to leave all my friends, and go to a new school, with new people, with new values" (followed by a low but pitiful moan).

So now I'm in middle school. My brother will come home from his first year of college in a month. I'll get my driver's license in what, four years? I've entered an episode of "Why should I do anything if Annie and Shanna can do it better?" And all's well, though extremely bizarre. I guess I've grown up a little. It's all relative anyway. Nine years is as long as forty years, depending on how long you've lived. I stole that from my dad about three years ago. You understand, none of this is really true. That's why there were so many revisions from the rough draft to here, because what I wrote today is true, but you'll read it by tomorrow, or the next day, and my whole life will be different. It won't consist of reading books with my parents. In fact, it doesn't consist of that anymore. It may consist of snuggling with cats late at night or ballet recitals. Is that how life is, a new draft for every day, a new view for each hour? Look, now I've gone and made my life consist of something else!

Found scrawled in blue ink in Rachel's handwriting on the side of the page: I can write so much more now. My dad seems like the wisest person in the world sometimes.

1989–1990

For Gram with Love

Over the fence
by an old rusty rail
came the whispery
twitch of a cream-colored tail.

Over the fence
by a big haystack
came the pat of a paw
soft and black.

Over the fence
in the tallest grass
came the twitch of a whisker
shiny as glass.

1989–1990

Ode to the Drip of a Faucet

Of the
translucent
sphere, a gem.
Let loose, after a gather of slowing power.
A drop of silver dew
or a tiny tear on a child's cheek.
Maybe, rain on a window.
Is it a witch's crystal ball?
All the possibilities of a tiny bit of water,
plummeting to the drain.

1989

I'm here for other children.
I'm here because I care.
I'm here because children everywhere are suffering
and because forty thousand people die each day from hunger.
I'm here because those people are mostly children.
We have got to understand that the poor are all around us
and we are ignoring them.
We have got to understand that these deaths are preventable.
We have got to understand that people in third world countries
think and care and smile and cry just like us.
We have got to understand that they dream our dreams
and we dream theirs.
We have got to understand that they are us. We are them.
My dream is to stop hunger by the year 2000.
My dream is to give the poor a chance.
My dream is to save the forty thousand people who die each day.
My dream can and will come true if we all look into the future
and see the light that shines there.
If we ignore hunger, that light will go out.
If we all help and work together,
it will grow and burn free with the potential of tomorrow.

―――――――――――――――――

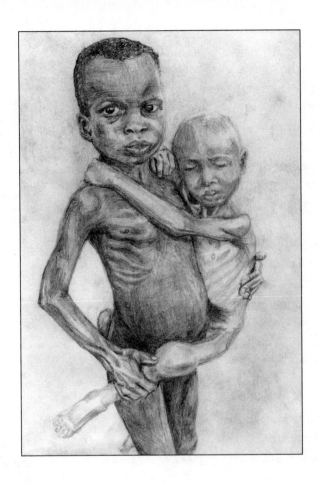

1990

I want to be a lawyer, a dancer, an actress, a mother, a wife, a children's author, a distance runner, a poet, a pianist, a pet store owner, an astronaut, an environmental and humanitarian activist, a psychiatrist, a ballet teacher, and the first woman president.

1989–1990

Little toy boat with a broken sail
Tossed by the swelling stream,
You are drifting slowly out of view
Like a silently waking dream.

I watched carelessly as you left the sand
Into the current,
Out of reach of my hand.

Behind your chipped paint
There's a man on your deck
Is he a ghost from a past shipwreck?

Did I tell you
The pleasure you gave me,
In the pond
Beneath the cottonwood tree?

Did I tell you,
Do you know?
That I didn't mean to let you go.

1990–1993

I hiked my bag up to my hip as I ducked
out of the crowd of kids around the exit
to the school. A little glob of loneliness was forming in my throat as I
watched friends moving toward the
buses. They went slowly, as if they
were hypnotized by some force I was
not a part of. I wished for a moment
that one of them would turn around

and just look at me, just take a little interest in their shadow. Which is exactly what I was. I decided it was hopeless. I wasn't meant to be noticed. I was meant to fight my own battles. Alone.

I turned and started home. Dry leaves sloshed around under my feet in the ditch at the beginning of the trail.

1990–1991

Maybe my world swirls around me
but one thing is stationary.
Friendship is a pillar of clarity
in my bizarre land.

1989–1991

Oh but the fall was filled with cobwebs,
Rotting images, and leaf skeletons.
Peppered with tree bark
And inconspicuous mushrooms . . .
But I noticed everything.
The lazy football games, the boys in the
    park,
The mysterious hazes, and a certain
    person across the room.
That year was drowning in purple-gray
    hills,
The kind that roll out from blue mountains.

1990–1993

A pinpoint of light
shining from the darkness.
Only I notice it.
What mystery does it hold?
Who loves that light?
What is this one sun, the one I see?
What secret is it keeping?

October 20, 1990

I slept so lightly
in the silence of an iced morning
that I was awakened by the frost.

1990–1991

I think weather was invented just to drive people crazy. The clouds are coming closer, reaching out until they get us—each a soldier for whatever sinister force is behind. They have got me bogged down.

1990–1991

Maybe if people stopped thinking of themselves and started thinking of the other sides of things, people wouldn't hurt each other. I wouldn't worry about people hurting each other, because each person would work till they discovered the right thing to do. People wouldn't cheat or lie. But would they just get depressed knowing so many feelings and troubles, caring about every little thing?

I guess people are happier not caring. Well, if people are happy ignoring everyone else, I can't stop them. I know I am not like that. I feel terrible when I lie in bed and hear people fighting, or when someone cries. I hate seeing war on TV. Gee, maybe I should try not caring sometime. Then I'd be unstoppable, untouchable. What a blast! Or would it be?

1990–1993

In second grade there were classroom rules hanging from the ceiling. The only one I can remember now seems like it would be a good rule for life. "Everyone must feel safe." Safe to be themselves, physically safe, safe to say what they think, just safe. That's the best rule I can think of.

April 12, 1993

There is a storm rising black over the hills. The charred bodies of soldiers buried there rise and march against the receding sunlight. The red glow on the horizon, like blood of young men. Proud men, unflickering eyes. Reflections of the fire that lights the darkness over the other horizon. Knees high, heads high. Empty air between the hands where stolen guns should be. Echoes of gunshots. They trample the bright white crosses, the flags of death. They hoist their own flags high into the sky, to flame and billow up against the dark storm clouds.

1991

Dear Soldier,

I guess I don't really understand the world, because I don't see why you aren't here. Why people can't make compromises. Why peace is still a vision, and war is our near reality. I must be ignorant, because I believe that it's unnecessary for forty thousand children to die every day. I know I am just a little sixth grader who writes poetry and worries about grades and makeup, but I worry about bigger things. I worry about the whales dying, about the ozone layer depleting, about the trees being cut down. I guess everyone worries about those things somewhat.

The ice has been creeping into the puddles with cold jutting hands. As I walk on the grass in my yard each morning, it crunches from the stiffness of the frost. The sky is a canvas stretched gray from one edge of the horizon to the hills. It is spattered with circling white seagulls glaring down with yellow eyes onto the earth. There is such beauty in the way the gulls turn their wings and soar in turning tranquillity.

There are a thousand things that echo through my mind when I think of this planet. Peace and cooperation are at the front of my mind.

1989–1990

Wind

His invisible eyes are two clouds,
Gray and filled by rain.
His deft fingers are waves, crashing at sea.
His swift legs are trees tumbling.
His nose is a brown leaf,
Twirling downward.
His light hair is a wheat field after a frost.
His lips are icebergs, hard and wet.
His chin is a sharp boulder,
Hanging dangerously over a cliff.
His hands are those of one who has been out in the cold.
Icy, painful to touch.
Poor man, he is not human or plant.
Just an intangible force.
Loneliness.

These are the hollow souls,
Crusts of helpless figures,
The crumbs that we toss to the gulls.
Skins and round watery eyes.
Horribly open, lucid and knowing.
How can the eyes of the ignorant
be so wise?

These are the forgotten ones.
They are lost in the invisible world of lists.
Here are our ugly siblings,
The ones who stand behind us and smile hungrily.
These are the ones we don't even glance at.
We fix our eyes just over their shoulders.

Bring on their hungry smiles.
We battle them with loose change,
Trying to send them back out of our minds.
We love them when they are far away and we are snug and warm.
But when they are close to us,
And we can smell their rotting breath
And look deep through sunken eyes into the eddying minds,
We choke with fear and distaste and pull away from the outside.

Here are the homeless and also the nameless.
Here are the people whom we politely ignore.
We are brutally well behaved.
Even when they speak to us, call to us, beseech us,
We do not answer or call back.

These are our sisters and brothers.
And that is what terrifies us.
They are us. And we could as easily be them.

1989–1991

On the first day of spring
The earth wakes from winter's slumber
The buds open like waking eyes
And when you look up
The heavens are in full bloom
With wisps of gentle clouds
Don't watch the world through a windowpane
The dust and glass mute the sunlight
Taste the dew on the thin blades of grass
Answer the song of birds
Wait all day for the haze of sunset
And sleep outside
For tomorrow it is summer

1989–1991

Song of a Masked Dancer

I am a flame red tulip tinged in yellow-orange
I am the stone that people sat on yesterday
I am the orca wearing black and white
I am the snow falling down over black sky
I am a misty reflection dancing on the sparkly water
I am the sand that feels bare brown feet
I am the ashes in the garden
I am lamplight late at night by a typewriter
I am a river running over me turning me carrying me
I am an autumn leaf gliding down at sunset
I am Lightning and Thunder, Fire and Rain
I am the morning dew on a wheat field
I am a dove journeying with the sooty wind
I am colored like the wind

I sound like daydreams
I taste like moonlight
I am everything and everything is me.

1990–1991

The darkness is infinite
As I leave the curtain's edge
It is filled with watchers
Silent judges

1990–1991

I will die with the night.
I shall go in the morning
in a white room
filled with pottery
and glass containers holding water.
I will lie on a futon
on top of a stone table.
All around me will be ferns
and flowers
and above my head will be a little tree.
I will be in a bay window
looking out on the ocean
and everywhere will be shafts of light.

1990–1991

When I was younger, I would ride the train to Iowa. With my family
and then with my mom. I remember eating Pringles potato chips.
We'd always pack a cooler with pop and crackers and Easy Cheese.

We'd go to the snack bar and the diner. And we'd look for prairie dogs and antelope. My sister Sarah must have been a little younger than I am now when she made up the nicknames "Worcester-sister-sauce" for me, and "Sister-wister-burger." We still use those once in a while. Sometimes we drove, stopping nights in Holiday Inns.

It all changed. Now it's usually three members of the family driving straight to Iowa or Minnesota. No rest stop except for food and potty-breaks.

There are the three heavens: the farm with Gramma and Grampa and the little town of Denison where you can still walk wherever you go; the lake in Aitkin, Minnesota, with the loons, and the Aitkin Bakery, and the used bookstore; and my gram and grandaddy's house in Des Moines.

1989–1991

Sleeping in the balmy atmosphere of early summer
The sun melts out across the sky
With the gentle ease of an earthworm
Waking suddenly, the sky is closing its gaping mouth
I am half sensitive
To what is around me
I don't know where I have come from
A world of half awareness and imagination.

1990–1993

Dear Mom,

Some might think in this day and age a girl's role model should be a career woman, someone working in an office or in a so-called "men's" line of work. I know those people are wrong. For me, you are the perfect role model. I admire how you take things you want to do, like playing your flute and writing music, and find ways to fit them into your life. I admire your ability to clearly say what you think and feel. If every woman were that assertive, there would be more respect for the women of this world. I admire your kindness. You are the only person I know whom I've never seen hurt another to get something you want. I believe *you* can get whatever you want without hurting anyone. What I admire most is not what you have done for yourself, but what you have done for me. I hope when I grow up, I can pass on to my children what I have learned from you about how to treat people. You have given me a wonderful life and shown me how to get that sort of life for myself.

People might think my mom not a hero because she hasn't done any- thing "exceptional." Well, you don't have to *do* anything exceptional. I know that you *are* exceptional. You have made me proud of you by working hard at everything you do and doing it well.

I love you, Mom.

Sincerely,

Rachel

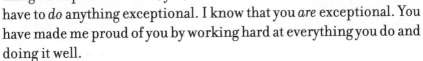

January 5, 1994

When my grandma was dying, my mom spent most of the years of her illness at her bedside. In the beginning, you couldn't tell that there was anything eating my grandma. I could act the same way I always did and pretend that there was no illness. But then she started losing weight and growing paler and quieter and more sad. She kept up the same game I did, pretending that there was no leukemia. About a week before she died, my sister and I came to Minnesota to see her at the hospital. My cousins were there, and two of my aunts. My uncle and two other aunts came up on weekends.

All of them knew how to act around my grandma. I did not know how to be sad for her, or support her, or love her when she was sick. The sight of her in that sterile hospital bed made me sick. The thought of an entity in her body, ravaging her, eluded my grasp.

The only person who seemed as helpless as me was my grandpa. He was never around, until she died.

My mom came back to our hotel in the night. I was completely helpless. I don't remember if I cried, but I do remember waking up in the early morning.

I heard my grandpa in the room and my mom and uncle. I kept my eyes closed for a long time, just lying there because I didn't know what to do when I woke up. That is probably as out of place and different as I have ever felt in my life.

Summer 1991

We pass her along like she is a rag doll. I feel her need to relax in my arms. I sense her longing to have company in the mourning. "I'm sorry, Mama," I murmur.

"I know," she says. "I know." She is sobbing now and both of our bodies tremble with the shivering in her shoulders.

"I love you, Mama," I say, reverting back to a child's voice in a blind attempt to comfort her. I am crying for her and how it must feel to lose your mother. I am crying because I cannot imagine losing someone I love as much as I love her. And my mom probably loves my grandma even more than that because my capacity to love is dwarfed and finicky.

My mother begins to tell Sarah about what she will need to do. I stop listening after I hear that we will leave in the morning and go back to my grandma's house.

I let go of my mom and sit down on the bed. It sings to me, calls me back to sleep. I am so selfish, how can I desert my mother and my sister by sleeping? I have already grown bored of being sad and I am ready to go back to being normal. I can't stand changes. Every time something ends it seems like I leave better things behind.

May 19, 1993

Death smells like homemade applesauce as it cooks on the stove. It is not the strangling scent of illness. It is not fear. It is freedom. Death is warmth as it melts into refreshing coldness. Death has friendly hands that gently guide you. They are calm and they do not push. Death is a long walk through a mountain meadow and somehow your steps seem to carry you down through the mountains and into the gentle swells of ocean. As carelessly as before, you walk down into the depths of the water. The fins of fish stroke your face.

Spring 1992

The darkness is warm in your house,
    warm and full of you and Gramma.
Thunder is filled with the gruff crackle of your voice,
    the wallpaper, peeling.
Mama told me about the people you talked with on the wall.
    one day, maybe you'll be on my wall.
The darkness, warm, and I
    wait for dreams in your big recliner.
Your breathing haunts me like a flower
    in the background of a painting,
    petals blurred together and into the canvas.
Somewhere you are riding your tractor through a bean field.
    there's no mud to hold you back.
Maybe it's because I can't hear your heavy coughs

that I wander into dreams so quickly.
   or maybe they're still here, but not as loud.
There is no absence,
   only warm darkness.
I know if I walked into your room right now,
   you'd be up on the wall between the little flowers
   talking to the people there.
There is no absence for you, either.
   the darkness is still warm.

1992–1993

There was an earthquake in the bathtub today. Rumors reached me that Mount Rainier might have erupted. I trembled in sudden coolness. Something that vast and indestructible rending giant boiling tears in its own flesh! But more than that, a dead friend. I would have mourned for that mountain.

August 1992

My face is lovely in the reflection in the windows. Smooth white moonlight stretches over the cheekbones in jagged lines and my eyes look almost black, except for the cold light of the passing stars. I angle my face up to the glass and the sky and watch my lips form the lyrics of songs on the radio.

The air that breeches the wide flat fields of Montana is cool and empty, so there is a voice for each glowing set of numbers as I flick the dial on the radio. The DJs are confiding this late at night that they know they share loneliness with everyone awake in the darkness. Even so, they aren't out here, cutting the breeze. Watching the stars move by.

Chris is driving. He is awake and alert but completely separate from me. We haven't talked since he bought me a Coke on the Idaho border. I'm alone with the classic rock songs that churn softly out of the speakers. I skip from harmony to melody, let the notes ricochet off the windowpane.

The singer is awake in me now, the softly voluptuous moon-voice I yearn for in the daytime. I sing loud because no one hears me, yet my voice goes forever above the short gray grass on the fields. My singer only wakes up when I'm alone. She is timid, like a hermit crab emerging, vulnerable, from its borrowed shell.

When I first started singing, she came readily and shamelessly. She was loud and loose and proud. But she was good enough to get the attention of my teacher, and he told me to get a voice teacher. From then on, I learned everything that was wrong with my voice. I memorized how to breathe, how to stand, how wide to open my eyes, and how to shape my mouth. And then, after helping me find all the faults in my voice, my teachers wondered why I acted wooden, and where my confidence had gone. I wish I had remained wild and terrible and free, because then I was unafraid.

1992–1993

I am a good, strong word giver
I am a jealous guard of my own secrets
Freedom is the rule
I am hungry for one good thing I can do

October 1992

What I'm Afraid of

bad grades
growing up and being mediocre
heights
being alone
things outside
my cat dying
falling, tumbling, rolling down, being out of control
pain
getting varicose veins
cellulite
wrinkles
other people being disappointed in me
sharks—pain—things biting
I'm afraid of being mauled by something
being permanently in one routine or one spot
I'm afraid that I'll hit my kid someday, or hurt someone I love
I'm afraid of being poor
I'm afraid of the priest at my grandma's church
I'm afraid of drowning, falling, pain
I'm afraid of my parents dying
I'm afraid of failure, embarrassment, disappointment, hope
I'm afraid of blind, ludicrous, idealistic hope
and I'm afraid of people knowing how bad I am.

October 28, 1992

What Makes Me Mad

people who don't listen
people who get too mad
mothers and fathers who yell too much
when people shove on purpose in basketball
the Anita Hill—Clarence Thomas case

the LAPD verdict
war
George Bush
most Republican politicians
chauvinists
death—death makes me very, very angry
hatred
the Ku Klux Klan
racism
people who are overly spoiled
people who don't care about the environment
people who don't take me seriously
people who don't ever think things through
people who are older than me but less mature
death

1992–1993

tom is the bus driver and every day he says the same thing
which is "so the gypsies didn't carry you off"
and then the bus door hisses like a nest of snakes.

the retarded kids sit at the front of the bus
and the kids with lighters sit at the back of the bus
and i sit in the middle of the bus with kelly
who trades me her fruit roll for my twinkie.

we go by the high school where shawna goes
where they only eat gum
but i eat cream cheese and cucumber because
i am still in my formative years.

miss hooper leads the pledge of allegiance and we
put our hands over our hearts all
except for billy who has no hands
but only flippers.

miss hooper passes out the little green books
about development and accepting
our emotions
she points to the faces
look at the man
the man is smiling
"the man is happy," says luke
happy is okay
"the girl is crying she is sad," says carrie
sad is okay
what about this man
his eyes are droopy
what about this man, TJ?
"the man is tanked," says TJ.

look at miss hooper
her face turns into a bulldog
miss hooper is frowning
miss hooper is perturbed.

then we draw faces
all kinds of faces
faces of feelings
except for billy who has no hands
but only flippers.

December 15, 1992

I want to be an artist or a
dancer. I would like to change the
world. I don't want to do drugs. I
may drink underage but I don't plan
to. I believe in finding who you are but
drugs sometimes become a definition
of people. There are people behind those
definitions. I won't drink to enhance myself

or to make myself more enjoyable to others because drinking doesn't enhance you. At this point I am still finding myself and developing myself and now would not be a good time to take drugs because I don't want to find a drug where a part of my mind or heart is supposed to be.

March 9, 1993

When I am an old woman, I will stop trying to look beautiful. I will quit wearing makeup and buying uncomfortable clothes because they look good. Maybe I will take up nudism. I will dance and play basketball and replenish my stock of Crayolas. I will write stories and they will be good, because by that time I will have real stories to tell, and I won't be just a sack of words.

When I am an old woman I will leave my clothes on the floor (if I wear any) and make someone else do the laundry. I will put plants everywhere and plant flowers in my yard. I will take up karate and learn how to flamenco-dance.

I will never, ever, ever cook. I will race my grandchildren and beat them and I will actually run when we play baseball.

I will get a cow and put it in my backyard and I will get a motorcycle and some leather pants.

1991–1993

She is loud. And confusing. She talks and tells stories but never about herself. Her true soul sunk deep inside her long ago, and she misses it. She is trying to bring herself back, but she has so many people inside of her she doesn't know who she is. And sometimes she wonders if she isn't just what is on the surface, and she doesn't want to admit it. She is afraid of pain, so afraid of pain that she won't risk it, won't hurt herself, yet she cries anyway. She cries every day and she is alone in the crowds. She aches to come out and stop being a plastic person. She cries at the moments when she should feel joy—

when the first daffodils peek up beneath the trees and when the sun begins to bleed like yellow paint into the sky. She feels trapped inside a small glass container and, lost, she stumbles through life. She tries to tell people but they don't understand her, and the last time she told someone that person forgot her in a few days and left her alone. She looks down on the world through a dusty windowpane, and reaches out to it but is thrust back inside herself.

1993–1994

The Dance

I pull off the damp sweater and turtleneck I wore to the game and put them on the floor of the car. My deodorant crumbles into white chunks when I take the cap off it. I pick up as much of it as I can but

there is still a fragrant layer of crumbs across my discarded clothing. I pick up the T-shirt I'm going to wear to the dance. It smells faintly of cigarettes from the last time I wore it. I neglected to wash it. This won't matter because I feel pretty when I wear it. This is the shirt that makes everyone gasp at how thin I am. Even though it isn't a compliment, people say it with hollow awe and then walk away. I can remember every exclamation I've heard while wearing this shirt. I know I have them all fooled because I'm not really so skinny. It's the shirt. It's an illusion.

I walk up the watery sidewalk alone. Outside the door someone breathes a mixture of wintergreen gum and hard liquor into my face. He fumbles with a package of cinnamon gum and stuffs two more sticks into his mouth.

"I'll get in," he brags. "Watch this. I'll hold my breath through the door."

It's too bad the stench of alcohol rises off every fold of his clothing. I don't stick around to see him kicked out. Once I feel the pulse of the music, I have forgotten him completely. To me, the power of music is stronger than gravity. The wild music of the dance entices me: *Come, come lose yourself. Forget how to speak except with your body. Dance.*

Sometimes, in the early morning when I listen to the halting euphony of the birds, I think that if just one more throbbing voice wailed out into the chilly morning air, I would rise to meet it, dancing and shivering into the sky. Dancing has always been my metaphor for life; when I do poorly on a test, it is for the same reasons I stumble after a pirouette. When something is beautiful, it is like the curve of a dancer's long neck or the airiness of her movements. When I am happy, I am dancing well. The first time I heard the phrase "ballet body" was the day the first bite of my young, fearless self was gobbled up by a greedy monster living somewhere inside me. I often wonder how something that defines me can be so devastating.

So I am drawn into the flashing lights of the cafeteria. I catch my reflection in the door and notice how pear-like my body is. Blinded by the strobe lights, I somehow find my way to some friends. I can't tell if they are glad to see me or not, and I feel empty. I wish I was inside the group they are dancing in, instead of on the fringes, so pointedly an outsider. Gradually, I move away.

The good thing about dances is the darkness. They aren't a showcase for fashion like the halls, and I can forget this body I loathe. I love not being able to see people's eyes, not needing to worry about the meaning of a glance. But you can lose track of who you are in between the darkness and the blinding strobes. As I move from one group to another in the crowded room, I feel my soul somewhere to the right or left of me, dancing in a group I haven't come to yet. This is not the only time I feel its absence; I feel it every day.

A slow song comes on and I get out of the way of the couples. I do it slowly, thinking I might cross paths with someone who would like to dance with me, but soon I bury this idea. Looking around, I can read the faces of other girls as we stand watching. We are silently wishing we were thinner, more popular, prettier. Some girls are watching the guy they wish they were dancing with as he holds someone else. I observe them all, and the ache dulls. Indifferent, I'm a little contemptuous of the other watchers.

When the fast music comes on again, I realize it isn't any better. It bounces against me instead of flowing through me. The language of my body when I dance to this music is angry and unintelligible. I'm ready to go home.

As I walk out the door, my reflection flutters up again on its glass surface. Now it wavers. What I mistook for a pear an hour before is only a faltering wraith. The gleaming eyes and jutting cheekbones are all that is left. I want to observe this shadowy parody of me longer; it fascinates me. Drenched in darkness, my face has taken on an enigmatic quality. It is almost beautiful. This reflected ghost does not surprise me; I have seen her before. She gazes down at me from the car window late at night, broken by the harsh glow of an occasional streetlight. This part of me, a half-hidden, mysterious fairy, is the part I can love. She is completely mine. She is mature and wise and feminine.

I've heard the beauty of a teenage girl described as tremulous. This is exactly true of me. The embodiment of my prettiness is the compliments I receive. I am a horrid, perverse goblin if nobody tells me otherwise. The reflection, the pale powerful shadow, is undauntedly stunning. Her beauty is the dignity of her face and the way her wisdom and her potential pours out her eyes. It depends only on the existence of an untamable soul.

Her haunting look interrogates me: *When will you learn what I know?*

When will you discover this power?

But with the question *When?* comes a promise. A promise that someday, and someday soon, everything she has will be mine.

The door swings shut behind me. I walk out onto the damp sidewalk and look forward to being home. For a moment I wonder again about that reflection. Who is she? Perhaps she is a dancer.

No one who's beautiful fits.
That's why angels sleep in the watery heavens,
 to protect themselves from demons.
Sooner or later trust pierces them, and faith,
 and they descend like spiraling leaves
 to this sad, hollow, destitute earth.
There were no gods to hold us up there
 with thick, brown fingers
 and our hands are too fragile to grasp their arms.
My god, this is a sick parallel to heaven
 populated by angel-husks.
The ghosts and wraiths use their rotten arms
 to drag the sparkling angels.
We drag each other because we are afraid to go down alone.
There is no such thing as bravery—
 it is just the ability to pretend the longest.
 How long have I been pretending?
Soon that misty, damp paradise will be empty
 and the carcasses of naïve cherubs
 will choke this supple earth.
We are all hollow death,
 filled with fragrant, hedonistic pleasure.
We are soldier-zombies.
 We are nothing but stagnant, liquid animals.
 We are goblins of selfishness.
So laugh when you say you are out of place
 among all of these bickering goblins.
It only means you are an angel.

———————————————————

1993–1996

I stopped thinking about my boyfriend for a period of time longer than five minutes. I played King of the Bench. I flew. I rocked like a baby. I danced. I giggled. Whitney is a creature of seldom changes. She is a good, steady creature. Meagan is open, quick to love. Ryan is forgiving and kind. Relaxed. If you paint a picture of us, we are all colors, and there is a gray, plastic, lightless blob of anguish over me and my dried apples and Rice Krispie treats. But anguish can almost be beautiful when you are folded up in it trying to spit out words. It is better than nothing. Better than nothing. Better than plastic. I knew he was plastic when his eyebrows melted.

1993–1997

the first of all my dreams was of
a lover and his only love,
strolling slowly (mind in mind)
through some green mysterious land

until my second dream begins—
the sky is wild with leaves; which dance
and dancing swoop (and swooping whirl
over a frightened boy and girl)

but that mere fury soon became
silence: in hunger always whom
two tiny selves sleep (doll by doll)
motionless under magical

foreverfully falling snow.
And then this dreamer wept: and so
she quickly dreamed a dream of spring.

1995–1997

i was born under the ram.
i'm an aries. a fire sign.
i was born with a fire in my belly.
i always talk in a very loud voice.
i used to be a ballerina.
i used to starve my little body and stretch a leotard over it
as tight and sticky as a popped balloon.
i used to ask tarot cards how to get a boyfriend.
i used to write poems about loneliness.

1993–1997

The day I was born. I have this image of that day that is made up of all the jagged fragments that my parents and my brother and sister and Claudia have told me. My mom is lying in her bedroom under her old, dirty white comforter with this splotchy, sleepy-eyed baby in her arms—only my mom's face is smoother and her hair is completely brown and long and it swirls around her on the flowered pillowcases. My sister is there, and she is small and chubby with huge, dark eyes that I have seen in thousands of old photographs. She sits on the floor under the window and stares at me, but refuses to touch the spotted little creature. And my brother is on the bed with his skinny legs bent and propped up on his elbows so that he can study me and stick out an index finger to stroke my damp head or touch my tiny curling hands. My dad opens the door and he is thinner and his hair is longer, and his glasses and clothes make him look like a *Dazed and Confused* stand-in. He leads Claudia through the door. Claudia has a tiny baby in her arms too, gurgling and plump with brown fluff-hair and muddy green eyes. Brigid.

1993–1997

When I learned to talk, I was fiercely possessive of my best friend, who came to my house the day I was born. When I hit the playground, with its competitiveness and its drama and its shrill, terrifying playground teachers with their shiny silver whistles, it was a matter of distinction to have Brigid-my-best-friend-since-birth at my side.

1995–1997

Bagel for Brigid

This is what it's all about from here on out, girl. It's all about everything going around in a circle, and sometimes you wonder what's at the middle of that circle, and you get scared it's just a hole. But maybe that hole is a window. To frame the things you see.

And that's what it's all about, really, looking out a window at all the things you can imagine, and being a little terrified, but still looking and planning and staking out a path.

And it's also about carbohydrates. Food. It's about what you gobble up at lunchtime driving back from Bagel Brothers. It's feeding your belly and your body and your mind and your soul so that you grow. So that you always grow. So that no aspect of you ever starves.

And it's about the simple pleasures that keep getting you out of bed every morning. Toasted with butter or jam or cream cheese and cucumbers. Simple little things that you know will be there when you wake up. Blankets. Sunlight on Puget Sound. Dew on cedars. Daisies. Somewhere, mountains. Somewhere, the ocean. The consistent things, the old things, like evergreen trees at dusk.

And it's something to feed the ducks with and the squirrels, and to share with me in Spanish class. Something of yourself to spread around. Something to share with your friends. You, girl, are the most beautiful thing I've seen all year. You have shared so much with me. Always divided ice cream evenly. Always played fair. You have so many wildflowers to give to the people around you. So much bagel to share.

And it's about something that comes from grain. From small, tiny little seeds. From flour. It's about things that are as long-standing and comfortable as wheat fields and grain. It's about making the most out of all your ingredients. Because you've got premium ingredients in that soul of yours.

It's about coming over to my house and eating one sometime soon. And always knowing that you're at the center of my heart. You're the guacamole on my veggie bagel sandwich. You're better than veggie cream cheese.

Spring 1995

I remember looking out the window on the flight from Anchorage to Magadan completely at odds with the fact that I was flying to Russia. I remember looking down at more ice than I had ever seen and I remember bright blue cracks of water running jaggedly across all that whiteness. I kept memorizing those blue lines. Telling myself what they looked like so that later I could write everything down. I couldn't believe where I was. I couldn't believe the blue cracks in the ice or the mix of languages bubbling up around me or the strange, vast country waiting for me at the end of all those blue lines.

Russia. Russia. It wakes me up in the night and takes the air out of my lungs and squeezes tears out onto my cheeks for no apparent reason. How do I write it down? How do I write about Russia?

I remember the exact moment when my sense of wonder came back. I don't know where it went or when it left or if I ever really had a sense of wonder in the first place, but I know when it came back.

April 18, 1995

Subject: Sorry I haven't written

The first time I had a chance to write I didn't have your e-mail address with me, so I wrote to Brigid and gave her messages for you— but I'm not sure she's read her e-mail yet. Then I brought your address and wrote you a really long letter but all the lights went out in the school midway through it and it got erased. I don't have any free time. I help out in English classes all day and we always have something to do after school. Lots of people invite us over. We usually get home around seven and eat supper at about nine-thirty and I never get to bed before eleven. I really don't want e-mail to be a major focus of my trip, so I hope you won't feel bad if I don't spend too much time writing to you. I am very, very happy here. I don't know the meaning of culture shock. People are incredible here. They take such good care of us, and it's because they are really interested in us—not just because they feel sorry for us. I share a room with Anyuta, which is really good because talking to her for about an hour every night has given me a better understanding of the way she is. We are really getting close. I love my family too. Larisa is really quick to laugh, and she feeds me the most unbelievable amount of food. I live better here than I did in the U.S., so don't worry about anything. Sorry if that's insulting, but you guys just don't treat me like an honored guest. I told Anyuta I'm going to tie her to a chair tomorrow so that she'll let me do the dishes. I love you.

    Rachel

Spring 1995

I'm sitting on the floor of my bedroom in good old Olympia, Washington, writing in a journal that has gone untouched for five and a half weeks. The last thing I wrote was scratched in dark blue marker in sharp strokes that ignored the lines. "It's hard to leave." That was a long time ago. I was terrified to leave Olympia and everything safe and dependable to me. But for five and a half weeks I awoke every day in Russia, ate breakfast in the tiny kitchen of our flat, walked between the pale buildings, and listened to the rumbling music of the Russian language.

Before this trip, I had spent my entire life with the same people. I had been in the same, safe reality for my entire existence. There are good things about my life in America—a house, a bedroom of my own, recycling bins, teachers who are my friends, cars with seat belts in back. But there are aspects that make me shudder: supermodels, malls, Slim-Fast commercials, our grotesque, gigantic homes, the O.J. Simpson trial, our lack of reverence for other cultures.

Some of these blemishes were present in Russia. The girls spent their time between classes in front of the mirrors in the entryway, adjusting and repairing their appearances. During dinner, TV was always flashing or rasping in the background. There were posters of partially naked women in full view in almost every apartment I entered. Maybe if I had understood the throaty Russian of the TV, I would have noticed the same sensationalism and irreverence I see surrounding O.J. Simpson; but none of those things touched me in Russia. I am sure some of them hurt the Russians, along with their economic situation, their disrespect for their president, and their doubts about opportunities for success.

On our way home, I stood on a balcony in Khabarovsk with other members of our group, watching the sun turn red and bleed into the bluish clouds. "Russia is heaven," I said to my friends and to the damp, worn buildings and the mysterious section of China we could see across the river. Then, after a pause, I admitted, "Except if you are a Russian." Russia is hell for its people, but they love it and are proud of it anyway. They make *you* love it with their strength, their joy, and their cheer.

So here I am, back in Olympia, Washington. I am happy to be here because I love evergreen trees and toilets that actually flush, moonlight on Budd Inlet and cheese bagels at Bagel Brothers, "my mountain," and my parents. Nevertheless, a giant, jagged section of my heart is still in Yuzhno, with the lights in the windows of the apartment buildings, with the *babushkas* wearing their flowered scarves and wrinkled faces, with the bleached birch trees, and with the teachers and smiling, giggling third graders at Yuzhno-Sakhalinsk School #2.

Olympia is safe, warm, and happy. It is my love.

Yuzhno is my passion.

Summer 1995

skipping stones
flat and hard
we pucker as we throw

skipping class
we smoked a pack
in a sunlit field

skipping beside daddy
in the dark and blue-light
nighttime downtown crisp

skip rope
skinny legs
wish I was that girl.

Pass over me.
leap and fly coldly
miss my shards. shattered.

skipping lazy eyes,
glance your sweet letters
sad my piteous writing

skip with a brown truck
farmer dark skin
chew spit skip.

bouncing on its flat belly
over water
gray determined stone

baby skip and twirl
your light flitting skirt
to this man here.

báby, skip life
store it on your hat
like a pin.

Summer 1995

Sometimes my voice goes thin. It quivers as if it has to stretch to cover all the words. Then whoever hears it gets uncomfortable and braces for my tears.

Sometimes my voice goes thin and most days I cry. I am not depressed. Really. I am happy. I am a death-blossom. A flower that thrives in the sweet wet dampness of despair.

Summer 1995

Empty country. Land devoid of its Kerouacs and Thoreaus. Devoid of the quiet consciousness that drove it and made it not only powerful but also kind, beautiful.

On that shore, the only calls I heard across that pure, frozen day were the voices of geese overhead and the congenial throaty Russian laughter. And always under every movement of my hand or turn of my head, as I fell asleep in our tiny, almost spartan apartment, as I walked in the mud and the refuse of the Russian alleys, the jarring, poisonous knowledge that I had to return to America. There was no call, only a twisted, false murmur.

What was it that tortured me? Why was my home and my country so terrifying? Supermodels and court TV and anorexia. Daytime talk shows. All very American. Our emptiness. How we've either forgotten or never learned our own history. How when a foreign student comes into my school, she will most likely be ignored and spend her lunchtime alone, or eating with other foreign students in some isolated edge of the cafeteria.

Summer 1995

Here was what I witnessed at the fair tonight: A girl was leading her 4-H cow on a rope, and I guess the cow got scared. It started bucking around in circles, and when the girl didn't let go, it whipped her around in the air and onto the ground. She hit hard and still held on a little until the cow broke loose, almost trampled her, and started running in Sari's and my direction. We ran for cover and watched the cow bolt through a big barn with a bunch of other cows and disappear. The girl didn't get up and a crowd gathered. Some guy came over and yelled, "Vern! Get the cart!" It was scary. Sari went over and looked at the girl and announced that she was bleeding from her head and her legs. I think it bothered me almost as much to see the way people gathered to gape at that poor girl as it did to see the cow whip her around like that. That is one thing I hate about humans. How we like to stand around and stare at our wounded, even if we are absolutely no help at all, just for the gore.

I love seeing my cousins and being in Denison in the house where my grandma and grandpa used to live. I love doing things like washing hogs. I hate seeing how my mom is when she is taking care of my great-grandpa. It's hard for her. I remember how hard my grandma and grandpa's illnesses and death were for her. They both died

of cancer and my grandma's, especially, involved a lot of waiting and watching. I don't know if you have watched anyone die. That is what we are doing, my aunts and uncle and mom more than me—watching him die. That sounds so pessimistic, but the man is ninety-six and he has a serious infection. He *wants* to die.

He is such a curiosity to me. Old people and babies frighten me. They are awe-inspiring.

Great-grandpa has aged so much since I last saw him. His hair is different and all perfectly white. He is so tall and so thin, with these enormous white hands, with long wrinkles. His hands are like long paws, big and long and slow-moving. Those fingers are so slow. Those hands just fascinate me.

He complained to my aunt once that everyone just comes and looks at him. They just sit there and stare at him. Well, that is exactly what I do. The first time I saw him on this trip I just sat and watched him while my mom talked, because he was such a fascination. I wanted to remember everything about him so I could write it down. I am horrible. I treat people like relics. I just love to watch them, especially the unusual ones. I am horrid! I am exactly like that crowd around that poor girl.

August 2, 1995

You will have a key to the secret entrance of my tower. See, my tower isn't going to have a door. It's going to have a long, dark passage underground to a secret hidden entrance. That way no one will ever see me go in and out. I will be the most astonishing legend.

There is this problem. None of my assorted ambitions involve a large salary, so I have no idea how I will fund my tower. Sadness. But I always have my dreams, don't I? And, hopefully, I can at least get a cheap apartment with a balcony for flowers and gargoyles, right?

Flowers and gargoyles and sometimes a way back to Russia. Those are my ambitions. And I will save you a bright purple La-Z-boy chair for when you visit my apartment. We must always be friends. It is a requirement.

So you want to know what I am afraid of. That makes me laugh because I am so good at pretending to be afraid. I pretend I'm afraid of losing friendships, and I pretend I'm afraid of hurting people, and I pretend I'm afraid of those horrible, lecherous men who stare at you like drooling goblins. But I'm braver than that, don't you think?

I'm also too brave to be afraid that I'm just tricking myself into the emotions I feel and treating the people I claim to love like puppets. Maybe I'm just too inhuman. I think about that as a possibility, but it just sort of puzzles me. It doesn't faze me in the least.

I have these petty fears. I am scared of my barn, and a little scared of heights. All those little things just anger me. I become really incensed when I am climbing a tree or something and I feel that weakness in my stomach. I resent that fear.

Nothing gnaws at me and rips at my mind as I am trying to sleep. I am sorry to disappoint you but I'm not afraid of anything. Nothing really terrifies me except the thought of never seeing Russia again, which would even be bearable if I die young. Things really hurt me. There is a lot that is agonizing. But pain is different from fear.

––––––––––––––––––––

1995–1996

That Bridge in Prague

I was the girl with a face-paint butterfly
spread across my face.
There was a swarm of people changing and mixing
and flowing across that bridge.
We heard the jingle of pocket change
flung into guitar cases and overturned top hats.
The river was like a huge lizard
oozing beneath our feet and a layer of cobblestones.
The street musician saw the butterfly's painted eyes and hollered
"Hello, blue eyes!"
as he strummed his pregnant curved guitar.
We slithered through cafés
in the strange harmony of languages.
We gulped and sucked the glass lips
of wineglasses on the brim of the river.
Drowning in the whispering ripples
and the dark heavy odor of gardenias.
Blinking as streetlights gleamed

on the river's dank, drifting body.
I shimmied and danced around some sparkly people
dressed in costumes,
and they giggled and danced with me,
and spoke at me in their throaty language.
The river lay quietly and traveled in its sleep.
It absorbed the mandolin and the tambourine and the voices
and the click of cameras and the drum of my feet.
And if all the cobblestones shattered
and the guitar cases tumbled
and the street musician went head over heels
and the wineglasses were carried along and crushed
in the belly of the river,
if we all went helter-skelter
like a bowl of peanuts to the water,
my face-paint butterfly would bleed off.
My skirt would turn see-through
and cling to my legs.
And if I managed to climb out,
the river would lick its lips and spit on me
and the city would wait for dawn.

1995–1997

If I die today

Silence the birds if I die today.
Let them only stare from the brass bars of their cages
and watch as my mother weeps.
Cover the flat faces of clocks with black cloth
and silence the alarms.
Hush the dirt-water of the creek
by whispering to it,
"She is dead, she is dead."

If I die today,
you must burn the papers under my bed
to charred leaves of ash.
You must silence my dead voice,
so it will not embarrass my memory.

If I die today,
you must drink milk from the carton, wantonly!
You must shriek and scream in the shopping mall
in front of all those blind dead ghosts,
and the placid, contemptuous mannequins,
and the mall gods who watch over everything
in their great bawdy underworld.
You must make a great loud racket. Such a loud fuss
to silence the birds and the sky and the rain.
You must be so crazy and free if I die today!
You must go to those cold-faced mannequins
and take off their tiny shoes
and find out if mannequins have toes.
And if they do
(and I imagine they have blunt tawny nails on them)
You must find out what plastic mannequin flesh tastes like.
You must kiss their shoes.
Suck on them with your clumsy tongue.
And you must do this right there in front of the undead shoppers
and the ladies behind the perfume counter.

You must cry out and tell everyone,
"She is dead. She is dead."
And do what I imagined.
You must walk through the grocery store
and take juicy bites out of apples
and then put them back.
You must kiss people you hardly know with passion
so that they stumble dizzily for a moment.

1995–1997

But I would say to my fellows, once and for all, As long as possible
live free and uncommitted. It makes but little difference
whether you are committed to a farm or the county jail.

—Henry David Thoreau

This is my absolute favorite aphorism because it is exactly how I feel.
I hate being tied down—to anything. That is why I'm never getting
married or spending too much time in any one city or in any occupation. Chains and boxes and leashes are not for me. The most permanent house I want to live in is a dark green Volkswagen van or on a
sailboat. I want to be a bartender for a while, and sing folk songs in
the tunnels of the London underground. I want to be a performance
artist and shave my head and paint my face green and dance around
onstage singing in Russian. I want to be a belly dancer and a painter
and a waitress and a hitchhiker. And the whole time I want to be a
writer. I want to live and live and live and never commit, whether it's
to a man or a house or a city or a high-paying office job.

One time on the ferry, I watched a Jamaican man talk to the general onlookers about his philosophy of life.

"I've been in Florida, New York, Europe, Africa," he said in his
lovely, lilting accent. "But you can't stay anywhere too long or it gets
bad. It gets stale."

The crowd standing on the ferry deck looked out on the still,
amber water. In the freedom of the breeze and the tremulous sunlight I thought, *Yeah. Right on, man.*

1995

America's Call

In April I walked along the edge of the Pacific Ocean and dipped my
fingers into the water. For the first time in my life, I was looking east
over the Pacific. My feet were no longer on the firm, familiar conti-
nent of North America. I was in Russia.

I have never witnessed anything as devastatingly beautiful as the long arc the water made that day as it rippled away toward America. My memories of Russia are a collection of vivid images: drinking tea in the tiny green kitchen of our flat, walking through mud and garbage between the buildings, a lanky cat looking down from a gray balcony, coal dust on the snow, curious unfamiliar faces turning to watch me walk by.

Before and after that brief flurry of vision and emotion, the rest of my life seems like a long barren plateau. I have never been so awake—painfully, poignantly awake—as I was in Russia. On that long gray beach, I dreaded the imminent return to my country. America did not call to me. It did not reach out to me and entice me back. It lurked upon the edges of my mind in dashes of fluorescent color. When I dipped my fingers into the water, blinking at the horizon, no echoing chorus of my country drifted across the ocean. The unbroken melody of the dreams of my people was buried beneath a low twisted murmur, the whine of cellular phones and infomercials, the chatter of tabloid talk shows and Court TV. This commercialized, empty soul was the thing I escaped in Russia, and I dreaded returning into the long halls of my home, filled with cool, plastic images of perfection.

When I did come back, it was as if I had been wide awake for a month and a half, awake in the world to blink and gaze at everything, and then shoved back into a numb stupor. The only thing my country told me when I returned was close your eyes. Go back to sleep again. I could not close my eyes to the incongruities of our nation. There is a tacky irony in all our comparative wealth. I gazed with wide, unblinking eyes at a country with much to offer and yet so tangled in commercialism and media. Our country has forgotten its soul and has contrived a harsh, gaudy personality. We have lost sight of our old dreams and ideas, not the conventions which bound women to the home and cursed African-Americans to subservience, but the awareness, thoughtful awareness, which produced Thoreau, Whitman, and Kerouac.

There is a throbbing, hushed call beneath the tackiness and gaudiness. That call was welling up a long time ago when Native

Americans carved homes into the walls of canyons and cut the images of animals out of their totem poles. That call lingered and reverberated as our forefathers penned the Constitution. That call fluttered into an odd, complicated melody as Thoreau contemplated life from the edge of Walden Pond and Whitman shocked his readers with *Leaves of Grass*. That call shook and trembled during the Civil War, World War I, World War II, Vietnam . . . but it prevailed. That call led some out into the streets to protest, others into airplanes and battlefields. That call led a few out into lonely wilderness, pen or paintbrush in hand, to try to find a way of recording it.

That call led me away. It led me to Russia, where the din of political diatribes and O.J. lawyers was quiet. Quiet enough for me to hear, gentle and faltering, America's call.

1996–1997

I am Rachel the fish. Swimming through a sea of phrases and parentheses and lowercase letters. A baby fish in a diamond ocean. Someday I will jump between the water and the sky and turn human, but right now I am a tiny fish, reflecting the world on mirror-scales.

I am swimming in this foamy ocean of shadows trying to decide which hook to bite, which sunbeam to leap into, which stretch of shore to build my house on. I am stuck below the real world in my flickering sea, and I am learning to be human. You learn from the bones here. I am swimming through the enormous white-bleached rib cage of my grandfather. His skin and his eyes and his coughing have been devoured by water, but there is an echo of him on the thin white bones. It makes me frightened to swim down here with the ghosts of my family. I see their faces above the water looking down on me, and I can even hear the threads of their voices. But as they stare down at me, my image is broken by their reflections, and like Narcissus they sit up there and talk to the pieces of themselves they think they see in me. It scares me to be among these bubbling voices. They are wondering why the last little youngest fish of the family is having so much trouble picking which Ivy League college to surface at, and making the decision to be a preppy kid who does her math homework and doesn't sneak off to smoke at lunchtime.

Sometimes I just like the feeling of the water. I know when I go up there the sunshine is going to burn my fins off and make me walk in line with the rest of the world. I like the ocean because it is three-dimensional. I can travel between schools of faces instead of checking in and out in a narrow line. I am especially friendly with hermit crabs. They fascinate me because they hide all their vulnerabilities in their shells. I have never known how to find a shell and then stay in it. I tend to wander out of the grotto when the sharks are attacking just to see what all the fuss is about. I hide my vulnerabilities by dancing around them in the water and changing my shape so that I am never one thing for too long. But I like to watch the cautious hermit crabs, and I respect them for their sensibility and their discipline.

I like the feeling of the water when it is crowded with voices. I am learning everything I need to know before I climb out and commit to being human. I am learning to speak German fluently. And I can read the Cyrillic alphabet and emit a shocking stream of Russian profanity. My Spanish is a bit one-sided: "Kisses." "I love you." "I adore you." "You are an attractive boy." "I am very hot." "Stop kissing me." "You shouldn't eat in front of the poor people."

I like the feeling of the water when it is filled with thousands of frantic fish bodies, moving in a massive horde toward some bread crumbs or water bugs. Before I climb out dripping on the shore and make a decision about whether I will ever be married, I am going to learn about all the different ways to love people. I started by reading books. I eat books for dinner. I am a book-eating fish. I've devoured *On the Road* by Kerouac, and *The Metamorphosis* by Kafka, and *The Sound and the Fury*, and *The Bell Jar*, and of course *Lolita*, which was terribly beautiful from the edges of the reeds in this paradise of water. Books are the best things to feed little fish if you want them to grow into interesting humans.

I like to watch the water bugs skid along the surface above me. It seems unfair that it should be so easy for them. Their bodies are light and empty and it is nothing to them to fly up into the sky or crawl along the trunk of a tree. The sunlight doesn't burn them like it burns me. They slide easily out of the water and become human. Sometimes I am jealous of the water bugs, but then I remember that their limbs are so light because they haven't eaten as many books as I have. They have not given themselves hopelessly to anything. So really they are just like the hermit crabs. Even though they are already in the adult world of air and light.

I have a little time left before my scales fall off. And so I paint my toenails turquoise and my fingernails gold and pull my socks up to cover my scraped shins. I clip plastic baby barrettes into blond hair which I cut myself. I throw my backpack on my back and fill it with novels and stolen lighters and homemade mixed tapes brimming with Janis Joplin and The Velvet Underground. I make up nicknames for things. Bob is the word for bureaucracy and the establishment and everything hypocritical and frightening. Parents are Ewoks because they wander around in the background of the movie play-

ing Ewok games with absolutely no idea what is occurring beneath their noses.

I am a Melville-Kerouac-tangential-William S. Burroughs-stream-of-consciousness fish. But like Quentin Compson, I spend my time in my chambers and wreaths of seaweed, listening to the click of a clock with no hands, knowing that time is not passing at all and that the sun can't really rise under the ocean. I think I am crazy and I wonder when I will break the surface and melt.

1996–1997

I didn't have to explain myself for my first four trimesters of high school. I got straight A's, enthusiastically attended pep assemblies, ate lunch with the same group of all-American high-achieving girls each day, and did my homework every night before going to bed. I went to every football game. I volunteered at the Olympia Crisis Clinic so that I could nonjudgmentally help kids who weren't quite as all-American and high-achieving as I was.

I got my first "B" second trimester of my sophomore year. Sometimes I did my homework the period before it was due, and sometimes I even ventured down the hall to eat lunch with the kids who wore flannel and ripped jeans and pierced more than just their ears.

Then I went to Russia. Aah, Russia. Former menacing Communist empire full of gorgeous people, coal dust on the snow, bland rectangular apartment buildings that looked beautiful in the sunset, sweet, smiling girls who shrugged their shoulders and tossed empty vodka bottles off of balconies, people who supposedly waited in breadlines squeezing my wrists and heaping extra servings of caviar and mashed potatoes onto my plate. Aah, Russia. That Russia. My Russia.

Suddenly there were contradictions. Imagine little Rachel standing in her coat and gloves in the doorway to a tiny apartment building and suddenly realizing, *Good God! The world isn't black and white!* The sky was gray and there was garbage in the street and the snow was black and the paint was peeling off of all the buildings, but it took my breath away. Knocked the wind right out of me.

I cried on the plane all the way home from the Canadian border when the sun started rising. Everything was dark and pink and purple. The mountains grew up out of the water, pink and purple, and the clouds stretched out, pink and purple.

It was the most beautiful thing I had ever seen, but it just could not compete with those stark rectangular buildings lined up beneath that gray sky. Contradictions. I cried all the way home over contradictions.

Third trimester of my sophomore year my grades took a nosedive. We all said it was because it was too hard to catch up after going to Russia. We all said it was worth it. But then, for some reason, I didn't go to football games my junior year and I didn't spend so much time with my all-American friends and my grades did not come up again.

That's where things become hard to explain.

Fall 1996

I don't have a bedroom right now. Our Japanese exchange student sleeps in my old bedroom surrounded by my charcoal sketches and pages ripped from magazines. After graduating from college my sister came back with her two yowling cats to claim the other bedroom. I sleep in the family room and fold my bed back into a couch before school every day. People are always walking in to watch TV while I'm half naked, and sometimes the cats pee on my clothes when people lock them in here because they are wreaking too much havoc on the rest of the house. It's an interesting arrangement.

There is no identity in this room. No rock collection from first grade. No row of stuffed cows on the top shelf. No green stain on the carpet where I spilled my watercolors. Every night I unfold the bed and lock the door so no one comes in to watch *Star Trek* reruns. I reach around behind the stereo until I find the two lonely refugees from my old room: my black Pentel Rock 'n Write pen and my *Essential Classics* opera aria CD.

Tonight it was the same routine. I slid the CD in and found a spiral notebook and now I'm writing. Tonight, I'm writing by candlelight.

The black pen and the opera CD are going to get me through this last year of high school. They are going to get me into college and through graduate school and out into the real world. Eventually they are going to drop a Nobel Prize for literature into my lap.

Granted, in a few weeks I'll go to the library and get a new opera CD and my pen will run out of ink, but the routine is always the same. First I hit *Play*. Then I curl up under the comforter, and by the time my pen hits the paper, a tiny bassoon player has crawled out of my stereo and begun a tune. Warm, low pizzicato of cellos, and then a man is singing in Italian, and I don't know what the words are, but his voice hurts. And my printing blurs into cursive and I forget the punctuation and all I can do is write.

There are words in me for every painful flutter of this music. There is a tone in this music for every emotion in my body. Flutes are dancing up and down playfully, but the voice is sad. It is sliding and writhing. And in this candlelight I feel things. I can see fireflies rising over the cornfield at my grandmother's house. I can see her crying and hugging us too tight before we get in the car and drive back to Olympia. I can hear her singing as she walks through the soybeans pulling weeds with callused hands.

I can hear my mom's voice breaking late at night in a hotel room when she told us Grandma died. And I can feel my mom. I can see her silver hair fanning out from under a hat when we had snowball fights on the days they cancelled school. I can see her lips trembling as she read the birthday card I made her last year. I can hear her at the end of a dock in Minnesota playing her flute for the mist and the reeds and the dragonflies sleeping on the lily pads.

It is a woman singing now and the voice is getting louder and I don't understand the words. The candle is trembling. I can see a man shivering on a frozen sidewalk in front of me. I can hear the gurgle of Russian running from his mouth and my friend's broken English as she translates for him.

"He says when he looks at you he sees himself the first time he was in this city. He says the Russian people are good. He says not to think they are bad because of the dirt or the garbage or because he has been drinking."

I can smell the alcohol on his breath. I can see the tears in his eyes. I can feel the boys in leather jackets squatting in a doorway watching us. I can hear his boots in the slush and coal dust as he walks away.

Singing about love now. Madame Butterfly looking out over the ocean and singing about the awful richness of love. And that voice. That voice rips me from my body and sends me into flames. Flames and words and passion and bright colors and more images curled up in this cave of blankets and candlelight.

This music makes me ache. This ringing human voice is stronger than the kitchen faucet dripping or my sister's cats fighting outside the door or my father's footsteps on the stairs. It's what I am about: my opera aria CD and my Pentel Rock 'n Write. Feeling things and making something out of them. Really feeling things, like my grandmother felt her grandchildren leaving. Like my mother felt her flute spinning across the water. Like that sad, drunken stranger felt the awe of a skinny American girl in the snow and coal dust of eastern Russia.

1996–1997

I write because in some secret compartment in my brain this little ironclad woman keeps screaming, *It's all you have!* I write because it's art and it's my first love, before Russia. My first, my truest passion. It swallows me, ego and all, in one enormous gulp. I don't write letters. I write disjointed chapters in my unending epic. The muse, the muse. She climbs into your body and moves your puppet limbs and eases the words loose from the walls of your soul.

I feel like I have been performing my whole life in this huge auditorium, but once in a while the houselights go on and I realize I have no audience. Nothing but hollow rows of folding chairs. And I don't care. I write it down because instinct tells me to. Sometimes I send a letter and my whole soul hopes they'll like it, because it's personal. Because I created something for someone else and dared to write a name at the top. Writing is brave. It is maybe the only brave thing about me.

Everyone gets scared. Sylvia Plath wrote, "But I think what I fear most is the death of imagination." The other night I just felt like I was drowning. I kept throwing my hands onto books full of quotes and words and my imagination could do nothing with any of it. I thought I'd finally lost myself. Silly, melodramatic girl! I was wrong. But it is still a shivering thing to rest your ear on the mattress and turn out the light and stare through blurred, salty eyes at a streetlight. I only get that scared when I run out of words.

Lately my whole soul is in chaos, passionate chaos. There aren't paintbrushes big enough for the things in me. There are no words that ring and pierce and reverberate. There's a peeling white noise in me right now. A very loud noise in my soul. I wish I had some purple paint and I'd roll naked in it and dance around and then you would understand that noise. I wish I had an empty auditorium and an enormous gong and I'd beat the very crystals off the chandeliers. I wish I had words, sweet, musical words, for the feelings in me. There are pages and pages of lined paper for me, and the tiny warrior-woman is waking up again and screaming, *Girl, write! It's all you have.*

Cut off an ear if you have to. Live in poverty and beg for food if, with your dirty face and your torn pants, you have a passion.

I think this is what alcoholics call a moment of clarity. All of a sudden I see the billowing sailboat trees against midnight blue sky, and I smell rain. My eyes are very blue and very sharp in the reflection of my lamp in the window. That deep-eyed wraith in the window looks powerful and free. And I am exactly alone, but not lonely, in folds of blanket. And I have been writing about an hour. Writing feverishly. This is a moment when I am exactly and only me.

1996–1997

Sometimes she wished she could write poetry across her face and go to school that way. She could see herself making the words on her eyelids with her crumbling black eyeliner pencil. She wished she could write on the walls, too, because lined paper has corners and edges and boundaries. She only thought this way when the words that leaked from her pen onto the paper were soft and floating and soundless. So that when she went back to read her own stories they were airy and voiceless.

Part of her longed for something dramatic to happen. This section of her consciousness waited with quick, frightened movements for her life to begin so she could write about it. Another part of her anguished over her helplessness in coping with the pools of murkiness and deceitful reflections inside of her. This part was afraid of crumbling in the light rain that fell almost every afternoon, and it was terrified at the idea of trauma. Somewhere in the gray matter and empty music between these two creatures, the creator in her danced about, evading her. So she chased it.

She awoke one Sunday morning when she was still waiting for her life to begin and kept her eyes closed. Outside of time, she could hear the voices of birds twisting through the crack in her window. There was no harsh light dancing on her elbows and she let them bask in the cool, tender kiss of the darkness. The night air was saturated with the fragrant dampness of the morning and it rubbed against her flesh idly.

She pushed the pressure out of her temples effortlessly and felt herself sinking deeper into the rumpled sea of blankets. The birds cried to her throat and echoed in the hollowness there. Wordless music shivered and stirred the empty darkness. Silently, she slipped out of the bed almost without disturbing the covers. The fluorescent green pulse of the clock danced just outside her vision and she was careful not to look at it. She crept downstairs in complete darkness and settled again in the window seat. She didn't fight the hollowness in her chest as she pressed her forehead against the wet glass. Her breath cloaked the pane and then curled back warmly against her lips. She turned her cheek against the moisture and tried to press her aching eyelids against it. Her eyelids couldn't be healed. It was as if her eyes were bloated and jagged and the dry skin of her eyelids had to stretch across them too tightly.

She had grown up believing she had some special potential. She had had faith that there was a special purpose for her. Now that idea was cracking and shaking before her. She let the ache of disappointment carve into her and the doubt devour shredded bites of her soul.

She leaned back against the rough pillows and fell asleep again, wondering if her life had already begun and ended and she had somehow missed it along the way.

When she woke up again her family was moving carefully around her. They talked loudly as if she were one of the pets sleeping there, 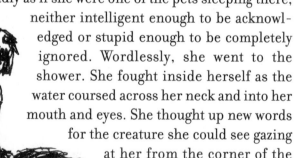 neither intelligent enough to be acknowledged or stupid enough to be completely ignored. Wordlessly, she went to the shower. She fought inside herself as the water coursed across her neck and into her mouth and eyes. She thought up new words for the creature she could see gazing at her from the corner of the mirror. A wraith, a goblin, an old woman, a baby. But she could think of more words for the way it behaved. Manipulative, melodramatic, hypocritical. Then she cursed herself for spending so much time thinking about herself.

Out of the shower she wrapped herself naked and dripping in a rough towel. She stared at herself again in the mirror and wondered what had become of the face that used to provoke whistles out of car windows and long stares in the mall. She didn't really mind not being pretty. Her face's hollowness was just a curiosity to her. Nonetheless she leaned in toward the bathroom mirror and wiped the layer of condensation away. She pumped a dollop of oily brown makeup onto her finger and began covering the vulnerable patches of blue flesh beneath her eyes. She hid the tiny scars on her forehead from when she had the chicken pox. She searched the cupboard for the small black eyeliner pencil. She wanted black eyeliner that day, and as she smeared the crumbling grease across her eyelid she wondered why her lips were pursed so tightly and why her jaw was locked spitefully. She thickened the line with vengeful determination. It was as if the black eyeliner was her weapon, her form of resistance. But she didn't know what she was resisting.

Fall 1996

It seems right now like life is too long. That is such a terrible way to perceive things. Looked through my photo album. Still Russia aches. Still. I cannot let myself remember too vividly for fear it will shatter me. All those faces. Those eyes.

November 1996

When I was born, on April 10th, there was a fire in my belly. A blood-red, scorching fire crackling happily in my belly. But sometime I realized that the fire in my belly wasn't always just warm and powerful and bright. I realized that most of the time the fire was too hot and too crazy and sometimes it crackled too loud and usually it produced a lot of unpleasant smoke. I was a very little girl then. I let the fire in my belly swell my head. People didn't like my big head so they avoided me. I tried to shrink my head by putting out the fire in my belly. For a long time my belly smoldered quietly without making any sound. But without the fire there was no heat to make me grow, so I turned gray and transparent like a blackberry vine that crept under the barn into darkness.

Then one day I flew far away to a strange, cold, beautiful place. And all of a sudden that place and the people there and years of silence made the fire in my belly burst and scorch me and melt me away to bubbling slime. Then I had to come back home, and there were no strange buildings and white trees to feed the fire in my belly, so it turned stagnant and ate me up. After a long time the walls of my belly grew strong again, and I stored up my fire and learned how to let it out of my mouth and my pen and my paintbrush. I sucked the fire back into me, and nothing remains of the charred rubbish I once was except for three pink roses on the backs of my hands, reminding me of the fire in my belly, and of the danger of burning myself away, and of the things I went through to become the person I am.

Fall 1996

It's the wee hours of the morning right now. I'm very sleepy and my whole family is upstairs asleep and I'm sitting beneath the only light on in the house. Sometimes I listen to see if I can hear them breathing in unison up there like some four-headed animal. I love to be all alone at night. What should I write about, crouched under an afghan with my eyes half closed in exhaustion?

I think I've used up all the people around me and now I need new people. Sometimes I wish I could just be crazy and sit in a corner smearing jelly all over my face and throwing it at all the people who talk about "potential." Sometimes I wish I would get amnesia and wander off to some new place with new people. When I get older I'm going to write gorgeous books. I'm going to write gorgeous books about all the people I've used up. It's going to be sad.

1996–1997

I started writing the other day in McDonald's, but the idea of being this weird beatnik chick composing prose between French fries didn't appeal to me so I stopped. I've decided that I'm going to spend the rest of my life traveling the U.S. as a prospective student at small liberal arts colleges. Either that or, like Courtney Love, I'm going to write some silly songs about how much it sucks to go to high school in Olympia, dye my hair the color of a skinned chicken, show my crotch a lot, and hopefully make big money.

I decided that I only like new people.

New people are better than old people. New people can't reject you. And if they do it's their fault for not giving you a chance. New people are curious about who you are, and they don't stop being curious until they turn into old people. You can be honest with new people because you have nothing invested. That's why I'm never going to get married or have children or stay in one place for more than five years.

I'm scared I won't get into Reed because of my grades and I'll end up at the UW with a bunch of ex-boyfriends from high school. I'm scared I'll get my first-ever bout of writer's block when I have to write my application essay. I remember when my sister was struggling with those essays and I thought she was nuts because even as a seventh grader I knew that writing was the most absolutely natural thing in the world. Now I know how she felt.

I'm listening to "Lisa Says" by The Velvet Underground. If I could time-travel I'd either go back to the twenties and hang out in Paris with Gertrude Stein and F. Scott Fitzgerald and Hemingway and Picasso and e.e. cummings or I'd go back to the late sixties and early seventies and hang out with Jim Carroll and Andy Warhol and The Velvet Underground and the whole Factory. I like this song. It's good to write to.

1996–1997

Alice was this little girl with yellow hair and white stockings. She was a bit impulsive. She dove into this hole one day after a rabbit and found Wonderland. There were lots of crazy things in Wonderland, like drugged out caterpillars and Mad Hatters who were perpetually stuck in the same hour for eternity. But overall, Wonderland was a groovy place.

Sometimes I think Wonderland is an airplane ride away. Over more frozen water than I have ever seen before, with blue cracks dividing it into big white chunks. In that Wonderland, teenage girls shrug their shoulders and toss vodka bottles out the window when they are empty. In that Wonderland, there is a layer of coal dust over the snow, and the cars, and the huge rectangular apartment buildings looming up against pink sky. Old women sit in doorways with scarves wrapped around their heads and watch everything with drooping eyes. Russia. My Russia. That was the first Wonderland. Rows and rows of windows with people inside them speaking a language I did not understand, under coal dust between mountains, on the edge of an ocean filled with white ice and cracks of blue. Russia. My Russia.

And poor blue-eyed Alice went into that rabbit's house and ate a mushroom that made her grow so big her face was squished against the ceiling. And she didn't understand how to get out of that house. And all the tiny little creatures threw rocks at her and tried to burn the whole house down because she was such an enormous freak.

Wonderland is different now. It isn't just Russia anymore. It is the crazy man I met downtown who gnashed his teeth and picked cigarettes up off the ground and helped me con the coffee shop into selling us a cup of tea for two hundred rubles. It is dorm rooms with black lights and four-foot bongs where everyone is speaking Spanish and singing along with Bob Marley.

And me. me. me. silly. silly. silly. Face smashed against the orange paint on the hallways at my school. Face smashed against the kitchen cabinets and the blue-flowered wallpaper. Jaw smashed against the place where highway 101 meets I-5 and the freeway streaks off to Portland or Seattle. Forehead smashed against the Olympic Peninsula. silly. silly. Poor Alice, shrunk until she almost drowned in a puddle of her own tears. silly. silly.

Soon. Soon everything will melt together and be okay. My mom won't be standing in my doorway asking why I smell like smoke and telling me she doesn't know me anymore. How can Mom understand sitting in a coffee shop with a crazy man smoking a cigarette he found on the ground? Mom. silly. silly. Oh Mom, there are some very pretty things amongst the caterpillars and Mad Hatters. Some very pretty things picking their way through coal dust and shattered vodka bottles. Some very pretty things in those clouds of pot smoke. Oh Mom, my stockings are dirty and the bow fell out of my hair, but I can still write pretty stories. Taking the garbage out in my pajamas, I still know how to gasp at the sunrise. Hitchhiking home, I still talk to the moon. Oh Mom, why say, "I don't know what happened to you"? silly. silly. Fell down a rabbit hole. Ate a mushroom. Went to Russia. Started talking to crazy men.

That's what I have to say about Alice. I don't intend to drown in my own tears.

Spring 1997

My name is Rachel and I'm here to teach you to talk to teenagers. I'm here to teach you to give up your adult language and speak the language of the Teen so you can trick us into thinking you understand us and then heal us of our petty sorrows.

The Only Way to Talk to a Teenager
A step-by-step guide

1. Use lots of hip, beat, cool words . . . like "jive" and "cheesy" and "funk."

2. Keep in mind that Teenagers are much, much younger than you, and they don't have the life experience to really grasp anything you tell them.

3. Whenever they seem irritated, elated, or confused, ask them if they are using drugs, which are almost always the cause of emotional extremes in Teenagers.

4. Make sure they know that Jesus is the answer.

5. Beware of the violent, predatorial nature that is always influencing every Teenager . . . always be on your guard.

6. And when, in their immaturity and corruption, none of the first five rules will help you, pick up your club, hit them over the head with it, and drag them back to the cave where they belong.

The Only Way to Talk to an Adult
A step-by-step guide

1. It is always best to scream profanities or not talk at all.

2. If they've passed forty-five, they are almost dead anyway, so there's no point in starting a conversation and getting attached.

3. Once in a while, just for kicks, come out of bathroom, sniff twice, stagger a little, and wipe your nose—so they will get all freaked out and think you're doing cocaine.

4. If you play your Beastie Boys loud enough, you won't be able to hear them.

5. Never forget that all Adults everywhere fall into these three categories: the Informant, the Mercenary, or the Judge, and they are all reporting back to your mom.

6. And when they are still there, babbling at you, dissecting you, and holding you down, pick up your club, hit them over the head with it, and then run like hell.

Okay. I'm Rachel. I'm your average, run-of-the-mill teenager. Sometimes I wear ripped blue jeans. Sometimes I wear polyester. Sometimes I take off all my clothes and swim naked at the beach at The Evergreen State College. Tomorrow I'm taking the last test I ever have to take in high school, so I can graduate next week and go to college in April. I'm just a little person. I don't believe in fate but my astrological sign is Aries, the ram, and my sign on the Chinese zodiac is the sheep, and the name Rachel means sheep, and hey—I often feel sheepish. I've got a fire in my belly. It's always been there. It used to be such a big loud blazing fire that I couldn't hear anybody else over it. So I talked a lot and I didn't listen too much. Then I went to middle school where you gotta be *cool* and you gotta be *strong* and *tough*. So I ate all my fire like this (gulp) and I tried real hard to be cool. But round about this time two years ago, I started to get indigestion. And luckily, luckily I happened to get a free trip to Russia and I saw another country for the first time. I looked backwards across the Pacific Ocean and from that distance some things back here in Olympia, Washington, USA, seemed a little weird and disconcerting. But I was awake in Russia, in the coal dust, in the snow. I was awake for the first time in forever with bug-eyes and a grin and tears of joy. And there was fire in me and outside of me and it flowed all around. And then I came back and I was awake. Finally awake, forever and ever. With warm fire in my belly to keep me warm.

But sometime when I wasn't looking, all the lights went out. And it was dark. And the only fires during those four or five months were the cigarettes . . . And then, blinking slowly in the dark, I was awake. I saw how things were, in the dark. Finally awake, forever and ever.

And after that I crawled along on my hands and knees for a while. I fell in love for the first time. Then crazy neurotic fire eventually burned that first love out. And I threw all my fire into falling instantly, madly in love with some other people. But of course that didn't work. And I kept crawling along. Just a little person. And sometimes the lights went out. Dark. And then I'd crawl along in the dark until I ran into something. I ran into people. I started trying, when the dark came, to find people in the dark. And the more I learn to find other little people to talk to in my little voice, the less dark it gets. And right now my fire is just a warm place in my belly helping me melt cold things and write stories and paint. And now I think I'm just barely starting to wake up, yawning and stretching and just beginning to open my eyes. And I think maybe that's what I'm going to be working on. Finally. Forever and ever.

So there's a very small glance at my very small understanding of the nature of things. Lately I've been thinking of writing a book called *Rachel's Myopic View of the World*. I've been painting little pictures for my friends. Sometimes when I think things are going to get dark, I make my hand into a little fist. And I close my eyes and I see a little tiny bright-white flame in my head. And that's my fire. That's what makes me write and paint. That's what makes me humble. That's what makes me strong. It's my little person. That's my language for it. That's how I describe it, and all of you have different words for it, in different languages. But this is my language and these are my metaphors.

See, I'm in love with a butterfly. And I chase it everywhere all by myself, out onto rocks and cliffs and into hot springs. Sometimes I get carried away and try to catch my butterfly and pin it down with a huge hatpin. And that's when I say, "I'm awake." Finally. Forever and ever. But that's just because I'm a little person who's scared of pain. Sometimes I try to make other people love my butterfly and chase it with me. But I can't. Because it's my butterfly. Sometimes it seems lonely and dark chasing my butterfly with my hatpin. But when I make my hand into a fist and think about it, I can't be lonely. Because there are seven billion different butterflies.

Today I talked to a friend who's heard that butterfly metaphor. I've been telling him for a while to stop trying to club my butterfly. So I called him this morning to apologize for dropping anvils on his butterfly, thinking it was self-defense. And he said he'd like it a lot better if he thought that his dragonfly was playing with my butterfly. And I said, "The bottom line is we're all friends." And he said, "The bottom line is we all are." So you learn something new every day.

I've been working at the Crisis Clinic for years. I've talked to lots of teenagers and lots of adults. And every single person, even the craziest of the crazies, has their own language and their own butterfly.

There's no language of Teenagers and there aren't six steps to talking to us. My story and my language is different from each of yours. But I can feel this, and I believe this is there in you guys, too. And that's what makes me able to talk to anybody. I just try. And I keep in mind that in the scheme of things, when some people seem way ahead or way behind or way out there, we're all really just sitting on my thumbnail, somewhere between complete egotism and complete awareness, chasing our various butterflies.

Spring 1997

On Wednesday, I went to Evergreen. I bought penny candy and a pack of American Spirits and I walked into the forest there. Down the path to the little wooden bridge over the creek. And I stood on the bridge and looked at a log that lay across the little stream. Someone had taken rocks from the stream and lined them up like little multicolored frogs across the log.

I took off both my boots and my socks and set them down on the edge of the bridge pointing up the creek. Then I jumped onto the bank and climbed onto that log and walked across it barefoot, nimbly, so that only one of the rocks fell into the water. I climbed over other logs and other rocks. I squatted in the pebbles and fished interesting rocks out of the stream for myself. I cleaned them and held them and put them in my pocket. Then I stood like Huck Finn with my jeans rolled up on a sturdy log, with my back to the bridge and my two empty little brown boots. I sang to the forest. I hummed. I made up waltzes and sang them in a husky voice. I belted out Russian drinking songs. Opened my mouth wide and sang loud and didn't notice when a young man came up behind me and listened. And after he walked over the bridge, I sang more. My feet never got cold in the creek water, and the wet pebbles, and the moss on the top of the logs. They never got cold until I picked my way back to the bridge and began to put my socks and shoes back on.

Spring 1997

Someone has taken rocks
and lined them across the log
like multicolored frogs.
Someone with blunt, brown fingers.
Feel the wakefulness of water in my nostrils.
See fading footprints in the mud.
I jump onto the moist bank
walk across the log barefoot
nimbly
so that only one rock falls into the water
with a plop
and I'm leaping and skipping toward the source of the creek
in silence
in anticipation
happily wet-ankled
and smiling.

I think my soul is nomadic. I've always stared upward at airplanes cutting white paths through the sky and wondered where they're going. I've always turned my head a little to listen out of one ear to the people speaking in Spanish behind me on the bus. I've always stayed awake all night on the long silent car rides across Montana and Wyoming, watching the muscles of hills in the moonlight, watching the lights of small towns fade into the darkness behind me, watching the infinite bald stripe of highway connect eastern horizon to western horizon. I've always been jealous of migratory birds.

I remember the smells of travel. The smell of gas station bathrooms. The smell of stale airplane air. The smell of redwoods. The smell of dry, red earth. New York City smells like motor oil and perspiration and hot dogs. The Great Salt Lake smells like rotten eggs. Prague smells like nighttime and gardenias. Iowa smells like drying cow dung and grass. Vladivostok smells like breathing, moving, musky bodies, but it also smells like the ocean. Yuzhno-Sakhalinsk smells like snow and coal dust and tears.

I remember the flight from Anchorage to Seattle on the way back home from Russia. Flying south over the Canadian coast, everything was dark. Flying south in that plane, my stomach started to ache, not the ache of motion sickness or indigestion, a deep spine-breaking pain, knotting itself around my belly and into my bowels and climbing into my throat. And in the midst of that pain, the colors of dawn. Beneath me the sun began to rise. A purple crease appeared in the blackness of night sky and violet light began to bleed up at us until we could see the flaming silhouettes of clouds. Then the water began to shine and I realized we were flying over Puget Sound. The water beneath us began to reflect pink streaks, and soon we could see islands in that water, and gradually we could make out the forms of evergreen trees on those islands, everything swept with the rose-light of dawn. Even the mountains turned pink with the sunrise reflected on snow.

And I began to sob. The sky turned blue and the whole full orb of the sun climbed out of the mountains. I sobbed in all that radiance, in the midst of the most glorious sunrise I'd ever seen, because it wasn't enough.

My mother hugged me at the airport and she was crying too, crying and hugging me and smiling. I didn't tell her that I was crying with the kind of confused rage and terror that our gerbil felt after a week of freedom when we found it behind the water heater, picked it up by the tail, and plopped it back into its cage.

I hated Olympia. I wanted to leave. I wanted to swim back to Russia across the Pacific. Olympia smelled like rot. Olympia smelled like the saturated white bodies of dead worms in a mud puddle. Olympia smelled like a cage with wood chips and gerbil droppings in it. And in the corner, on the motionless metal wheel, the matted fur and stiffly curled claw of a dead thing.

There were the trees, but there were the vast raw clear-cut scars. There were people, but we all knew each other's stories and forgot how to be curious anymore. There were mountains, but I couldn't look at the Olympics because they looked like the mountains in Russia, but farther away. Big boats came into Budd Inlet with Russian writing on the side, and some of the sailors got off and drank beer on benches in Sylvester Park or squatted in doorways like they squatted in the doorways of their homes. But the big boats were gone after a while, and I was still standing on the sidewalk in the town I grew up in.

Maybe it was finally the trees who told me to stay. Or maybe going to college in my hometown was just the path of least resistance. Maybe it was the need to be near my mother without being in her nest. Maybe going to Evergreen was just the best way to be different from my economics-major-high-achiever-khaki-and-high-heels-Yalie-corporate sister and brother. I don't know why I stayed. But one day I knew I had to. It was the same day I demanded detention for skipping class, instead of making big sad eyes and blaming it on depression. It was the same day I decided I wanted to be an artist and a writer and I didn't give a shit if I was mediocre and I didn't give a shit if I starved to death and I didn't give a shit if my whole damn high school turned and pointed and laughed in my face. So I tried as hard as I had ever tried to do anything in high school and I graduated early, tooth and nail, applied to Evergreen, found a dorm room, and I moved. And now Olympia smells different.

Olympia smells like trees. It smells like huckleberries squished on my thumb. It smells like rain, evaporating off rooftops, oozing over the streets, simmering in puddles on the soccer fields, scooting down into the moss and over the arches and coils of roots. Olympia smells like garlic and tofu cheese on the pizza that Neil pulls out of the oven with a wild grin. It smells like salt water. It smells like a cloud of pot smoke rising up from the hip joint of Cooper Point. It smells like the cedars, the serene giant draping cedars talking silently to the middle of my belly. It smells like bare feet and mud. It smells like half-empty beer cans stacked on a table on a Wednesday at noon. It smells like the little bouquet of dandelions, daisies, and bleeding hearts someone left outside my door this morning. It smells like my mother, across town, in the backyard with the parsley, counting the thirty days since she's seen me and wondering when I'll call home.

In a year or two, or maybe next winter, I'll go to Brazil. I'll leave. But when I leave I will not be escaping. I will kiss the trees goodbye one by one. And I will smile across the water at the Olympics. I'll ride out Evergreen Parkway to Cooper Point Road and turn right. I'll ride up over the rises and dips of that road that I've been riding over all my life through the cedars and past the barn. I'll lean out the window when I pass my old high school and scream "Ha Ha Ha! Fuck You! Fuck You!" just for old times' sake. I'll get on Highway 101 and when it reaches I-5 I'll either go north towards the airport or south towards Mexico.

When I leave, I'll leave laughing. I'll come back to talk to the trees and to play chess with my dad. I'll come back to see my mother, who will talk to me like I'm a woman instead of a little girl. And to my college friends. And to swim naked in Puget Sound at night. And I won't be afraid to come back, like I've always been afraid before. I'll cry, but I'll be smiling, and I'll hug my mom.

I've always crushed the flowers while staring at migratory birds. Now I am learning to notice the smell of the trees.

Spring–Fall 1997

His eyes are bright Crayola-crayon sky blue. He's still got the same green and black pair of shoes on his feet that he was wearing in the parking lot the day I met him. He has at least 650 different laughs. He can smile with just the corners of his lips and the corners of his eyes when he has a secret or when he's full of mischief. It makes me wonder if he's thinking about something funny, or if he has a secret, or if he's just sitting there listening to the breeze floating in and out of his ears.

This place could be a fairyland sometimes. When the full moon is breathing down milky light from above the tops of the cedar trees. When there is just a flaming sliver of the sun above the western horizon and shadows grow like slithering tentacles across the field. When you can see shadows of people materializing and dissolving in the mist under a streetlight a few dorms down. This place could be an achingly green, glistening, lichen-covered heaven with pinkie-sized brownies nested in every stump and trolls down beneath us digging tunnels through the earth. The raindrops sound like elf-drums.

Maybe that's what made Neil wander his way here from the East Coast and nestle in under the Douglas firs and the roofs of Evergreen's dorms. Maybe it was the elf-drums and the ten thousand raindrop-prisms refracting the harsh light of Reality and speckling it with rainbows. Even his name sounds like an elf name: Cornelius. Mostly his friends call him Homie. Mostly he calls his friends Homie or Hoss or Cuz.

My understanding of Neil's story is a confusing series of gaps and bright dabs of color, dappled with doubt as to which stories are truth and which are fiction. I don't know how much of the ambiguity is his subtle guardedness and how much is the acid he used to take and how much is his addition of fantasy and humor to everything he says. He tells everything in vignettes. He lets information out in tiny spurts and it has to be caught and sifted and distilled.

He left home when he was thirteen. He avoids direct questioning about things like that. Like what he means when he says his mom was crazy. Ask him a question he doesn't want to answer and you'll wonder if he even heard you, or he'll answer with something vague as his voice gets distant and he looks away and changes the subject to *The Simpsons.*

He lived in a tree on the coast of California for a year. He showed me a photograph of it, crawling and spraddling its way along a hillside. He lived in the woods for a while when he came to Evergreen, and he knows which plants to pick and which mushrooms to eat. I think in his eyes, living under a tree seems easier than getting a job and an apartment.

He fits in here, where they had to cut trees down to make room for buildings instead of planting trees around the buildings as sterile landscaping. He fits in, sheltered by water and fresh air and tree trunks. Spent part of his childhood canoeing alone in the woodsy part of New Jersey. There were blue terrapins everywhere, he says, and I can imagine his round eyes reflected in the water. Those eyes still get wide when he talks about blue terrapins. Elf eyes. I wonder what the turtles thought looking back up at him.

He even has elf-drums of his own. A big one the color of sun-dried tomatoes and another big red one with stickers all over it. There are butterfly stickers. A sticker that says "Pussy Eating Vegan Dyke." A sticker that looks like the "Enjoy Coke" logo but when you read it says "Enjoy Life" instead. A big obvious sticker that says "Support your local fools."

His hands are callused and hard and brown from playing the drum. When he plays, he tilts his head to one side, his eyes get cloudy and they don't focus on anything. It's as if the tiny pure goblin inside of Neil turns his body off so that it can speak directly through the drum with no distraction. He can make eight thousand different noises with his hands on that drum. His hands—brown hands, rough hands—move so fast they look like giant moth's wings. Neil says he thinks all the sounds are already in the drum, wanting to come out, and his job is to find them.

He says there are three real ways to make people feel good. You can give them good beats to dance to, you can give them good food to eat, and you can heal their bodies. He doesn't pay rent, living in the dorms with friends. But he plays the drum, turns on Bob Marley and

dances around like a chicken, cooks overflowing woks full of potatoes and garlic and tofu (rarely cleans the kitchen), and is always
willing to trade a back massage. In this mossy, mist-cloaked unreal-
ity, Neil is surviving just fine on currencies other than money.

Once he grabbed the Fool card up out of a deck of tarot cards and
explained it like this: "See, the Fool can dance on the edge of a cliff
and not fall off . . . because he's held up by the force of his own
bliss."

He laughs a lot, hysterical wild-eyed crazy laughter. He says once
he and a carful of friends got hit by another car and flipped over
while driving through the redwoods. "When we got out," he says, "I
was cracking the funniest jokes ever. The world could be about to end
and I'd be cracking jokes."

He'll come running into the room, eyes bugged out, with a wide-
mouthed expression that is half laugh, half gasp of sheer terror, and
shout out his latest observation, or something crazy that happened,
or act like a monster and try to strangle people. We laugh. We all get
bug-eyed expressions of our own. Or sometimes people won't be
quite as willing to laugh, and we'll watch him bemusedly and somebody will say, "What are you doing, Neil?"

halloween '98
neil as hobo

In the middle of a giggling, ludicrous debate he says, "You get joy from laughing at the fool's pain!" And he laughs at his ingenuity, but I think maybe there was a little honesty behind that comment.

The way I see it, there are some people you think are cool, people you admire, people you think are smart, people who are witty, people who are talented. You wish you could be like those people. You try to impress those people. You show them how cool, smart, witty, and talented you are.

The way I see it, there are other people who make you feel good. With those people you never think about being cool. You never feel honored to be in their presence. You never try to impress them. They don't wear their talents like costumes. Those people can teach you a lot if you pay attention to them.

Neil. Sleeps till at least two in the afternoon. Is addicted to cigarettes, coffee, and *The Simpsons*. Rarely combs his hair. Makes hackey sacks out of hemp and popcorn. Says "I'll be back in a minute," and doesn't show up till morning.

Laughs at people's jokes. Gives everybody hugs. Remembers to call up and scream into the phone when he hasn't seen someone for a few days. Furrows his brow when something seems not right with someone and says, "Hey, buddy, how're you doing?" Opens up people's notebooks and writes things like, "Funky loose comet star sweet wet air animal on light don't stop now, we land of planet fall still luck."

Knows how to cultivate mushrooms, where to find the best sage, how to shine abalone with the oil from your face, how to rub the backs of knees until they feel like marshmallows, that garlic is a good remedy for almost anything.

Gives his friends back massages to heal their bodies. Cooks them good food to eat. Gives them beats to dance to.

Neil makes you feel good.

1998–2000

My Mother

This woman knows the smells of corn and soil
and milkweed leaves and bleeding hearts and soap
and garlic sautéed brown in olive oil
and salads made with pears and cantaloupe.
With silver hair her face is like the moon.
Showed me all the music in the stars.
Taught me how to keep my voice in tune
when we would sing together in the car.
I feel her always watching, seeking me.
It seems we're walking on adjacent trails.
I think her eyes still tint the things I see
but both of us are blinded by our veils.
I think I'll tear mine off after a while
and pray that when she sees my face she'll smile.

Winter 1998

Dear Mom,

I'm sitting in L.A. at dawn, looking out at a stagnant swimming pool and a rainbow of flowers. I had a dream about you last night. You haunt me because I see such a light coming out of you, but your light is a different color than my light. And I want to whisper, "Don't be scared," and I want to pretend that I can become your idea of me. But I can't.

I know I scare you. But being on a tightrope, with a safety net and a costume, doesn't work for me. I want to paint my face with the color of your eyes but I don't want to wear your costume. When I look at you I can see music. I can see a song playing on your face, in your voice when you talk to me, when you talk to my friends. And I'm grateful. I fall down and sob over that song. I cry with gratitude because you can make that song for so many people.

I have to do things that scare you. I'm sorry I scare you. I hope I'm not ugly in your eyes. But I want to write and I want to see. And what would I write about if I only stayed within the doll's house, the flower-world I grew up in? What kind of a writer would I be? What kind of seer would I be, if I stayed in the prism I grew up in? I would hear the bird-voices like kazoos and xylophones. I would see the rainbows and sparkles in everyone's eyes.

But I wouldn't be able to accept ugliness that was different than my ugliness. I wouldn't be able to see pain that was beyond my pain. Our pain. I would be beautiful. I would be strong like you and I would have a smile like yours. And that strength and that smile are mountains and cornfields and daisies and milkweed. And I shudder and I sob at the beauty of all that.

You brought the soil with you from Iowa. You brought the bare fecund soil and you passed it on to me. You gave me a love that was so unconditional, that is so bare and poignant and forgiving and brown and soft like the soil . . . that I have to plant things in it. I have to plant cacti and palm trees and sticker bushes and daisies and pumpkins. I have to let the wild ginger and ferns take root and grow there.

You gave me a potential. I grew up with faith. And letting in everything that I can let in without breaking myself is the only justice I can do to all that soil. You gave me a flower bed and a cornfield and a lake and a whitish-gray house and cedar trees, and I won't let those things break apart. You gave me a planting ground, and because it's so dank and warm and solid, I have to challenge it with the hardiest and the most fragile plants I can find.

I love you, but I'm growing out of what you gave me. I'm saving it inside me and growing outwards. Thank you. Thank you. Let me fight my monsters. I love you.

You made me. You made me.

Winter 1998

I was standing ankle-deep in sand
staring at the place where my feet disappeared
anchored like cement boots.
and the waves were angry giants waiting to eat me
and the sky was the ceiling of a shopping mall
and the only sound was bubbles popping
as all the ideas in my head exploded
and turned out to be empty.
and when thin water scudded up against my shin
I wondered if I lay down
and opened my mouth
would it wash out all the mud and sludge
within my drooping belly?
and as I struggled to find something tortured
to scream at the muddled universe
a hermit crab crawled up and pointed a claw at me
and said "Why so defensive?"
and thinking about that one took a moment
and I shifted my eyes from side to side
and shifting them noticed all the gulls
diving and dancing in the salt air.
and then I heard songbirds
behind me in the brambles
and so I decided to whisper a question
instead of shouting a curse
and I whispered timidly.
breathed it out

like kissing my dad's forehead goodnight
expecting it to pop
like the other bubbles
when it hit the air.

Spring 1998

Something in me is very mindful of the behavior of water. It might be that I grew up where a creek emptied into Eld Inlet and I spent my days chasing snakes and floating toy boats in rivulets until the tide brought salt water in to cover my playground. It might be the conversations I had with bluegills beneath the swimming dock at my grandparents' lake cabin in Minnesota. It might be the understanding that we all come from creatures that crawled out of the ocean; we're made of water, and in some sense our thirst and the water in our bodies is the factor that makes us like plants, like animals, like each other. At any rate, I dream of rivers. I take hours in the bathtub. I shout, "Hi, Mama!" when I arrive at the ocean. I get parched and neurotic when there are too many consecutive sunny days, and I sometimes inexplicably weep while washing the dishes. Water is my symbol of transformation and cleansing and emotion. So it makes sense that an image of water was the catalyst that set me to work, translating my values about my role as an artist into action.

I was in Top Foods in early April when I was beginning my contract on the artist in the community. I was walking through the meat section and all I could think about was this article I'd read about the infrastructure in Moscow. The city is heated by boiling water flowing through underground pipes. Because of the economic depression in Russia, the pipes can't be repaired. So the pipes burst and sections of soil become saturated with boiling water. People, little children, walking along the sidewalk in Moscow fall through into sinkholes and die in boiling water. I was crying in Top Foods, surrounded by every variety of dead cow you could ever want, carrying around this image of boiling to death. And the whole opulent array of Top Foods seemed like a big pink bow on the head of everything that is unjust and frivolous and neglectful about those of us with power and money. And it made me sick to my stomach to think about how self-satisfied I was that morning at having written a nice little poem about raindrops on cedar trees and having a whole quarter to talk to artists about their lives.

I started the collaborative art project with the resolve that I can't exist in a bubble of creativity and poetry and raindrops. If people in Moscow can learn to live in a minefield, then I, with my senselessly privileged existence, can translate creativity into action that counteracts the monster neglect.

I began to read about the National Endowment for the Arts, looking for a cause that I felt strongly about. In the 1998 *Arts Education Policy Review*, composer, public radio producer, and NEA grant panel member Daniel Gawthorp comments, "We need to change the focus of our attention from a distant unconcerned Congress to local communities, and start changing people, one at a time, by the strength of our examples and our convictions. We need to quit demanding leadership from Washington, from the very folks who got us where we are now, and start exhibiting some leadership of our own . . ." Gawthorp's article made me think about personal accountability. Thinking it over, I realized that the most powerful actions I can take toward societal improvement will have to start very close to home, arising not from the need to leave a mark on history, but from empathy and sincere understanding of the places in my life where neglect exists.

The first time I went into the Successful Choices class at Capital High School, I spent a lot of time talking about my convictions about the importance of art and the need for youth to speak out on their own behalf in order to improve the community's view and support of them. Then I asked some questions about what they wanted from the community. Most of the responses to my questions were "drugs and alcohol." I found myself getting responses more from the teachers than from the students. I was nervous and I felt like I had to talk in order to demonstrate my own intelligence, that I knew what I was talking about, that I was in control of the situation.

Upon leaving the classroom, I felt this immense amount of pressure. Pressure to be a role model. Pressure to have an impact. When I took a step back and thought about it, I realized that being a role model and having an impact are not things you can contrive. They just happen. It became much easier to work with the students once I took a deep breath and acknowledged the fact that I do not have any answers to the questions that I was asking them.

This quarter I started out wanting to prove myself. I made conclusions almost before I asked questions. Specters of children falling through sidewalks kept reappearing in my head and whispering, *Why isn't this you? What are you doing that is so important? What makes you deserve so many advantages?* And my ego couldn't stand to pause and hear the silence after those questions, so I started shouting out, *I support the arts! I build community using art! I work with at-risk youth! I help! I help! I help!*

Spring 1998

This quarter started with boiling water. If I lived in Bosnia or Rwanda or who knows where else, needless death wouldn't be a distant symbol to me. It wouldn't be a metaphor. It would be a reality.

And I have no right to this metaphor. But I use it to console myself. To give a fraction of meaning to something enormous and needless.

This realization. This realization that I will live my life in this world where I have privileges.

I can't cool boiling waters in Russia. I can't be Picasso. I can't be Jesus. I can't save the planet single-handedly.

I can wash dishes.

1998

Things I'm doing and working on as a result of spring quarter 1998:

1. Write three pages every morning.

2. Spend two hours a week alone, consciously taking the artist in me on a date, looking for things to play with and observe and reflect upon.

3. When I feel blocked, stuck, or frustrated creatively:

• Write down the feelings of self-doubt in detail, without trying to be constructive, so I can get them out and then move on.

• Find old pieces of writing or old pictures and go back over them.

• Take the biggest creative risk I can think of and try something totally new.

• Think of universal qualities that are important to me like grace, loneliness, humility, compassion—whatever—and try to express them through images.

• Write about why I love writing.

• Think of the things I am thankful for and write or make pictures of giving thanks.

• Give myself permission to write the most atrociously terrible, mediocre thing that has ever been written and then fill two pages, without stopping to read what I am writing.

• Make lists of words and sounds I like, things that make me happy, things that make me sad, people I have met, places I have visited, foods I have eaten—whatever.

• Write about the things about me that are false and the things I want to let go of—then identify the things that are left.

• Write down all the questions in my head. Don't bother trying to answer them.

• Go back and read the books that have inspired me, like *Letters to a Young Poet* and *The Artist's Way*. Write down hopeful quotes.

4. Continue working with the Successful Choices class at Capital High School next year. Develop a video project with them that expresses whatever they want to express about themselves. As I

am working with them, focus on learning and sharing rather than teaching. Focus on asking questions and listening rather than having answers.

5. When my mind gets so cluttered that I am having trouble working effectively and listening compassionately, take the time to sit and listen to the thoughts in my head and my emotional reactions to them without trying to make sense of everything and without being swept away. Sit by the tracks instead of riding the train.

6. Focus on supporting the arts in my personal interactions with the people around me. Honor the everyday creative and artistic acts of my friends, my family, and the people I run into in the course of a day.

7. Support cultural/intellectual diversity and ecological accountability through my habits as a consumer. Buy coffee at Batdorf & Bronson instead of Starbucks. Buy books at Traditions or Orca instead of Barnes & Noble. Shop at the Food Co-op. Spend money on postcards by local artists and pieces by acquaintances who are pursuing art, instead of buying posters of masterpieces by dead people to decorate my house.

8. Avoid using creativity as an excuse for being disorganized, neglecting my physical health, being late, engaging in unnecessary drama, smoking cigarettes, and other instances of weakness. Defy negative stereotypes of artists by addressing these opportunities for improvement and using my creativity to develop more stable habits and routines.

9. Go to Belize this summer. Get some perspective. Learn about art, education, and survival in a very different setting. Have an experience there that will fuel my writing.

10. Take the Contested Realities program next year. Use it as an opportunity to develop video as another tool for creative expression, to continue working with youth and to analyze my sources of information more objectively/critically. Learn about current world problems and political economy so that gradually I can find informed ways to take action outside my immediate sphere of influence.

11. Stop mistaking self-sabotage for humility.

Rachel, you are desperate for a space of humility and purity of intention within yourself. When you get to that space in a healthy way you'll have more perspective than you've ever had before. It isn't supposed to be easy. It may take a long time. Try to cry. You don't need to control. Try to remember that humility is important to me because it's a comfort and a reality, not because it's a virtue.

May 10, 1998

Mama,
Happy Mother's Day 1998

You are my poet—
    maker.
You're the cannon I
    shoot from.
I keep your eyes
    in my shirt pocket and
    try them on to look at
    daffodils.
I am the bun that
    turned into a kumquat
    when I came out
    of your oven.
Sometimes for a minute
    I understand what
    God is when I'm looking
    at you.

Thanks Mama.
Rachel

August 1, 1998

I've been thinking about all of you fishing off of your island at the top side of the globe as I go fishing off of my newfound paradise in the Caribbean. I arrived by speedboat two days ago at Tobacco Cay, off the coast of Belize. It's about five acres in area, and only five families live here. Once I step off the dock and slip on a snorkel, I'm instantly immersed in the landscape of coral reefs. I've come face to face with barracuda, gazed across mountains of brain coral and lacy, purple sea-fans at bear-sized tarpin, and stalked spotted eagle rays weaving through small herds of parrot fish. I especially thought of y'all today as I went out fishing. I caught a fish that would demolish anything that hangs out in Cedar Lake: a barracuda a little more than two feet long. It was lucky I had an experienced fisherman at my elbow—otherwise my pole and I would be somewhere at the bottom of the ocean, trailing limply through the reef.

Aside from the fishing, I've been writing myself into a stupor and filling up microscopically-written journal pages with conversations with the ocean and pelicans and palm trees. After my group leaves, the solitude may lead to irrevocable insanity. If I come back to the states wearing a headdress of barracuda teeth and talking like "Nell," I hope you'll all be committed to nursing me back to normalcy. I hope all of you are having a good time. I miss you and look forward to spending time with the numerous wonderful branches of my family when I return to temperate regions. That is, assuming I turn down the offers of marriage and come back (you'll be proud to hear I've been told I'd be a good farmer's wife). Just kidding mom . . . breathe deeply. I hope you're all making do as best you can without me; I imagine it must be very, very difficult. Hee-hee! So goodbye for now. My dinner is ready. Big wet kisses to all.

the amazing rachel

Summer 1998

Dear Mom, Dad, and Sarah,

I'm sitting on the deck of the Swinging Armadillo Bar and Hammock Lounge with a warm breeze pouring in off the ocean. After our first week here, the beauty of sweltering sun on gentle Caribbean surf turned into the beauty of lightning illuminating huge blue clouds in the night and frequent squalls bringing in violent bursts of rain. I can see Venus hanging in the southeastern sky and my friend Goody pointed out the Big Dipper to me last night, which is almost indistinguishable here because of all the extra stars. When it's clear, I watch the meteors and dim satellites inch their way between the stars. A few nights ago we went to a new national park a little to the north to look for birds and crocodiles—a mangrove swamp where a river empties into the Caribbean. We paddled in canoes with two Garifuna guides through this maze of dark channels and tangled mangroves forming slow-growing islands. Much to my disappointment, we didn't encounter any crocodiles, but trails of phosphorescence skidded out from our paddles, miniature reflections of the shooting stars overhead—and flocks of egrets and pelicans and white herons rose out of the trees as we slid by. On the way home there were fireflies.

Being here builds up the population of flora and fauna and creature friends I store up in my brain to fuel poetry. I have particular things in my brain that are my angles: fireflies, meteors, pterodactyls, white herons, phosphorescence, manta rays—I'm madly in love with those things (I forgot cedar trees—of course cedar trees, always cedar trees). I can't really explain it; maybe everyone has some sort of symbolic cartography of their soul complete with dirt roads and plant life and marine animals . . . or maybe this letter will just make it that much clearer that something went awry genetically and produced an inexplicably loony third child. I think Cedar Lake (even the loons on the lake) and the amount of geographic soul-area it has in the people in our family shows that I'm not the only sorry, sentimental fool who invests in places and animals with almost religious significance, and if it is a genetic malady, it's been present for generations.

Summer 1998

Came back from the cays today and wound up in a hotel room in Dangriga, watching cable television and waiting for my stomachache to go away. Happened to flip on C-SPAN.

I gather the U.S. has dropped cruise missiles on Afghanistan and Sudan. I gather Clinton has admitted to having sex with "that intern." People are calling in from all over the U.S. to comment. And half of the people don't even seem to know that missiles were dropped—they're fixated on Clinton's tawdry sex life. One man actually quotes *Wag the Dog* to explain what's going on—like that's where we're gonna get the real inside information. A young boy voice calls up and is obviously reading a little prepared speech about Kenneth Starr being evil for embarrassing the president and keeping him from protecting the U.S. from the fascists. Everybody is conjecturing about the timing of the attack and calling for the president to resign.

And nobody says a word about how sad it is that people in this world have missiles dropping on them.

1998

This is my last night in Belize. Back in Hopkins. Back in the village where a new thatched temple has gone up and the palm trees stand in a line with their heads thrown back, gaping at the sky. This village of children, bobbing heads in the waves, riding three to a bicycle, singing, "If you're happy and you know it clap your hands." Pastel houses on four skinny legs. Red gravel streets. Lightning. Fireflies over the savannah. Blue fire in the water at night. Bundles of cocaine falling from the sky out on the horizon. Out toward Tobacco Cay.

I meet another beekeeper this week and realize I have to let my story go now. I wasn't expecting to meet another beekeeper, but he looked at me while he told us the rules, and I watched a giant bumblebee walk up his forearm while he lectured us in his basement. I'm not entirely superstitious. Mindful of meteors. I take my cues where I can get them.

He is a beekeeper. And he lives in his own Imaginary Tahiti and makes other people follow the rules there. He says you can do anything in five hours or less . . . if you know what you're doing. If that is true, I can let my story go without snapping under the weight of it. I need time limits. Stories are dangerous.

Colin.

I had heard of him. We always had a web of mutual friends. I recognize him in dreams, and in the daylight tell Eric, "I dreamed about your friend Colin the other night."

"I'm sorry," Eric says.

The first dream comes years before Colin and I go out the window together. I dream he is my date to a party. I dream we are too drunk to stand. The mothers of kids I went to preschool with arrive to slap joints out of people's fingers and watch us with angry, sagging eyes. Only I know they came for Colin. I beg him to run away. He will not leave and he clutches my arm so that I cannot leave. He leads me inside the party and we drink together, while the mothers wait to pounce on him.

The second dream comes only a month before we meet. I dream that Colin has been hired to kill me and my best friend from childhood. He drives a van with curtains and tinted windows. He drives us out into the hills while I plead with him. "Colin," I say, "I know you are a good person. You do not want to do this." He never says a word to me, but in the end he doesn't kill us. He shrinks us into finger-sized people, carries us into the crawl space of an abandoned house, and hides us in the bowl of a cobweb-laced toilet. Years later a stranger finds us there, still alive, but finger-sized, and transparent-gray as deep-sea fish that pop if they go near the surface.

Stories go rancid inside you if you don't let them out. They take root, bits of pencil lead that break off in the palm of your hand. Your skin curls across them and they disperse up the network of your veins, from fingertip to elbow to throat, and turn to poison. I have been hoarding this story. Terrified. Now I have a time limit. Any day now I might disappear under the gangrene of too many hoarded stories. If Colin dies it will be from a constellation of rotting stories buried inside his skin. A wild red iron fish fighting to get out.

Of course it'll be the bees that do it, finally. But that is the simple truth. I think the bees are just operatives of all those angry stories. I'm getting ahead of myself. "Oh, Colin," I whimper. My story is a comedy.

Eric buys five or six bottles of liquor. I never drank with him before. Just read poems with him and smoked between the nurse logs behind the community college.

We drink on opposite sides of his split-pea-soup couch. Our toes tangle on the middle cushion. Eric is a tall, lanky creature with a fierceness that hangs all over him like extra clothes. His presence is tentacled. I am drunk when the cluster of strangers comes in. It is dusk, that summer kind of dusk—high and thin and scented of smoke. We don't turn lamps on. The strangers' faces are blotted out, replaced with stars of reflected sunset and strips of shadow, like badly developed photographs. Colin comes in with them. Colin is like the shadows of them. He is quiet, a silhouette. There is a fluttering quality, as if he is made all of cheap fabric that the breeze passes through. I recognize him, surprised at the awkwardness of him. Wax paper. An animated piece of origami. He was more solid in the dreams than in real life. He could be just my hallucination.

I go to him. The others forget to talk to us. Our conversation trickles beneath theirs. "I'm Rachel."

"Pleasure to meet you, Rachel."

His voice like hinges. The slow whine of something opening and closing again. The others talk somewhere far above our heads. "I've had dreams about you."

"I'm sorry."

Our dialogue isn't so important. The important thing is the proportions of it. From the moment I introduce myself, it is as if we are two baby rattlesnakes whispering to each other beneath a thatch of sage. Eric and his cluster of guests are an army of cowboys on horses in the open desert. Our conversation is infinitesimal—a hiss lost in the wind. To us, their conversation is so big, so high above us, that it's nothing but weather patterns. Words so loud they aren't words anymore, just the indistinct drumroll of thunder.

We are all very drunk. When I notice the other people again, Eric is fighting with a thin curly-haired guy. They are locked up around each other. They tumble to the floor, roll together, rise again, and flail out against the walls. They move together like one palsied animal.

Colin looks at me. "I'm getting out of here."

The window is situated in the wall only a few inches from the door. The door stands open into dusk, waiting for us. I like to think we slither out of Eric's house, scuttle out unnoticed beneath their feet. We don't. We are life-size again. Anyway, it's impossible that we slither, because Colin doesn't take the door. He reaches it, veers, and springs out of the open window. Without thinking, I jump out after him.

I fall and I fall and I fall.

Outside, shadows weight the air. I scamper across the street to sniff the irises. I take his hand and lead him across parking lots to the bowling alley. His hand is cool and damp and it hangs in mine without ever committing to it. Inside the bowling alley, I show off for him. I steal someone's ball and heave it down the lane, bare feet stripping the wax off the wood floors. He tilts his head and watches me. There is something about his lips that I will never be able to put to words. A child's ripe pout and the traces of a smile. No matter what he feels, Colin always looks amused. *Oh, Colin, oh my Colin of the innocent face.*

I tuck my feet up under me in the plastic seats and interrogate him. He tells me he used to be a beekeeper. He tells me he's allergic to bees. "It's like that, you know. The more times you're stung, the worse your allergy. So finally I just stopped."

I want to know what it means to be a beekeeper, and he tells me the stories of trucking around the country. Different seasons in different places. Crates unloaded by forklift in the night when the bees aren't active. Alfalfa pollination. Almonds across California. Buying queens that come stapled in tiny packets like cheap jewelry. Suits and masks and smoke to calm the bees down.

Colin has a doll's eyes. Blue as a bad fairy. They do not twinkle, blink, widen, narrow, smile. I am a fisherman. I troll for stories. They come to me out of air. Strangers next to me at the lunch counter. I reel them in. I go hunting for challenges. The wild red iron fish that hides beneath the bank. Colin's eyes leak no free stories.

It isn't every day you meet a former beekeeper. And it isn't every day you meet a beekeeper who's allergic to bees.

Everyone is gone but Eric when we come back. Eric is surly. He pulls me aside in his kitchen and tells me he wanted to hang out with me alone. "You're a fuckup, Colin," he says occasionally throughout the evening, and, "You're always gonna be a fuckup, Colin."

Colin is skinny as kindling, loosely put together; we could scatter him apart if we blew hard enough. I fight Eric off with my eyes. He turns on the TV and he glares at me, as I scoot closer to Colin on that split-pea-soup couch. In the end I fall asleep with my head in Colin's lap.

"Can I touch your hair?" He wakes me up to ask if he can touch my hair. Eric is gone. There is one lamp on. I sit up. He takes pieces of my hair. Plucks up just a strand at a time. Holds them loosely, sets them back against my cheek. *Oh Colin. How could I resist? How could I resist someone with doll's eyes who wants nothing more in the world than to touch pieces of my hair?*

He asks if he can sleep next to me on the couch. "Only sleep, nothing else. I promise, Rachel."

We fall asleep crammed together on the couch. Or at least I sleep. I wake occasionally in the night and his fingers are still moving, unraveling strands of hair. Holding them, and setting them down again. I wake up in the morning and he is watching me with his expressionless doll's eyes. He pauses for a moment when my eyes open. Quizzical, he holds on to a section of my hair for a minute before he regains himself, and drapes it carefully across my cheek.

This first morning I wake up drenched in the smell of him. I am stained with it. The smell of lemon soap and Camel Filters. *Oh, Colin. I am stained with it. I am stained with it.*

It's a few days later when I let him kiss me. We are out dancing. I discover that he dances like a slow marionette. A heavy marionette. A praying mantis. I run out to dance next to him so he will not stand out. So he will not have the feeling of being onstage. So that no one will laugh at him. Maybe it is because he's so skinny. From the very beginning I try to protect him. Maybe that fluttering quality or his child-lips. I stand between him and the wind. I use my body to create a lee. I wait for the wild red iron fish to make its way out. I clear out a calm place.

He stretches his neck to kiss me. I am embarrassed. I kiss him anyway. He has the strangest kiss. He takes a very dainty bite out of me. It's a half kiss. It teases. He licks the edge of an ice cream cone, then withdraws. I wither. It is the kiss of eternal withdrawal. *Colin.* I fall and I fall and I fall.

He tells me he will try anything. He is blank pages. All he knows is beekeeping. And he can't keep bees anymore, so he'll try anything. We go to the Thai restaurant with mirrors all over the walls. We whisper about the other customers. "Something suspicious about that man's tie."

"Mmm. Very suspicious." *The creak of his voice. Something opened carefully and quickly closed again.* "She's watching us over her newspaper."

They are all spies. Colin and I, we're onto them. Always poised to make a run for it. We shift our eyes back and forth over the soup bowls, leather shoes, half-empty water glasses. Yes, half empty. "Those shoes are the shoes of a Commie."

"Pinko scum."

He sleeps in my bed every night and plucks at my hair. In the mornings I watch him sleep, and grow jealous of his eyelids. They are wide as tulip petals. Iridescent. Made of insects' wings. I want to slip inside his eyelids and spy on him. I still haven't seen an emotion in his blue doll's eyes. He sleeps with his back to me. He curls away on my bed to his own private sleep that doesn't involve me. I climb over his back in the morning and take an inventory of his sleep-features. I count his eyelashes. He sleeps with his lips blanched upward in amusement. He sleeps always at the brink of a laugh.

Time limits change the whole landscape. I have borrowed Colin for a moment; a twitch of his jawbone becomes a catastrophe.

After a week of sleeping side by side, I take off his shoes one night and make love to him.

His shoes are always spotless. Black suede with thick white rubber soles. I would have ruined them in a day. Later he will explain about his shoes. How they are a trick. A disguise. The one thing about him that stays clean. I turn on the lamp and kneel on the floor of my apartment. He sits on the bed, watches me without moving his eyes, tilts his chin to one side. I pick at the knots with my fingernails. I unravel the bows. We are silent. I unweave the laces halfway down the tongue. I poke my fingers in by his ankles. I draw out his feet. I pause to arrange his shoes, parallel, beneath my bed. I remove his socks. The rubbery smell of foot sweat with undertones of lemon soap and Camel Filters. I unearth his feet. Long ridges of tendons divide them into exquisite triangles. I hold his left foot in both hands, and when I place my thumb just there, just exactly there between the hills on the sole, his long toes curl and uncurl rapidly.

I have discovered the only section of Colin's body that shows its reactions. I fall and I fall and I fall. I am holding back tears. I kiss his toes, every toe. I kiss the hairs on his toes. I kiss the miniature sunsets in his toenails, I kiss his heels. I am weeping into his ankles, the too-apparent bone structure. I am wiping my tears off with the hair on his shins. I am kissing his calves.

We roll together, two stick bugs, all skinniness and elbows until the angles fall off. In the end we are dragonflies, never anything so delicate. He sleeps with his back to me and I curl up around him with my ear between his shoulder blades, listening for a heartbeat.

In the morning I tell him we'll get fat together. It'll be beautiful. Two huge, billowing fat people. We'll have a contest. We'll start eating like swine. He narrows his eyes. "We won't even get out of bed to go to the bathroom."

"We'll eat chicken-fried steak and piss through tubes."

I discover him sleeping in my bed in the afternoon. I drop the groceries on the floor and clamber for his neck and cheeks. He wakes a little and shoves at me. The onions have rolled out across the floor and come to a rest under the rocking chair. "Colin, your neck tastes weird."

"Mmm."

"What's on your neck?"

"Almond honey."

"What?"

"Beekeeper's secret. Most people don't like it. Too bitter. Bees eat it, though."

"Why'd you put it on your neck?"

"Beekeeper's secret. Best thing for a sting."

"You got stung." Silence. "Are you okay?"

"Yes."

"What were you doing, Colin?"

He opens his eyes for one moment and looks at me, closes them, curls away from me. I feel something turn over inside me—an eel that I never noticed living in there. "I was just walking. It just got me."

"On the neck?"

"Just a freak thing, I guess."

I watch him. He doesn't move; he is folded up like origami under my blanket. "Was it really?"

"Yes."

"Okay," I say. *okay. okay. okay. okay.*

I retrieve the onions. I put the groceries in the refrigerator. I climb next to him on top of the blankets. I play with his hair. I forget to eat all day. We do not move from the bed until morning.

He hates coffee. Mornings when I go out for coffee, he brings cans of Coke. I discover his love for sweet things. We drink strawberry milkshakes together. He asks the waitress for extra whipped cream. He brings me cartons of caramel-laced ice cream. The fullness of his lips smudged with ice cream. He buys gas station cotton candy. The smell of it makes me gag as we walk along the sidewalks. He buys Skittles, gummy worms, marshmallow Easter candy past its expiration date. He buys two scratch-off lottery tickets on his way out of the diner. He rubs them with a quarter right there at the cash register. He doesn't wait to get to his car.

In bed at night I make fun of his knees and he makes out with his elbow. Of course his knees are gorgeous, knobby, rail-thin. Mesas rise out of his legs. I am piecing together the cartography of his body. I am bewitched. But I make fun of his knees. "Good God! Those are the most grossly deformed knees I've ever seen."

"You be quiet or I'm taking my elbow and blowing this joint." He closes his eyes and delivers the inside of his elbow an impassioned kiss. "Oh, sweet elbow."

"Damn slut elbow . . . Put those knees away somewhere, would you?"

He starts to giggle. We giggle together. I am waiting to catch sight of the wild red iron fish inside of this Colin. I believe in it. I stalk it.

I come home and find him in my apartment. He twitches. He expected me later. He sits at the edge of my bed, folded at right angles. A praying mantis. I greet him. He doesn't speak to me. He looks across the room at the crack where the wall meets the floor. His knee twitches. "Colin?"

His eyes zigzag across the crack where the wall meets the floor. "Colin?"

"Colin?"
"Colin?"

"Colin?"

"Colin?"

"Colin?"   "Colin?"   "Colin?"
                    "Colin?"   "Colin?"   "Colin?"

"Colin?"

"Colin?"

"Colin?"

"Colin?"

"Colin?"   "Colin?"

I want to cry but I can't. After the night when I cried on his feet I
will not be able to cry again until months after Colin has disappeared. I remove my shoes. I stand in front of him, barefoot. I kneel
down so I can interrupt his horizon, the crack between the wall and
the floor. I crouch there, barefoot. I stare at his glass doll eyes, with
my eyes tight and stretched and aching. I go closer. I touch him. I
touch his earlobe. His forearm. Try to wrap my arms around the vine
of his torso. He shrugs me away. He is stronger than he appears. I fly
back and crouch in the path of his eyes. I want to cry but I can't.

I writhe. I start when the streetlights flicker on outside my window. My apartment turns dark. I blink across the room at his silhouette. Finally, I hear the soft explosion of his spit. It snaps against the
floor.

I go to the light switch. We both blink at each other, our faces crin-
kled up. When my eyes adjust, I look where he spit. There, encased
in bubbles, is a yellow jacket. It shudders, wriggles seizing legs.
"Let's go get some ice cream," Colin says.

Now I begin to understand what it is to jump out a window with
a beekeeper. I understand now that there is a time limit. I understand that I have stolen Colin. Stolen my time with Colin. I take what
I can get.

I do not sleep. I memorize him, close my eyes, and memorize him
again. Some nights he comes late to my apartment with gauze taped

to his arm from emergency room needles. I freeze at the buzz of a housefly butting against the windowpane. Every morning I inventory all the parts of him. Round nostrils. Upturned nose. Eyelids. The cracks between his toes. His Lincoln Log thighs. I am perpetually losing him. He begins to apologize. He kisses me goodbye in the morning. I am frozen in my bed until he returns in the evening. I taste his whole body for traces of almond honey. I beg him to come with me to a frozen place empty of bees. "It's all I know, baby. It's all I know."

When I was a kid I would hide in the closet at my best friend's house when my parents came to get me. My friend would hide there too and we would hiss at each other to be quieter beneath rows of jumpers and OshKosh. When we were in kindergarten, we went to school in a church, and every day when spelling time came, we sprinted down into the sanctuary and hid under the furthest pews. We cackled down there. It was better than any kind of candy.

Everything between Colin and me unfolds beneath those church pews. One morning, I sense the sunlight outside and stand up on my bed to open the venetian blinds. I tease him about something, maybe laugh at something he said. The mattress throws me. I let go of the blinds, tumble over backwards, bounce off my bed, and land on the floor in an intricate reverse-somersault. I try to keep talking without missing a beat. Colin laughs, sitting up in my bed with his knees tucked close to his chest. He convulses with it. He closes his eyes against it. He bends his head down and wraps his arms around his legs and hugs himself. Holds himself as if he is afraid that laughter will shatter him. He curls up with it, ducks his head down, closes his eyes as if he wants to savor it, not let any part of it escape from him. I laugh too. The two of us. Him with emergency room gauze dangling from his elbow. I who can't leave my bed or eat during the day.

Colin's laugh startles me. My own laugh startles me. Stripes of sunlight sneak through venetian blinds. Origami people clutch themselves together against the floodwaters of laughter. *I can't say it right Colin. I can't say it right my Colin.* We stole this laughter in the morning. When you work within time limits, laughter in the morning is like the recession of a glacier. It turns epic.

I stay in my bed and watch the stripes of light change through the venetian blinds. After he is gone a few hours, and I can no longer convince myself that I'm asleep, the mariachis creep into my apartment with their mean guitars. I hear them laughing outside my door. But they frown as they parade in around my bed. Sometimes they fake sobs. Cover their teeth with their yellow nails to hide their laughter. They cuss in Spanish and glance at me to be sure I don't understand. They strum their guitars with flourishes, cock their wrists and bow their lips down like the painted frowns of circus clowns. They sing to me for hours. Infinite dirges. They slap rhythm on the bellies of their guitars, sometimes on the walls of my apartment, sometimes on my thigh exposed from the edge of my nightshirt. They sing Colin's name, dangle the *l* in front of me. Pat my head. Wail with grinning eyes. In Spanish, they sing how I will never kiss Colin's eyelids again. Never arrange his shoes beneath my bed. Never trace with a pinkie the long scar down the length of his back from neck to tailbone. I know that they are laughing. Kiss eyelids. Hahaha. Arrange shoes. Hahaha. They make a joke of it, and it is a joke, and I get nauseous.

When he comes through the door, folds his coat, sits on his bed— the mariachis dissolve. I bury my nose behind his ear and smell that he is real. I squeeze his fingers. I bite them like I am testing a piece of gold.

I remember the window. I discover I never climbed back in again. I live in a world outside the window. With Colin. We are not getting fat. I fall and I fall and I fall. Some nights I taste almond honey on his fingers or his ankle and shrug my shoulders. I have no influence in this world outside the window. I am weaker than insects. I resign myself to being a witness. I take on the task of memorizing him. I repeat his jokes to myself until the words don't make sentences to me anymore. I have little energy for writing them down. I am witness. I am eyes and ears. I am a recording device. I am a series of questions. I even look for metaphors to approximate the taste of almond honey (sweet pavement, dirty mincemeat, earthy cough syrup, the taste of carnival funhouse music).

Some nights I discover his face swollen, his eyes red, his breath snagged somewhere in his throat. Some nights I scream. I scream (*Colin I love you Colin Colin I love you I love you Colin Colin*) and I tell him to leave. He lies on my bed with his sweat and his swollen face. "Baby," he says, "Baby. Baby, baby. Hang in there. I didn't know I could feel anything before. Baby. Baby."

This smells of the mariachis to me. We can't be honest when we tell each other how we feel. Our honesty is in lifting up each other's hair, opening each other's eyelids, and scouting out the spies at the Thai restaurant. Sometimes he even pretends to cry. His voice folds into a whimper. He crunches up his face. I pretend to comfort him. This is all a lie. The worst part of this lie is that he *wants* to feel something; I know he wants to feel something. We are terrible actors. The world outside the window is very fragile. We invent meaning. Admitting a lie could reverse gravity. We are origami people.

I try to distract him from the absence of bees. This is great fun. We play Scrabble and he beats me again and again. He lays down eight-letter words. I pout. He calls me the Scrabble Master. I lose repeatedly. Sometimes I tip the board. I call him Rain Man. We develop a haiku game and berate each other through poetry until three a.m.

Five. Seven. Five.

We are two twelve-year-old boys. We go to the pizza parlor and play Ms. Pac-Man competitively. I tell him I'm the Ms. Pac-Man Master. He gets the all-time high score. I call him Bobby Fisher. We play more Scrabble. We play ten million stupid games. These games are my treasures. The games are my victory over the bees. I become a master thief of time.

We go through August and my tongue never sticks to almond honey as it trolls his body. I begin to believe his eyes are changing. Maybe not doll's eyes anymore. I wonder if there will be a time when I will be able to rest. A time when Colin will wake up first and memorize my eyelids. I wonder if there will be a time when I won't be a decoy stealing Colin from the bee trucks. Forklifts at night. Smoke to daze the hive. The mail-order queen stapled in a packet.

We drink together and yell things at passing cars. I always try to start street fights. Colin hides behind the dumpster and yells, "If I were you, I'd beat her good!"

We crack up like kindergartners on our bellies beneath church pews. We make out in front of old ladies in the easy chairs at the bookstore. I watch the sky and note the meteors. Eric calls to tell me he doesn't respect me anymore. "How could you go for someone so obvious?"

I say, "I will not eat green eggs and ham," over and over again until he slams the receiver down and never calls me again.

One night we're in my bed arguing about the definition of erudite. "Obscure," he says.

"Wise," I say.

"You're wrong," Colin says.

"You think you're pretty smart, don't you there, Rain Man. You think you're pretty erudite. You're like the Erudite Master."

He does a strange thing. He throws his arm up over his head and hides his face in his armpit. I try to pull his arm away and look at him. I laugh. He curves his neck deeper beneath his arm. I laugh. I try to unravel him. He giggles. He tries to disappear into his armpit. "Where are you going, Colin?"

"Tahiti."

This is how I discover Imaginary Tahiti. Colin tries to escape there through his armpit.

Picture the glimpse of coconut palms and umbrella drinks I caught sight of through Colin's armpit. If you could smell the Pacific, and see the colors of the little parasols in the two glasses, inches from you at the edge of your bed, would you have a choice? Would you have a choice? *When did I make the choice, Colin? With Eric? At the window? In the bowling alley? Did I make a choice?*

September is hot this year. It is the only month without rain. We go searching for leftover blackberries against the fence behind my apartment. We drive along the water in his car. He is in love with the stereo. He plays the Dead and tells me stories of kids they picked up on the highway in the bee truck. I kiss his neck while he drives. I understand that the question is not, *When will we be happy fat people without preoccupations with bees?* I understand the question now. *Where are we fat people without the preoccupation of bees?* I know where. Umbrella drinks and extra large hammocks. We have to dive in through his armpit.

I accept the rest of my life as stolen time spent outside the window with Colin. I am a witness and I am a distraction. I do not mind a life of stuffing him with blackberries and watching his lips turn purple with the juice of them. I can live forever against the threat of bees. In the other place, Colin and I live in round brown bodies that jiggle. We float forever in green salt water. We sleep in the sand. He sleeps facing me and curled toward me and I wake to find him drawing my eyelids with a shell in the sand. Imaginary Tahiti is a real place. More true than my town, and my apartment, and the Dead filling up the inside of Colin's car.

I peer with the corners of my eyes at a honeybee darting among the blackberries. They are almost all withered now. They turn to black dust after a while if nobody picks them. Colin divides the leaves in search of more. I try to place myself between him and the honeybee. Colin is taller than me. Taller than me and thinner than me and he sees the honeybee. "Relax," he says. And he looks down at me. He feeds me the last blackberry.

Things improve. September passes and I forget what almond honey tastes like. One night Colin falls asleep with his fingers enlaced in mine. Now the mariachis only come when Colin is late. Occasionally in the evening. Never in the afternoon. Things improve.

I make buckets of pasta for him. I squeeze honey into the sauce. He buys bags of Halloween candy and orange-frosted pumpkin cookies. We begin to compete at getting fat. "You're the Fat Master."

"No, no, you're the Fat Master."

Things improve.

He dresses in my clothes for Halloween. He buys a blond wig for ten dollars off of a trick-or-treater who knocks on my door. He brings me a gray fedora with a red feather and a gray trench coat, in case I want to be his date. He cackles while he shaves his armpits. I straddle his lap and paint him with eyeliner. He kisses me, one halted kiss. Colin's kisses never change. Sneaky kisses. Kisses that make me flail out, clutch his face. His kisses disappear before they're finished. The kiss of eternal withdrawal.

We drive out to a party. We talk strangers out of their bottles of wine. I glance at Colin engrossed in conversation with two women on the couch. I wander within earshot. He's squeezing his sock breasts and telling them they only wish they had what he has. We leave. We laugh as we shiver in the car. I tell him I love him. He looks at me. "Oh, Rachel. I love you so much."

So much, Colin. So much so much so much so much so much so much.

He drives and laughs and I search for meteors. The road is dark. I stretch to kiss his neck. He speeds. I laugh. I can see every streetlight as it bounces off his eyes. The road is dark. *So much so much so much so much so much so much.* Our hands are sandwiched on top of the gearshift. I laugh. He laughs. I laugh. He speeds. The streetlights laugh, dark. *So much so much so much so much so much so much so much.* It bounces off his eyes, meteors. He speeds.

I do not recognize the sound at first. Busy searching for meteors. It could have been the engine. Just the tires pushing away the road. I laugh. He speeds. He laughs. He knows what it is before I do. His eyes shift in the streetlights. The sound, at first, is dark. I laugh. Eyes shift. *So much so much so much so much so much so much.* It bounces, it speeds, I recognize the sound. Buzzy meteors.

They rise from beneath us, a garden of buzzing. The road laughs. We are inside a hot hailstorm. His eyes. Dark. Our hands, sand-wiched. Stung. Stung. Stung. A garden of engines shifts. Our hands stung. Eyes stung away. The road speeds, pushing. *So much so much so much so much.* They rise, stretch to kiss his neck, buzzing. Stung. Stung. Stung. Stung. Stung away the road pushing. They rise beneath us hot meteors. The road shifts away.

We float forever in green salt water.

So much so much so much so much so much so much so much.

When my face hits the windshield, it kills three bees, crawling on my lip, my nostril, and my eyebrow. When I wake up, I will discover what bees taste like. The bees in my hair and ears escape through the cracked glass.

The other driver will find us, two sleeping stick bugs.

I tell the police officers the blood on my face is costume blood. I will not remember saying this in the morning. When I get back to my apartment, I look for Colin in my bed. I look in the bathroom. I look in the kitchen. I pull back the sheets and look beneath them. He is skinny. He could fit under there. I do jumping jacks to prove to myself that I don't have a concussion. I have a concussion.

Colin comes at dawn. He is sorry, but it doesn't matter anymore. He has ripped holes in my fishnets. His face has turned to lava rock. He has grown fatter in the night. He tells me there were pieces of my hair hanging from the windshield. I feel my head for bald spots. He tells me he cried when he saw my hair in that windshield. I wonder how long he hid those bees from me beneath the Dead filling up his car. I do not ask him. We can't be honest when we tell each other how we feel.

When we wake up he shows me his knees. He peels the gauze off and shows me thirty-one stitches. I count them with my pinkie finger. "Good God. Those are the most grossly deformed knees I've ever seen. Put those away somewhere, would you."

We laugh a sore laugh together. I bury my nose behind his ear and smell antiseptic, rubber gloves, lemon soap, and Camel Filters.

In the late afternoon he shows me, for the first time, his little jar of almond honey. It is the color of old women's shoes. I spread it all over him with my thumbs. His body has a new cartography now. I discover I have memorized him all wrong. He dabs almond honey on the stings on my back. He does this the same way he kisses me and plays with my hair. It is the rippling touch of baby-hands, ghost-hands, a half touch. I do the rest of my stings myself.

In Jackson, Mississippi, there is a facility for worn-out beekeepers. Never would have guessed. Colin makes plans to leave. His parents ship him a new laptop computer to bribe him not to die. I have no laptop computers. I am a bribe. I am a distraction. I am eyes and ears and a series of questions that falls apart abruptly and ebbs into silence. I am a giggle catapulted out across the floor of a church.

In the days before he leaves, Colin takes his laptop computer everywhere he goes in a little briefcase. I tell him he will unleash millions of stories and we'll get ridiculously fat with all the caviar we'll buy with his royalties. Colin takes to wearing the trench coat and fedora whenever he goes out. He hobbles, bowlegged because of his knees. I walk between him and oncoming traffic when he crosses the street. Once I almost pee my pants downtown laughing at this ridiculously skinny, hobbling kid in his oversized hat and coat, clutching his little briefcase.

I decide to buy him dinner the night before he leaves. I make reservations. I try to comb my hair over the bumps and down around the welts on my forehead. When he comes to my apartment, I notice an angry sting at the corner of his lips that wasn't there before. My story is a comedy. I am the stupid man in the British sitcom who steps in the same pile of dog shit every time he leaves his house.

As we walk down the sidewalk I am silent. He gets nervous. He tries to hide it. He asks if I'm okay. It gets too much to handle when he starts throwing himself into piles of leaves. "Come on, baby! Jump in the leaves with me."

"I have too many bruises." I wait for him to brush off the leaves and then I tell him to go home. "Take your fucked-up face and just go away from me."

"It's our last night."

"You should have thought of that before you fucked up your face."

I walk by myself to the restaurant and eat alone. This is how Colin and I leave each other.

For several months he calls me on the phone almost every night. The nights when he does not call, I believe he's finally left for Tahiti without me. In these several months I am scared he'll be hit by cars, laughed at on the dance floor, inadvertently stung by a honeybee. I start to pray. I pray to goddesses. I pray to Buddha. I pray to Antonius Saint of Travelers and Lost Things. I pray to the bodhisattvas. I pray to the moon. I pray to Jesus Christ.

I make trades. I will give away my ability to write if Colin stays away from bees. I will never lie if Colin stays away from bees. I will become a Christian if Colin stays away from bees. I cut out pictures of palm trees. I talk dirty to him on the phone. I listen closely to the static on the line in case one of those crackles is Colin's wild red iron fish emerging to swim with me.

I run out of money because of too many days when I didn't leave my bed. I get a job working in the mountains. I wear overalls. I learn the names of four different kinds of wrenches and three kinds of hammers. I learn to use chain saws. Power drills. I learn to drive a Bobcat. I shovel snow as if there is nothing else so important. I come home and sleep until it's time to go to work again. I stop writing entirely. I start letters to Colin but I fall asleep on the pages after a few lines. I wonder if this is the monkey's paw, the flip side of the trade I prayed for.

In the end, we just lose each other's phone numbers. I call him on his birthday. I have to call his mom to get the number. I don't write. I eat and sleep and watch the mountains. They change very slowly.

In March when the daffodils combat the rain, out of nowhere I dream of Colin. I dream I see him at a party. He tells me he is healthy now. I cry and kiss him. I kiss him and kiss him. I pull away for a minute and I notice the tiniest puncture on his mouth, just where I have been kissing. I pull away further and realize that I have missed something. Colin's body is a network of bee stings. He is dying in front of me. He tells me he has decided to die of it. There is nothing I can say. He doesn't care. He says goodbye and drives off.

I scream after him, "I see now you never loved me!" and "I never loved you either!"

He is gone.

Now we go to visit this man in his castle and I watch a hairy bumblebee walk up the bare skin of his arm. He tells me five hours or less . . . if you know what you're doing. So I know it's time to let the story go.

I try to call Colin before I sit down to write. His roommate answers and takes my message. Colin doesn't call back. I call and leave a message on the answering machine. Colin doesn't call back. I call in the

night when his roommate told me I could reach him. The phone is off the hook.

All the possible explanations for a busy signal. Maybe my dream was right and he'll be disappeared soon. I do not wonder, because I know. We are always there with our umbrella drinks, dipping our toes into the surf. It is not a question of when. We are there at this moment, more real than springtime, laughing at the thin girls in their too-tight bathing suits.

I can eat now. For the first time ever I have hips. I do not drink too much and leap out the window with strangers. I am mindful of meteors, but they are aesthetic.

No dreams of assassins. No bees spat on the floor. Never the panic of unfamiliar laughter.

There, story. Go away now. I want to write other stories. Not fragments of the same story for two years. My trade was rejected. I can write again. I want writing. Silence. A comfortable chair.

Never the shudder of long naked toes.

The stars still fall and I resent them. They streak from Orion to the rooftops as I depart the gas station with a bag of Fritos. They fall on the freeway. They fall on the mini-mall parking lots. I want them frozen, suspended. I want them to fall on Colin. Standing in the mud flats next to me.

April 1999

Urgent Confidential Report
Wall Street's NEXT GREAT SHOCKER

The real shocker is not another 1,900-point Dow drop,
the dangerous frenzy over Internet stocks, or the coming "Y2K
    crisis."
It will confound the bears,
crucify the bulls,
and affect everything you own!

Interesting pre-Y2K events:
fell in love with Colin
got a job
tried to write a book
Moscow sinkholes
war in Kosovo
China's nuclear ability
shooting in Colorado
gray whale hunts
May 5th-ish—climbers stuck on Rainier

1998–1999

Once upon a time when you and I were dolphins
We always searched for manta rays
the ones as big as underwater airplanes.
I said they were angels who would give us wishes
and you said you would ask for a shell
like the giant hermit crabs who retract
from the disruption of our tails.

Do you remember:
We played hide-and-seek in the coral

and you swam against the current
through melancholy purple sea fans
and knots of paisley brain coral
into the darkest underledges
of reef architecture.
but after I counted to a hundred and nine
I could always
find you.
do you remember.

We swam to the belly of the ocean
and shocked the blind albino creatures
who had never heard of colors.
and Kim was there and
Bram with his same eyes
and he made us laugh until
the clown fish scattered in a panic
and Neil too
and Arwen was the spotted eagle ray
black with a million golden eyes
and the porcupine fish frowned up
at the sound of
dolphin laughter.
When we were dolphins.

And we never fractured the coral fingers
when we chased between them
because when we were dolphins
we still knew how
to be gentle.

Do you remember:
When you and I were dolphins and I asked
"Are you going to get tired of me?"
and you looked through water at me
and a hum filled up the ocean

all around us
and between us
and even the porcupine fish smiled
and I turned pink inside
and I wasn't afraid.
When we were dolphins
and knew how to kiss
using only the power of a sound.

Do you remember:
before the catastrophe of fingers and eyelashes
before the awkwardness of words and legs
when you and I were dolphins
and I was not torn
and you were not broken hearted
and things flowed simply under water
and you could turn me pink
with a sound.

May 1999

Dear Gram,

I'm sitting at the Spar Café in downtown Olympia having my Friday ritual of coffee and hours of doodling and writing. I decided this week that I'll have to officially change Friday into letter-writing day, because (as you and my friends in other states and countries have probably noticed) I'm not very disciplined about writing if I don't have a specific time dedicated to it.

How are you? It seems like it's been a very, very long time since I've seen you. I'm committed to being in Olympia for work until early October, so I won't see you this summer, but it sounds like a Corrie sojourn is brewing for your birthday or Christmas. I plan on traveling the country after my job ends, so I'll see you in December—and maybe even show up at your door some other time next year, toting a backpack and in desperate need of a shower.

I've just passed the six-month mark with the Washington State Conservation Corps. I'm pretty astounded at my own tenacity. Manual labor is about the last thing I have a natural talent for, and managing to stave off wanderlust for a whole year stationed in Olympia is perhaps even more contradictory to my nature. During the last six months, my upper arms have for the first time ever grown larger than my elbows. I've planted a few thousand trees, helped place a few thousand sandbags, become proficient at using chain saws and all sorts of other tools I'd never heard of before, and managed for the most part to be financially independent. It's been more of a challenge than anything I encountered in fourteen years of school. When I finish, I'll get a $5,000 educational scholarship, which I can use anytime in the next five years.

When I'm not working, I sleep, eat, and try to narrow the spectrum of possibilities for what I'm going to do with the rest of my life. I've been remarkably successful with the first two, but the spectrum of what I could do with my life has only become broader and more contradictory. I think a lot about the conversation we had last time you were in Olympia. I remember you said that when you were my age the roles for women in society were a lot more limited, but that in a lot of ways it was less confusing to pick a path for yourself and do a good job of following it. That makes a lot of sense to me. Do you know that in a lot of preliterate societies people were given names that delineated their roles (like Joe Fence-Builder or Bob Tiger-Hunter) and they just identified completely with their job and did it well? Sometimes I think I'd be much more productive if my name was Rachel Soup-Maker and all I had to do was make the tastiest damn soups ever for my village. I wouldn't spend so much time racing back and forth between creative writing and teaching and journalism and psychology and film and sociology and ecology and ethnobotany and international relations and the list goes on and on . . . I remember when I graduated fifth grade we had a list of questions for our yearbook. One of them was, "What do you want to be when you grow up?" Everyone wrote something like "doctor" or "astronaut" or "Spider-Man," and then you turned the page and there was my five-paragraph manifesto on the million things I wanted to be, from wandering poet to first woman president. That was real cute in fifth grade, but when it's ten years later, I'm going to be a junior in college, and I still don't have the conviction to cross "Spider-Man" off my list—well, you can imagine it gets a little nerve-wracking.

Right now I'm trying to concentrate on small things like paying bills, growing muscles, and writing letters to people like you, who deserve them. I read a lot of *Letters to Doris* last weekend. That was nice. I love getting insight into my family's relationships before I came along (and before my dad came along, for that matter). Letters make me feel connected to this continuous richness of family. I want you to know that all the work you've done to pass on pieces of family history is much appreciated.

Gram, thanks so much for the birthday card and the $25 you sent. The money will go towards my days off like today, and the weekly luxury of strawberry milkshakes and French fries (which I'm convinced are integral to my creative process). While I'm writing belated thank-yous, thanks also for the mittens, scarf, and hat you sent for Christmas. It's too warm for mittens now, but the scarf and hat are still part of my regular equipment for tromping around Olympia on rainy days. The waitress at the Spar still sometimes asks me where the mittens are when I come in without them. I reassure her that they'll be back in October, part of my signature ensemble.

I'd love to hear what you're up to, and would write back on the next Friday. Take care.

Much love,
Rachel

1998–1999

Some Things Not Entirely on the Up-and-Up I've Noticed at the Park

Every morning at 5 a.m. when I wake up, and every night at seven o'clock when I'm too exhausted to hold the drool in, I raise my eyes and hands skyward and thank the Good-Lord-Jesus-in-heaven-above for this job. I know I'm lucky beyond measure to be working and living at Mount Rainier.

That said, let's just all take a deep breath and admit that there's something a little shifty in the National Park Business (note very intentional use of the word "business"). You'll have to excuse my complete ignorance and youthful idealism but the phrases "national park" and "conservation corps" tricked me into thinking our work at Mount Rainier would be supportive of nature or that we'd at least curb our ingrained will to dominate and alter nature for the four days we're up here. So far, the most ecologically meaningful thing we've done on work time was picking up garbage around Longmire. I'm not exaggerating—I was ecstatically prancing around grabbing M&M wrappers and broken PVC pipe and joyously singing, "Conservation, conservation, hallelujah—finally some conservation!!!"

The activities that really started to border on the farcical were our little cosmetically "touching-up nature" projects. As I rake up the less desirable parts of nature, I like to fantasize about imaginary Mount Rainier Fashion Rangers scrupulously picking out the sauciest possible combination of natural elements to accessorize that big old beautiful mountain up there: "Hey, Ranger Ted, these trees are elegant yet understated—but imagine if we made it appear that they never dropped those unsightly twigs and leaves that smudge our clientele's Airwalks and Tevas."

"Wow, Ranger Joe! What a saucy, saucy idea!!! And these old-growth snags look a little past their prime. Wouldn't it be saucy if we called them hazardous and cut them like cartilage in a nose job?!"

Saucy! Saucy! Saucy!

Shoveling Cougar Rock has also led to some interesting revelations about the subtleties of nature. Namely, snow melts. But wouldn't it be saucy, saucy, saucy if, for the sake of our patrons' comfort, we made it appear that snow in the national park only falls in large angular drifts at the borders of tent pads and picnic tables and never, ever, ever where it might bother our honored guests? Heads up, guys, pretty soon they're going to change Cougar Rock to Kamp Kuddly Kougar and start leaving mints on the tent pads.

Speaking of Kuddly Kougars and wild animals made important by thinly veiled domestication—have you ever noticed that there's something seriously not right about the animals around here? For instance, they're not animals at all. They're little overfed muggers addicted to processed food and sunflower seeds. Miniature junkies. They couldn't survive in the wild. Luckily, they don't live in the wild. They live in the national park where dysfunctional, attention-starved humans trade corn nuts for their attention in an attempt to befriend something other than the computer. The other day a stellar jay came up to me with a syringe and yelled, "This is AIDS blood, bitch! Gimme some Tostitos before I infect your ass!" No joke. Junkies, I tell you. Miniature feathered junkies. Watch out.

I think it's pretty apparent that I'm a little disenchanted with Walt Disney National Park here. I don't like feeling like we're just helping to keep up this very benign façade of wilderness. Every time we drive past that one "hazardous tree" they took out in Cougar Rock, I look up at how they cut it with the chain saw "to speed up the decay process." And it's kind of funny how the oh-so-ecologically-considerate-hurray-for-decay cuts they made have the added bonus of tricking the tourists into thinking that tree just benignly fell of its own accord. And the question arises: "Uh . . . hey . . . don't you think when you took a chain saw and lopped off the whole damn top two-thirds of that tree you were probably doing enough to speed up its decay process!?!" but it's so saucily, saucily benign, how can you really question it?

And when we're pulling up shrubbery to transplant into campsites—and we're told, "Just make sure you make it look like you were never there" . . . well, I'm sure those well-disguised holes amongst the old growth will be grown over in no-time-at-all by salal and huckleberry, but something about the "make it look like you were never there" smacks of deception.

My folks have this story they like to tell about when I was a wee little preverbal babe riding in a car seat. My first word was "cat" and my second word was "Krih" for my brother Chris, and then sometimes from my car seat I would reach one arm out in front of me and yell, "Mah-nis-neah! Mah-nis-neah!" . . . and they had no idea what the hell I was talking about (except maybe the sinking premonition that their youngest child was possessed by demons and would be screaming nonsense for years to come). Well, as my coordination skills improved, my parents realized one day that when I flung one arm out like that, I was pointing . . . and as my pronunciation skills improved, "Mah-nis-neah!" turned into "Mountain is near! Mountain is near!" And they realized with relief and parental pride that even though I got the name wrong, my occasional seizures from the backseat were not the result of a budding mental illness. I was just really fucking stoked on that mountain.

When I was a little older we started taking off to the wilds on weekends. And I have some very vivid memories of wandering in national parks with my mama. I remember discovering the buoyancy of pumice somewhere up near St. Helens. Testing it in water to prove that it really did float. And I remember my mama explaining carefully, "No, Rachel, no, you can't fill your backpack with pumice and take it home to the wading pool." And goddamn, I wanted that pumice, but my mama very persistently explained that nature didn't intend pumice to be in my wading pool. So I left it.

I remember hiking up out of Sunrise with my parents and my friend Brigid . . . and we stopped on some crag somewhere to eat our granola bars—and there were ground squirrels everywhere. Brigid and I just yearned to feed our granola bars to the ground squirrels. We wanted to feed those ground squirrels the way I want to smoke a cigarette after nine cups of coffee. But my mama was there, and my mama had read the signs about why we don't feed the wild animals. And even though the hikers next to us let their kids feed the ground squirrels, even though we just wanted to feed one single ground squirrel one single granola bar—out of all the ground squirrels and granola bars in this world—we ate our granola bars and continued up the mountain.

I could go on and list a myriad of instances in which my mama prevented me from making a hat out of moss in the Hoh or from ripping anemones out of tide pools at Kalaloch. But the general theme of all of them is this intense sense of care and respect my mama had for every little section of soil our feet made contact with. And this trust, that the national park gods who made those "Don't feed the squirrels" signs were benevolently watching over everything, meticulously protecting every sprig of sorrel and gently pointing us up the designated paths.

As human beings, we're all a bunch of addicts. Addicted to cars, sex, video games, coffee, electricity, Styrofoam, the Internet, sausages, attention, cigarettes, Chap Stick, opera, crack, tourism, paper, chainsaws.

I guess some part of me thought that working at Mount Rainier would mean four days a week when I wasn't an addict anymore, where under the benevolent guidance of the national park gods I would tiptoe through the undergrowth counting spotted owls and replanting social trails. So this rant is the result of the sinking realization that the best of what we do is mitigation, and the worst of it is very similar to the work of custodians at Disneyland—and the national park gods are about eighty times less benevolent and conservation-minded than my mother.

Like good addicts, we cover our tracks and minimize the problem (Make it look like you were never there . . . speeding the decay process). Like good addicts, we're in denial (I work for the national park! When I kill plants it's for conservation! My gasoline smells like roses!). Like good addicts, we point fingers at bigger addicts (goddamn tourists, feeding the deer—they check their brains at the gate!).

A junkie I know told me that throughout his drug-abusing career he believed there was a part of him that was still pure—that had remained untouched by his addiction—that he could come back to and draw strength from when he decided to be clean. Funny thing was, when jail and multiple overdoses finally forced him into rehab, he got clean and realized that there was no such place in him. No untouched place. Someday this country's gonna get tired of getting high on all the extrinsic values of nature, and we're going to want to go clean and sustainable as a whole. And as we start hopping on the mass transit and tearing down the dams, we're going to look for some untouched place within this junkie country to draw inspiration from. We're gonna look toward the national parks that Roosevelt assured us would be waiting—and we're going to see a whole hell of a lot of overfed ground squirrels, deer, and gray jays (probably also foxes and bears) running down neatly sawed hazardous tree trunks and flattened social trails and paths, staring right back at us and waiting for corn nuts. No untouched place.

So the same junkie I mentioned earlier goes to rehab and his mama comes out for "family week." During family week, family and junkie tell each other all the ways they've hurt each other over the years. Then, at the end, they share a good memory they have of each other. Well, said junkie's mama tells this story about when he was very small and she showed him the trilliums in the backyard. Like all of us, he wanted to pick the trilliums. Very carefully his mama explained that when you pick a trillium it doesn't grow back for seven years. But if you leave them they grow up again relatively soon and you can see them again and again. That not-yet-a-junkie little boy left the trillium and with great enthusiasm said, "I can't wait! I can't wait for them to grow up again!" and then his mama carefully explained that the season was almost over and no more trilliums would be coming up. Undaunted, he replied, "No next year! I can't wait for the trilliums next year!" And as far as I know, that's as far ahead as that junkie ever thought in his life.

I'm sure I don't have to explain to you the way your natural surroundings weave their way into your psyche. We've all seen sunrises and moaned to ourselves over them. We've all seen the mountain on some particularly spectacular day and gasped something similar to my "Mah-nis-neah! Mah-nis-neah!" And somewhere, indisputable proof of my junkie friend's ability to think ahead towards beauty.

1998–1999

Mount Rainier, Mount Rainier, please explode suddenly like a Chinese friendship pagoda and kill us all. No warning. Please, Mount Rainier. Evade the seismic charts dot-dot-dotting your movement as if you were as simple as the electricity in a human heartbeat. Be stealthy.

Please kill us at dinnertime—so that later they unearth us in an archaeological dig with our forks poised and our dopey cattle facial expressions still intact. I want the archaeologists to slice layers of embalming volcano dust away from us and find our elbows still glued to a very expensive picnic table and mummified pierogi hanging out of our mouths and I want them to chisel pumice from the intricate furrows between our eyebrows.

Catch us at dinnertime, please Mount Rainier, so that the archaeologists, upon sweeping dust from our faces with toothbrushes, inspect our furrowed brows and our urgent horse-flared nostrils and laugh and laugh and laugh. "Why, this one has an enormous piece of onion in its teeth!"

"Why, this one spilled sour cream all down its shirt!"

"Upon examination of their faces, it seems they are either a crew of displaced circus clowns or a horde of blabbering intellectuals."

Maybe they will take another look at our listless fish-mouths, all open and limp as if we had all been shot with Novocain before our demise, and hastily rebury us. "Lord knows we don't need any more pretentious intellectual fossils, Doctor."

"Good Lord bless us, Jim, we don't."

"Already have an extensive, monotonous collection of horse-nostrils and slack-jaws."

"What with liberal-democrat-man they found last year in the ice."

"And that tourist bus the lava caught in Mexico."

"And that aging-hippie-man cluster they found frozen in leaking refrigerator coolant."

"And the presidential-motorcade-tribe they say got caught when the Rockies finally had enough and swallowed I-90 in one gulp."

They will carefully measure the parabolas of our expressions—and the angles at which our spoons were frozen as we pointed them at each other emphatically. "The depth of these dimples definitely point toward self-congratulatory laughter, Doctor."

"Mmm . . . and the upward slant of these ocular cavities combined with the extreme clench of the thumb and forefinger on the spoon suggest a rhetorical question."

"Aah . . . this is positively the Rosetta stone of a raised eyebrow of superiority."

"I'm afraid we must conclude these are no circus clowns, Jim."

"Terribly sorry, Doctor."

They will cluck with their tongues and shake their heads as they shovel the volcanic residue over us.

"The number of people who appeared to have had words like *paradigm* and *conservative* and *postmodernism* on their lips when the natural disasters swallowed them . . . it's astounding, isn't it, Jim?"

"In my opinion, that element of our ancestry is best left buried, Doctor. Bad for species morale knowing our primitive forefathers ran around in their own heads like gerbils in cheese-mazes."

"Couldn't even pause their yabbering long enough to hear all the trees snapping down around them."

Maybe they'll use MacLeod's to tamp down the rubble above our heads. Maybe they'll unzip back-to-pack and pause to piss before their march back to camp.

"Someday we'll find circus clowns, Doctor. Someday."

"I hope so, Jim."

September 27, 1999

Subject: Because I Don't Love You Anymore

since you deserted us i found a new dad who never complains when i borrow his clothes and stocks the refrigerator with beer for me and my hoodlum friends and bought me a Ferrari and my own chauffeur

so i never have to get my driver's license and lets me make life-size dinosaur sculptures in the yard.

that is why i never write to you.

actually, dad, that was just a little joke, but i think it is important that i fill you in on some sketchy things that have been going on up here. don't tell mom who tipped you off, but the mailman's been coming by a lot more than usual, and staying for a real long time, and wearing really racy high-cut mailman shorts. and mom's been dressing real trampy. i just thought you should know.

　your loving daughter,
　Rachel

1999–2000

Had a dream about falling, falling to my death off of something dusty and smooth and crumbling like the cliffs in Utah, but I kept holding on, and when each new foothold or handle of rock broke, I reached out as I fell and grabbed a new one. I didn't have time to think about anything—just react as if I was playing an adrenaline-filled video game. And I heard *I can't die. I can't die* again and again in my head.

　And I felt guilty.

Seems somehow positive compared to the dreams I used to have of tumbling, thinking, *This is it, I'm going to die.*

1999–2000

You create what you see in your head. Every day since your fingers were agile enough to hold those oversized Crayola crayons.

　Your first memories are drawing pretty ladies and telling yourself the stories of the pretty ladies. At the kitchen table. On the hearth. Almost always on the floor—between the feet of the family. Annexed by height. As unnoticed as the house cat. As a child you were a chameleon when you wanted to be. Epic political debates went on a few feet above you. Searing fights. Budgets were planned. Relatives' illnesses were discussed in a complicated secret code—but it didn't matter—they could have spoken plain English—they could have shouted that Great-grandpa was about to keel over and Cousin Bo was gay. You would not have noticed. You sprawled beneath them. You drew. You colored. You made up epic adventures about your Playmobil. You were a different species. They were as far away as the red-tailed hawks that sometimes soared over the yard in search of baby chicks or salmon from the creek.

You create what you see in your head! You tear apart cardboard boxes. You buy a hot glue gun. You have ink-stained fingers from ages four through twenty. When you are alone, you leap and twirl and lunge the dance of what you see in your head.

January 10, 2000

Woke up this morning around 4:30 or 5:00 a.m. to Sarah's groans of pain. By ten-something it got unbearable and Kelly came to take her away to the ER. I spent several hours falling asleep for ten or fifteen minutes in between her bouts of vomiting and heating up beanbags in the microwave. I can't imagine being in Sarah's body today. Cramps so bad they made her vomit, IVs, and enemas of something that glows. This has been the first time I've really been here while she is sick. She said she wanted to die, the pain was so bad. Could barely speak through it. She crept out to the car folded over herself when Kelly came to get her.

I have a lot of respect for Sarah—for the way she's made her life enjoyable, challenging. I think it must be scary—being aware all the time of how little control you have over your body. Being subject to searing pain inside you—pain that comes without warning and makes it impossible to sleep, or eat, or even drink water.

I spent the day doing housework. Took the ornaments off Sarah's Christmas tree. Unwound the lights from the porch railing and the crab apple tree—dragged the tree outside and tossed it down the hill through the rotten maple leaves and stale blackberries toward the creek. I unpacked the dishwasher and transferred armloads of laundry from hamper to washer to dryer to living room chair. Sang scales while vacuuming up leftover Christmas tree needles—and scrubbed coffee stains off the kitchen counter.

All of this amounts to very little, of course, because I still have neither a driver's license nor a job, which are the two things I really needed to hurry up and get upon my return to Olympia. Oh well, one step at a time.

I made $24 today, and could probably get more if I told Sarah how long I actually worked.

Talked to Mom and Dad on the phone. Both seemed panicky. Mom wanted me to assess whether or not she should come home. I was touched that Sarah asked to talk to Mom this morning. Both she and I, more than Chris I think, tend to revert back to childhood at certain points. Not necessarily a bad thing. We do have a very involved mother . . . overly involved sometimes. This means we have to claw our way toward autonomy sometimes. Kick and scream and yell to get some space to grow in . . . It also means we let her take care of things we are capable of doing ourselves.

But I think both of us have a sense of this huge depth in the feminine side of our family. Power. We have a certain power. I think Sarah and I favor our mother. Chris favors Dad—he says he's the most even mixture of the two of them, but that's a lie—he favors Dad. He favors Dad's side of the family maybe even more than Dad does. Sarah and I favor Mom. We are the ones who pay attention to the labels on the Christmas tree ornaments, the names, the years, the history behind our Christmas decorations. I believe the women in the family are the ones who slow things down. Savor the one-at-a-time epic of unwrapping Christmas presents. Sarah and Mom are the best about remembering to buy presents, acknowledging birthdays, wrapping things without too much tape or extra paper. Sarah and Mom are the ones who even wrap gifts for the cats.

I think I am the most refined mixture of my mother and father. I am the purest parts of both, the distinctive blend. I am the most accurate record of the shared experience of my family. My face is a calendar of forgotten pits—the hen that pecked a scar into the apple of my cheek, Smokey's chain stretching across the backyard, before grass had grown over it, when there was still a rocky driveway. The scar on my eyebrow that Bart licked blood from when I fainted and hit the VCR.

I am falling asleep now. Cara is casting a spell on me with her purr. It didn't help at all that I've been awake since five, and I just ate my one meal of the day, which I will digest like a garden snake over a period of months as it slowly moves across my silhouette, stretching it in the shape of my pasta meal.

I'm exhausted. Somehow I have to get better at budgeting my time. I think driving will certainly help. Oh, oh, sleep.

1997–2001

She is older sister
Capricorn girl
had a blond-haired doll named star
gave me back massages
painted my face with mood lipstick and blush
curled my hair
without burning my forehead with the curling iron
played light as a feather stiff as a board
She is brown-haired chocolate-eyed
tried smoking only one time
and threw up on the rhododendrons
doesn't like seafood eats kraft macaroni and cheese
cried during bambi
had terrible braces
fell in love only once
led me through haunted houses in the tattered red barn
sang alto in the school choir
loves her cats like children
doesn't need a sickness
got ripped off by the tooth fairy
She is scared of garden snakes
because our older brother chased her with them
proudly stated once that her name means princess

and mine means female sheep
went to bible camp
sold girl scout cookies
She is the one who introduced me to victoria's secret
did my hair before ballet recitals
held the bobby pins in her mouth
danced in the background in school plays
president of her class three years in a row
never thought about being a cheerleader
listened to her geometry teacher call her stupid brunette
remembers the characters on days of our lives
She is feet on the ground
held there by cleats
brave stuck moral
held there by heaviness
by air
telling me stories
holding my hand
wondering why I don't call
She is the one who still calls our mother
the one who knows how to knit
the one who could handle economics
the one who listens to confessions
the one who divided ice cream evenly
She is older sister
Capricorn girl
had a blond doll named star

January 11, 2000

Lately I've been thinking of writing about my mother. Cindy Corrie.
Thinking about her dresser drawers. I almost cried invading her
dresser drawers in the Caymans. Folded long-sleeve T-shirts, colored belts from those pyramid-sales parties she went to in Olympia.
I could write a history of my family according to discoveries I've

made over the years in cupboards and drawers. Unfinished baby books in the commode with bits of hair taped into them. The Sorry box in the drawers under the window seat—held together by duct tape—dust-covered faces peeling off of the elated WASP family on the top. There is extra spice in the spice-rack—duplicate containers of oregano from houses I lived in and moved out of, taking the seasoning with me. The place mat drawer has been disassembled and shipped south. The history of meals served on the living room table. There's something forlorn about our place mats in another country. They miss the mismatched candlesticks. They are afraid of the lion lizards. These are my mother's things—those place mats are hard-earned. The loosely woven straw champions of twenty years of survival of the fittest. Place mats that defeated cranberry juice and oyster stew and candle wax and salad dressing. Those are sturdy place mats. Displaced and ill at ease under unfamiliar bowls.

Something about the prefurnished house is insulting. Ironic. Opulence is not this family's forte. We are not graceful entertainers. We are burrowers, we are accustomed to a network of paths across the floors of our house. We are jungle creatures, at home among towers of paper foliage.

There is an insult in the uncarpeted rental house. It shouts at us. The silk plants turn up their noses at the thought of half-yellow houseplants, the ones that drop leaves all over the kitchen floor, the ones that bloom psychophrenically and die in the shower when left in my care.

It's too easy. It's insultingly, mockingly easy, this new shiny home in the Caribbean.

It took years of work and the very slow evolution of table manners to preserve those place mats. They're too tough to be served under packaged rum cakes.

There are even board games in the new house. But recent-release games. No Sorry. And nothing in that house is held together by duct tape.

My mom put stolen hotel shampoo in my shower down there. I take it as a subtle nod to the fact that with all its well-placed knick-knacks and framed prints, that house is as cheap as a Missoula Motel 6. It has not earned its cushions. It is empty of stories. There was no saving and pooling of nine-year-olds' Christmas money to afford the mugs in those cupboards.

Alien.

Sterile.

March 31, 2000

Subject: You read it here first . . .

Poppy,

You wonder why you never get your own personal e-mails. If I so much as give you a "heads up" in one of my e-mails to Mom I have to prepare myself for the mockery and neoliberal jabs at my progressive education that are always the thanks I get. Down, Oppressor Man!

Incidentally, at this point, the neoliberal jabs are pretty close to the mark. Yesterday I attended my first program lecture. Our guest speaker was, I think, a physicist. But his side occupation is dreamwork. Classic example of the weird juxtapositions in Evergreen faculty. "Hi, my name is Dr. Jenson. I'm a Harvard grad with a Ph.D. in political economy, but on the side I analyze the paintings of my pet donkey, Aphrodite." Yesterday I learned all about remembering dreams, recording dreams, encouraging dreams, lucid dreams, precognitive/prophetic dreams, co-dreaming, and nightmares.

It's a good thing that you, Chris, and Sarah all appear to have stable salaries, because I am steadfastly pursuing a track that guarantees I'll never get paid more than three Triscuits and some spinach.

So far I like my class. The reading is very interesting. The schedule is completely indecipherable. And the teachers wrap themselves in paper, sing in German, and yell insults at us to help us get a grasp on Dadaism.

Chad is in my class. This lends to the whole surrealist atmosphere of it. When he told me we were in the same class, my first plan was to wait until he came into the classroom and then start screaming, "Why are you here?! Stalker! Stalker!" every single day. Then I figured out that he knows our faculty and appears to be good friends with them, so this no longer seemed like a good idea. So now I've been doing my best to completely ignore him, taking care not to speak to him, look at him, or acknowledge his presence in any way whatsoever. This works okay except that my internal dialogue consists of *go away. go away. go away. go away. go away,* and that makes it hard to concentrate sometimes.

Yesterday he came over and talked to me, which was probably the nicest thing he could have done, because otherwise the ignoring thing would have gotten more and more uncomfortable. Of course I regard it as further proof that he came to Evergreen just to stalk me. This was our conversation:

Chad: So how are you?

Rachel: (glaring suspiciously out of the corner of her eye) I have to go pee really bad.

Exit Rachel.

Anyway, Evergreen is my college, not his college. He had his chance to go to college. It's not my fault he picked the wrong one. Luckily, I'm more popular than he is, and can get all my big strong friends to kick the crap out of him. And I can get away with it by telling everybody it was my Dadaist performance piece for surrealism class.

So how are you, Papa? Do you miss me? Are you ever going to come back to Olympia to visit? My car is leaking gasoline. If this continues I will need to know where to get Groucho Marx glasses in order to avoid being tarred and feathered by my fellow Evergreen students. Actually, I think I am going to try to patch it. I also got pulled over because there are holes in my taillight and whenever I brake, a blinding light shines out of it into the eyes of the drivers behind me. I don't see what's wrong with that. It seems like a definite bonus for when I get into car chases with stalkers who follow me home from surrealism class. It's kind of like having my very own Batmobile.

Tonight, I am finally going to take Butch and Claudia to dinner. If my ATM card doesn't work, there's going to be trouble, because Butch has been fasting since Monday in anticipation.

Please e-mail. I love you very much. I also love Mom. I hope the sea has given up trying to eat you and that you are well on your way to flying around the world smoking Cuban cigars.

Rachel

———————————————

2000

Every morning I wake up in my red bedroom that seemed like genius when I painted it, but looks more and more like carnage these days. I blink for a minute. I get ready to write down some dreams or a page in my diary or draw some very important maps. And then the ceiling tries to devour me.

I really meant to paint it—that big white ceiling. I was thinking about painting it gold to contrast the red, or painting a fresco on it, or writing notes of encouragement to myself up there, or making the mother of all very important maps.

I wriggle around under my comforter trying to find a ballpoint, a Crayola, anything fast. But sometime between the time I finished writing in my diary last night and the time I woke up, I managed to lose every single writing utensil I've ever had in my possession. I can hear the ceiling spit and gnash above me. Waiting for me to look, because if I look, it can eat me.

And I struggle for some socks and some boxers so I can make a run for it—but I haven't done laundry in a month and the other girl who lives in my room when I'm not here—the bad one who tends the garden of dirty cups and throws all the clothes around and tips over the ashtrays—the bad other girl hid all my pens while I was sleeping.

And I try. I try to look at my fingers. I try to look at my journal flecked with the spittle of the ravenous ceiling. I try to look at the floor with all the fashion magazines left by the bad other girl, to find one pen—just one pen. But I can't imagine where any pens might be, and trying to imagine, I get off guard for a minute and my eyes roll up towards the sky and I'm fucked now—I'm fucked—'cause there is no sky. There's that ceiling up there and it has me now—'cause I'm looking at it and it's going to rip me to pieces.

2000

I am a creator of intricately decorated bedrooms. Each time I move, I spend weeks painting, gluing things to my walls, choosing the precise pictures of goddesses and art postcards to arrange on my walls. This is a labor of love, and I become completely immersed in it.

There have been two or three times when I have awakened or returned home to find one of these rooms transformed. The pictures on the postcards are tangled and perverse. The colors of the walls are hideously gaudy. The goddesses are defiled by my crooked cutting job or are themselves crude. The very fact that I glued things to my wall fills me with astonishment and shame. I discover that every well-chosen arrangement of elements is an obvious and overwhelming sign of my own maladjustment: That vase is ostentatious. The woman in that picture is lecherous. The paint job is clumsy. I glued things to my wall. My God, I glued things to my wall.

I wonder why I didn't notice the awfulness of my room before, and become ashamed that other people have seen this three-dimensional diagram of my own faults that I could not read. I am inside a terrifying mirror.

When good art goes bad.

I am building the world myself, with you in the back of my mind. I'm building the world myself and putting new hats on everybody one by one, before I go out, so wrinkled, I have to grab the great big flaccid flaps of my eyebrows and lift them off my cheekbones in order to see. Before I go out, I'm gonna have people in tutus. Cops wearing sombreros. Stockbrokers with horned Viking hats. Priests with panties on their heads.

In the world I'm building, everybody shouts hello to everybody else from their car windows. People have speakers attached to their chests that pour out music so you can tell from a distance what mood they're in, and they won't be too chicken to get naked when the rain comes. Football players get paid in hamburgers, senators get paid in scalps, first ladies carry handcuffs and bullwhips, and presidents wear metal collars. Hella big metal collars with hella tight leashes. And you get money for counseling the dandelions.

But most important of all is *Let's Make a Deal*. In my world, nobody goes on *Let's Make a Deal* and leaves with the cell phone or the hot tub the host hands 'em to begin with. No half-steppers in the world I'm building. Half-stepping gets thrown out with rapists and sugar-coated Cheerios. In the world I'm building, we all take what's behind the door on *Let's Make a Deal*.

Spring 2000

Graveyard Shift

Sometime between eight o'clock when I laid down to rest and 10:20 when I got on the bus to go downtown, a rain came in and wet the street a little. The rain brings out the smell of dirt trapped in the grooves of the concrete. There is a wet-dirt, industrial sort of smell in the night. I think it's funny that we live in this environment where rain doesn't smell like rain anymore—it smells like other things: trapped dust, metal, motor oil. Sometimes in the woods or the mountains, I can smell rain alone—a different smell—the smell of laundry left out on the line through a storm and a dry spell. Here, though, rain smells like the things it releases from the buildings and the pavement.

There is an acoustic guitar riding in the first seat of the bus. I do not sit with the guitar. I sit alone, and ride all the way downtown without speaking to the guitar or making eye contact at all.

As I get off the #12 bus, the man sitting behind the guitar asks the driver, "Can I ride with you to Plum Street?" I get off the bus, and as I wait at the crosswalk to head up the hill and buy my gas station coffee for the night, I see the bus pass with the man's silhouette inside in the second seat. I tip my head at him, because I remember that on the bus he was a good-looking man: a black man with a shaved head and a jaw like whale bones and long seed-shaped eyes. A nice man who laughed when I almost sat on the guitar. He had the nice kind of man body too—a nice neck that flows into shoulders that are strong but not huge. Strong things inside smooth things. Lately, at the pizza restaurant and the grocery stores, I stand in line behind these big guys with necks like redwood stumps that shoot straight out of their pelvises: no aboveground roots. They have those big huge shoulders with the circumference of my waist. When you're down in the redwoods and you see how they shoot right out of the ground like that, it seems like a miracle they don't tip over. That's what I think, in line behind these really big guys—their necks and heads could come unrooted in a wind storm and tumble down and hurt someone: widow-makers.

I like these nice, skinnier men who don't threaten to topple over on me. You get too big and it seems like you're a tank or something—impervious to the landscape. You could roll right over me and I'd be yelling for you to stop, but you wouldn't be able to hear me through all that shoulder. Some of us are a different kind of animal, like deer and coyotes, the kind that stay in the trees and observe things and know how to wriggle. The man sitting behind the guitar on the bus seemed more like someone who would wriggle around you if you were in his way—not mow you down like a tank. So I tip my head at him, and I think he tips his head back through the murky window.

The bus is retired now. Headed for Plum Street. So that's where buses go at night. They stop being city buses and go to Plum Street for a couple of beers and a good night's sleep. They stop being city buses and go to Plum Street and become normal citizens like the rest of us for the night. I thought maybe they slept standing up like horses in the stalls of the Olympia Transit Center, until more people came to ride them in the morning. Buses have personal lives on Plum Street. You learn something new every day. This is a town full of secrets and the way to discover them is to work graveyard shifts.

For a minute I am worried about the guy with the nice kind of man-shoulders. Does he know that he's riding a city bus that no longer exists as such? What happens to someone who rides a nonexistent bus? What is the ride to Plum Street after the last bus downtown at 10:20? If no buses run after 10:20, what are you up to if you find yourself on a bus at 10:45? Defying the laws of physics. Time travel is what you're up to.

I cross the street, and the bus and I part ways at right angles. I never saw the guitar get off the bus so I imagine it is still riding the nonexistent bus up to Plum Street—not speaking and not making eye contact with anybody.

Spring 2000

#41 Bus

The guy at Tony's Variety, probably Tony, asks me if I need some carton tins. I don't know what the hell he's talking about. I like this guy though—he sells cigarettes cheaper than any place other than Frank's Landing. I don't know how he does it. They're up over five dollars most places.

One of the things you learn when you do respite is where to go to get deals on cigarettes, how to drive on back roads from the Westside to the borderlands between Tumwater and Lacey so you can cash a check at the Pit Stop, and which pharmacies are open the latest. People in the mental health system know how to get deals better than anyone, know the buses better than anyone, know the secret parts of the town better than anyone. Now I know where the runaways from Aberdeen used to camp in the woods. Who the vicious landlords are. Which convenience store owners are truly friendly. The people at the Puget Pantry are the winners. Secret town. I get obsessed with this phantom, spiderweb town within a town.

Tony's Variety fits in here somewhere. Any place that has deals—or has bars on the windows—or unexpectedly gives you free stuff—is part of the secret town. There's a lot of one-size-fits-all slutty lingerie in Tony's Variety. And those ugly fimo and metal pipes. And lighters, that when you hold your thumb against the bathing suits, they melt away and show you some model's goods.

Tony must know a lot about the secret town. Apparently he had me pegged for someone who needed carton tins. He was right, I realized, when I saw what they were. Big metal pencil boxes with American Spirit advertisements all over them. He loaded me up with two of them without really waiting to see if I wanted them. I *did* want them—but I wondered how he knew that.

———————————

2000

What I have—
a house cat.
small hands, crooked toes, knees, elbows
thighs, a throat and a belly.
dirt under my nails.
six lost journals underneath seats
in trains across the country.
a Buick. questionable.
eight black ballpoint pens
sharp teeth
beady eyes
and hope.

What I want—
a garden with pumpkins
and bare earth to turn over and
turn over.
hardwood floors for sock ballets.
air and raspberries.
sometimes in the morning
danger and stolen kisses
from a sneaky mystery lover man.

2000—2001

Mama, I don't want the car.

In the end I think I'll say it was the salmon that saved me. Nobody ever thinks to ask, "So what saved you?" when they scoot in next to you on the bus, though. So I'll say it to myself as I wait at the bus stop, in the bathroom spitting toothpaste flakes across the mirror. "I was saved by the wild salmon. I was saved by the wild salmon." My room-mates will become disenchanted and I will be forced to live alone.

"Trevor, today is the beginning of a brand-new life!"

I hop around in my socks in the kitchen. There's something nasty on the floor near the refrigerator and my foot gets snared for a minute before I yank it back and head for the coffeepot. "Today is the beginning of a brand-new life, Trevor. I'm going to clean my room."

Trevor leans on the stove in his pinstriped pajamas. His hair is funny and his voice is thin from sleeping. "That's good. Maybe we can work on the living room, too."

I ignore him and scamper back to my bedroom. The pellet stove is broken. It's November. I have to wear layers.

"Today is the beginning of a brand-new life. Today is the beginning of a brand-new life." I chant it to myself as I pull on long under-wear. It cracks me up. It's a joke with myself. I'm trying to stave off boa-constrictor boredom. This is the twenty-eighth day I will go to work this month, for at least a few hours, which is good. This is the sixth month in a row I've worked almost every day, which is good. At work I am never bored. In a month I will have enough money to pay my tuition for the rest of my time in school. I will work less for two years, finish school, go into the Peace Corps. Sometime soon I will write every day again if I can just put my mind to it. I will have a clean room. I will plan my escape from Olympia to a foreign place. I will finish the novel. I will get bigger biceps from lifting weights at Matt's house. I will do my laundry regularly. Sometime soon I'll be able to call myself an artist. But this is not a brand-new life. This is just part of the plan.

I return to the kitchen and breeze past Trevor to the coffeepot. "Do we have any travel mugs? I gotta do some errands."

The DNR guy said the salmon follow the stars. How do they make it back to the very same river to spawn every time? Smell? Ocean currents? Studies have shown they follow the stars.

What studies? This sounds like a miracle to me. Show me these studies. I think you're onto something metaphysical.

He couldn't cite the studies off the top of his head at that lecture. But I believe they are around. I believe wild salmon follow the stars.

I felt guilty that day. The DNR guy explained what they needed to spawn. Loose gravel. Dead logs that crash into the streams and nestle in there, so that there are slow deep places. They need pools and undisturbed gravel beds and shade so that the water stays cool. I kicked the toe of my Red Wings into the floor, gently, again and again. It was a big room of us in our work shirts and our Carhartts watching the DNR guy. Arlin elbowed the guy next to him and they snickered about something he drew on his folder.

It was a big room of kids who had gotten used to planting a couple hundred seedlings a day, or pulling Scotch broom, or doing in-stream work to make those pools—making fake logs because the real logs weren't always left behind. I think most of us cared. Arlin didn't care. He played hangman with the guy next to him. At least several of us cared. We raised our hands with their sunburnt backs to ask questions: "What about the salmon from Norway? Can we eat the salmon from Norway?"

At least several of us cared, but we were used to being outside for ten hours a day with our shovels and our Pulaskis. We weren't used to lectures. We were used to safety reports. Tell me how to cut this notch without the blade snapping back in my face. Tell me how far apart to drill the holes for the rebar. We were smart, but we had biceps—even I had biceps. We'd been excavating campgrounds from the snow all week at the mountain. Our biceps were getting antsy and wrestling with themselves inside our skins. It was hard to care where the studies came from. We were hungry for the evening when we could take out the rowboats.

From the time that the mama swishes her tail around in the gravel and makes a divot, from the time she releases the red from inside her silverness and her pink insideness, a lot of the babies die. You have a lot to contend with if you're born a fish baby. Herons. Runoff. Shadeless streams getting warm as bathwater. The Grand Coulee Dam.

I traced small triangles on the floorboards with the toes of my Red Wings. I felt guilty. The DNR guy said salmon have disappeared from forty percent of their streams. Disappeared. Poof. Fleets of salmon Houdinis spontaneously effervescing. Something metaphysical. Could you get one and do a demonstration? Poof. The DNR guy showed us a graph of population over the last fifty years: human vs. salmon. It looked like an X. First the salmon were ahead by a mile, but then we started closing in on them. In the middle of the X we were even, so there was a war. The war was the salmon's fault because they had a monopoly on the water and they were hoarding it. They were also pink and everybody knows what that means. The humans won because we were better educated, and because the salmon had a big-time societal problem with being addicted to spontaneously effervescing.

I felt guilty because of what I did to the babies.

Mama, I don't want the car.

The smell of wind laced with rotted fish will always be the smell of December at home. In the winter we could smell them rotting all the way up to the house. I would go down sometimes and look at their weird, flat eyeballs and try to pierce through their bodies with sticks. If it was a still day, or the wind was headed north, we didn't smell them as much. But you still knew the salmon were up into the creek to spawn because of the gulls. That was something I could watch from my window. Seven thousand and ten seagulls. They shifted above the trees like the edges of a curtain of ocean. I imagined a big, invisible woman dancing in a skirt of white beads. You could track her movements by the settling and unsettling of folds of seagulls. I sat in the corner of my bed by the window and observed her: now she swivels her hips and white beads swoop out wide to the left; now she shakes crumbs out of her skirt, and white beads billow and fall and billow again.

I went outside to load in the firewood and there it was again. The smell. One year the septic tank stopped working and sewage started to emerge from the earth under the apple tree. That stank too, but in the winter I could have friends over—

"Eww . . . what's that smell?"

"That's all the salmon down by the stream, stupid. They're just done spawning."

I lived down by the stream. Our house was through the woods up some steps. I lived down by the stream.

In the winter I had to pull on rubber boots to go down and examine their carcasses, but in the summer I went down barefoot and there were only bones. I hated to stick my feet in the rubber boots because there were dead animals in there. Sometimes there were moldy socks that squished like dead mice. Once, a banana slug. After I achieved a certain amount of autonomy, I started to ruin tennis shoes by wearing them down there in the wintertime. Eventually I abandoned my shoes by the steps in the woods and went barefoot even in the frost. I didn't care if I caught cold. Everybody knows what you get to do if you catch the flu. I took catching the flu very seriously. I stalked the flu.

In the summer I went barefoot through the woods because I was not afraid of blackberries. Brigid came with me and sometimes I told her to go barefoot to toughen her up. "What if there are blackberries on the steps?"

"Look at the ground and put your feet down slowly."

"I don't want to."

"You're going to have soft feet."

It was a certain kind of torture when we came up dripping after the sun started to fall. The two of us trudged up shivering, wanting to run because we'd drenched ourselves, and taking one slow step at a time, methodically scanning ahead of ourselves for anything thorny. Those walks up were miles long. We were emigrants setting out toward the bathtub, and we had to walk even slower to keep from spilling the tubs with the little people.

The little people. They had little plastic hair caps that were very good for chewing. All the women had stiff plastic dresses that made them look pregnant. "Let's get the little people and go down by the stream."

"Okay. Let's make a picnic."

But those hair caps. The men had little triangle bangs and every single one of the women had a pixie cut. If you pulled hard enough with your teeth you could snap those hair caps right off the little people and then you could stick your tongue inside their plastic heads. If you stuck your tongue inside a little person's head and sucked really hard with your whole mouth, you could create a vacuum and the little person's head would seal itself to the tip of your tongue and you could wiggle it around for a while like your miniature conjoined twin until it fell off. I only did that when I didn't have any friends over. Some of the hair caps were black and some brown, but none of them were blond. And you know, that really bothered me. There were no little people of color until I was too old to play with them and none of the pirate little people were women. Those plastic pregnancy dresses would have gotten in the way when they were pillaging.

The little people lived in dwellings etched into the interior banks down by the stream. These banks were inside the stream channel. Reeds and scraggly grass grew on them, but when the tide came in they were covered up by feet of water and you could only see the curled tips of the reeds floating in bales at the surface. I didn't know that I lived in an *estuary*. It's a pretty word. If I had known it, I would have said it all the time so the kids in my class knew that I was important. I didn't know that I lived in an *estuary*.

When I got a butterfly net for Christmas, I used it as a fishing net in the gaps between those interior banks. They were Swiss-cheese banks. The creek ran under and through them, and if you ran too fast, you could plunge through one of their holes into it. I used my butterfly net to make giant aquariums for the little people's houses. They could have mason-jar aquariums taller than two of them put together, with fish in them the size of their heads. Sometimes the fish would die in their mason jars while the little people were away on boating trips.

Brigid got sad. "Is it dead?"

"Yeah, I think it's dead."

"Do you think it was sick?"

"Maybe."

"Do you think it starved to death?"

"Maybe."

Sometimes Brigid would purse her lips and get ready to cry. She was that way about animals. She expected them to live. Those times, I would dump the fish out quick into the fast part of the stream. "Maybe it'll get better if we let it go."

"Let's say it'll get better."

One time we were playing shipwrecked princesses and I ate one of those fish. "Let's say all our food sunk in the boat and we have to eat what we can find."

We stretched strips of seaweed out on rocks to dry them. I caught a fish with my butterfly net and set it on the rock too. It was about the size of a thumbnail.

"It's going to die," Brigid said. She pursed her lips.

"We have to eat what we can find." I was serious about the authenticity of shipwrecked princesses.

"You're not going to eat that."

"Yes I am."

And then I had to eat it because I said I would, and I dropped it into the back of my throat without letting it cross my tongue. I swallowed it fast. It was like nothing.

"Gross," Brigid said. She sat in the rushes staring at me with a knotted mouth.

"What's your favorite animal?" I said.

"Pigs."

"Do you like sausage?"

"Yes."

"Sausage is pigs."

Then Brigid wanted to go home. We had to trudge up those steps, soaked with creek water and mud, setting each foot down slowly.

It's strange to look back and discover a cruel child behind you. But I didn't know that I lived in an estuary.

It's been more than a year since I started my job. Exactly a year since the Buick broke down for the first time. It seemed metaphysical. But I got it going again. I needed it for my job. I needed it for crisis respite and I needed it to drive home from graveyard shifts.

Mama, I don't want the car.

Live for a long time in the place you were born and strange things will happen to you. You forget what it's like to discover. In order to survive, you seek out ways to discover things in miniature. Instead of becoming worldly you become intimate. You see every tragic refraction of the place and it sees the same in you.

Sometimes, downtown at a stoplight, I look left at the bank and right at the furniture store and try to guess how many times I have waited since birth for this same stoplight to change colors. A thousand? Six thousand? Higher. Twelve thousand? Higher. A hundred thousand. A million. Six trillion. A google. Googleplex: a google of googles. Infinity.

When you are fifteen, your mother and father turn into furniture. Where once they were animate and sometimes startling creatures with whom you interacted, a bookshelf and a divan now blend passively into the carpet. They continue to speak to you:

How was school today . . .

You left your underwear in the . . .

I'm making potato soup for you tonight . . .

Did you notice my tulips . . .

Why are your eyes so . . .

Did you finish your . . .

I love you . . .

but you have HEARD it, so you get one of those hearing aids that tunes out background noise and you turn up Alanis Morissette and you wait for something to happen. You begin to lay plans for your escape. It's strange to look back and discover a cruel child behind you.

Live for a long time in one place and traffic lights, buildings, bodies of water, freeways turn into furniture. I see my neighbor from the apartment-three-years-ago in the bookstore. I reach around him to pull some novel off the shelf and my nose is a few inches from his cheek. I look directly into his eyes on my way to looking at something else, and I don't say hi to him. I don't say a single word. I don't even nod. I pay for my book and go about my business. There are only so many times in a day you can ask someone what they're doing these days.

I know the names of everything. Plum Street turns into East Bay Drive at the intersection with State Street by Lew's East Bay restaurant and Capital Christian Center, and if you continue north along Budd Inlet you will reach Priest Point Park, or even further, Burfoot Park, where you will see cedar trees, Doug fir, vine maple, bigleaf maple, Oregon grape, skunk cabbage, evergreen huckleberry, red huckleberry, salmonberry, snowberry, sword fern, bracken fern, lady fern, deer fern, horsetail, possibly gooseberry but probably not bear grass, which grows at higher elevations, or eelgrass, which grows in Padilla Bay. And that is Safeway and that is the Capitol and that is City Hall and that is the Lemon Grass and that is the statue of John Rogers and that is Capitol Lake and that is Tumwater Falls and that is the Deschutes River and that is a fish ladder and that, my friends, is what we call a hatchery out here in the Pacific Northwest, where our fish are what we call anadromous, which means that they transit between the ocean and the river, which is a lot more than we can say of me.

So it's important to move. There are a number of different ways to do this:

"I better get going. I have to get home and clean my room."

"I'll call you next time I'm in town."

"Do. I hope I get home."

"Do you want me to follow you?"

"No. It's too embarrassing. It's making a racket."

I don't get my room clean. The engine roars and keens a loud rhythmic objection as I turn onto Capitol Way. It's been making that sound all day. But whatever metal animals have been ramming against each other in there, they're going bald now. The sound is less cushioned, more tenor, and I expect it can be heard for blocks. I get to the crest of the hill and that whacking noise accelerates and there is also a lot of noisy air and it dawns on me that, no, the Buick isn't going after all, that sound is something else. *My Buick is metamorphosing into a helicopter.*

And then it stops. Turns itself off in the middle of the dark before the bridge. Instant rigor mortis, so the steering wheel resists me even pulling it over into a driveway. Today is the beginning of a brand-new life.

In the Buick I could drive from work to Matt's house in twenty minutes and smoke a whole cigarette in the time it took to get home. A lot of times after that I would walk inside and barf. I was working long hours then and going to school, and all I ate was Coca-Cola and mochas. That last cigarette would be the thing that threw me over the precipice into the land of barfing. Sometimes I would turn off the engine and open the door and lean out and barf right in the driveway. Matt would be asleep and all his blankets would be damp with sweat and it would be like slipping under a washcloth. Or he would still be awake playing computer games. And his face would be blue with light reflected off the screen. "Hey lady," he'd say without taking his eyes off the blurry people running around shooting each other on the monitor. I would go lie down and fall asleep while he finished his round.

The worst would be when there were people over and they'd been up all night drinking and I could hear them deciding that it was time to take some acid. That only happened once or twice.

"Do you wanna do some *L*?"

"I don't know, man. What time is it?"

"I don't know. I'm gonna get spun."

Then I would hear them giggle. I would curl my hands up to keep from scratching the walls. I hated that giggling. They were my friends. I was so happy when I found these people. They were different from the people before them. They were my friends. And they were great in the afternoon. They were fine. Who else did I know? My mom. My coworkers.

Those mornings after graveyard shifts when I lay there and wrenched around from the leftover coffee in my body, and from the flipbook of things I had to do before class evolving in my head, and from that giggling in the other room, those mornings I thought: *Boy, can I move.*

On one side of town there is a blackberry patch and a street with different-colored pastel houses, and some of them are as old as the town. On one side of town I stay up through the night and watch the traffic lights blink red and yellow, that "out of service" blinking, and watch dawn evolve without being able to see the sun come up. On one side of town I scrub the inside of the microwave until there are no red spots from the Pizza Pockets. No red spots. That microwave is the cleanest microwave you've ever seen. And I ask people when they wake up if they want some tea. "You're having a hard time sleeping? Do you want some tea?"

On one side of town I collect secrets, a long series of everyone's stunning secrets:

I used to be thinner and I loved to go dancing . . .
They were bad to me in Phoenix . . .
I am a wanderer, you know? A wanderer . . .
I think there's someone in the basement . . .
Do you know what I wish . . .
I'm scared to go to sleep because of my dreams . . .

"Do you want some tea?"

On one side of town I "assist in establishing healthy sleep patterns." I am the guard of Healthy Sleep. On one side of town I am part of a houseful of people straining to gain some control, straining to be able to sleep through a night and not wake to find hallucinations piled up and gnashing from the corners of the bedroom. And then I drive twenty minutes and smoke exactly one cigarette and I am in Opposite Land, where everyone is doing their damndest to avoid healthy sleep patterns and get them some good hallucinations. *Boy, can I move.*

 They were my friends. I waited virtuously for them to change. I wasn't about to just abandon them. I was a model of tolerance and loyalty. Judge not.

I fumed. I hated them. I wanted them to be punished.

Matt was patient and he gave good back massages. He did my laundry for me. It's as good a reason as any.

The riparian zone on either side of dawn is where things are revealed. Once I had to wait at the coffee shop for the buses to start running so I could get home from work. They don't come until nine on Sundays. I got a steamed milk and sat on the bench and chain-smoked. A guy with dreadlocks sat next to me. He smoked too. "Isn't it horrible when you see someone jogging in the morning and you're chain-smoking and drinking coffee?" he said.

I looked and there they were, gorgeous and alien, like a pair of exotic antelope. They floated past. Every part of them was golden and every part of them moved in deft unison—ponytails, calves, forearms, and thighs. Seraphim.

After keg parties we could climb up on the railing of the Mill House and watch the sunrise reflected on the Olympics. We didn't watch the sun itself. We watched the Olympics change color. "Is the keg tapped?"

"It's tapped."

We'd lie around on the couches on the porch and hug each other, satisfied with our work of the night. We were a lot of kids who cuddled all over ourselves, nestled into those moldy couches. We'd tell ourselves the story of the parties over and over again until they were myths. "Did you see that kid get on the table?"

"Fuckin' off the hook. We thought we were gonna have to tie him down."

"You should have seen your face, man. You were like, 'Do you need a glass of water?' Shit, mon."

"Shit, mon."

And then giggles. We all talked like reggae stars once in a while. It wasn't so bad then. I didn't have anything better to do. I was so happy to find these people. They were different from the people before them. We could stand on the railing and see the first pieces of dawn on the Olympics and not even notice the burnt old pieces of the mill across the street. We could climb up on the railing in our bare feet and get high enough above the leftover mill that we couldn't even notice it anymore.

Someone said there were some hippie kids who lived in the Mill House before we showed up and they got tired of looking at the mill every day so they cast a voodoo spell and burned it down. We knew everything. We were on the right side of things and we celebrated that by staying up after dawn.

We hooted in our bare feet at the sun rising on the Olympics. "That's beautiful. The hot springs are up there, you know."

"Good morning, hot springs."

Later someone told me that mill was a cooperative.

I find Matt outside the coffee shop and we walk down the street together toward the bay. "We could climb that tower."

"I don't want to climb the tower. Too cold."

"You can wear my shirt."

"I don't want to take your shirt."

And right then he knows what's going to happen. It means something when I turn down a clean piece of laundry. "Do you want to talk about it?"

"I don't know what to say." I don't want to tell him that since the Buick went last night I realized that to stay with him would be whoring myself for his Chrysler LeBaron.

"That's okay."

"We have to really try to be friends."

"Okay. I might need to keep my distance from you for a while."

"Okay."

A sea lion fishes out in the ripples. I see its head come up, a dark spot like a beetle on top of the water. When it dives under again there are rings. It's down there under the water somewhere, but the only evidence is rings.

Matt stares out towards the dark silhouettes of the mountains. "Wow."

"What are you thinking?" I ask, suspicious.

"Nothing really. I'm just enjoying the moment."

I think he's saying this to make me look neurotic. I'm sure of it. I try to breathe deeply for a minute and concentrate on the seagulls. Matt smiles to himself. There always has been this mysterious part of him, too. "What?" I ask.

"Whenever I find myself at the end of a relationship, the world just seems so much bigger all of a sudden."

"When I find myself at the end of a relationship, the world seems cold and it has a lot fewer cars."

This is the beginning of a brand-new life.

"I'm getting the fuck out of here."

"Where are you going to go?"

"I haven't decided yet. Away. Melaque."

"Where's that?"

"Mexico."

"What part of Mexico?"

"I don't know. Maybe Madagascar. Aaron was saying Madagascar."

"Melaque, Mexico, Madagascar."

"Yeah. Anywhere that starts with an *M*."

"Costs a lot to fly to Madagascar."

"But it's full of crazy animals."

"Come down from there. You're going to kill yourself."

"Nope."

"Come down from there."

"Nope."

"It's too cold out here. I wanna go inside."

"Nope."

"What are you doing up there anyway?"

"Waiting for a falcon."

"You're going to kill yourself."

"Or a tiercel. They're the same, you know. But they're different. One's male."

"Well, I don't see any coming. Maybe you should get down."

"Nope."

"I think it's almost dawn."

2000–2001

I wake up early one day with errands to run and decide I will bump into Colin and his new hoochie-ass girlfriend. I shave my armpits. I dance around in front of the mirror in the tight shirt I got in the little boy's section of the Salvation Army. I smear on Chap Stick. "Fun life," I say, "Fun life."

I'm going to pass Colin and his hoochie-ass girlfriend on the street and they're going to be terribly jealous of my fun life. I imagine I live in a Mountain Dew commercial. I am always on the beach with a bevy of sinewed friends and we're always dancing.

I meander through downtown. Drive in expanding rectangles on extra streets. They are here somewhere, most likely in a shadow, ensnared together. They'll drop the spoons in their strawberry milkshake when I slide past. Free as a bird. Fun life. Toucan Sam.

They are not at the coffee shop. They are not in the grocery store, on the bridge, at the magazine stand. I drive to the school, embarrassed at myself. Dolled up for no reason.

Of course he emerges from the library. Sans hoochie-ass girlfriend. I shove my hips out in the sun and make six-guns. He makes six-guns back at me. This town ain't big enough for the two of us. "Hey-hey."

"Hey-hey."

"What are you doing here?" I ask.

"Reading up on some young anarchists. Those kids in Oregon are smashing up stores now." He pronounces his words like rubber bands stretched and snapping . . . *yyy-oung aaann-archists*. I perform a dance beneath the conversation, like I have to pee. (fun life. fun life. fun life.) He's wearing sunglasses. "How are you?" His voice

144

shifts. He's uncomfortable. I grin, sunshine on the apples of my cheeks.

"Well. I'm well. Meeting some people." (I'm always on the beach with a bevy of sinewed friends.) "How are you?" I stretch *Howw arre* and snap *you*.

"Good. Got a job scrubbing toilets."

"Nice!"

"My friend from North Carolina went home."

"You had a friend here from North Carolina?"

"You know—Leslie."

Sunshine on the apples of my cheeks, sticky in my eyelashes and I'm on the beach and I'm always dancing. "Shit, Colin! What happened? But things were going so well!"

He shakes his head. Laughs at me.

Spring 2000

Backyard

I mow the lawn with the gasless push-mower. I do it barefoot. There's hurt in my wrists. The apple trees are blooming. The mower needs filing and crushes the grass flat more than it actually mows. I dance around to Magnetic Fields for Colin between runs at the lawn. Some of the dandelion stems refuse to be cut or to lay down—and they stand there beheaded, no matter how many runs I make. Colin doesn't want me to sing Magnetic Fields or to dance for him.

It's getting on into spring. The bluebells are up around the edges of the house. It's getting on into spring, and it isn't as miraculous now as when the first snowdrops came up. I mow the lawn and sometimes the mower won't budge—gears dogged with twigs and plaits of grass. The sun shines and Colin reads political economy in the green lawn chair, and I sit on the cement of our back porch and smoke, and the push-mower doesn't really cut. It just pushes down the grass like a hairstylist. Colin doesn't want to see me dance ballet in my boxers in the backyard.

This is the first time in a long while I've gone out without long pants. My legs are white, sickly, from being hidden all winter. Colin doesn't want to see me dance but I dance anyway, in my boxers, like a stripper humping the push-mower.

And Colin laughs. Finally.

More flattened chunks of grass rebound up again while I'm busy dancing. It's getting on into spring now. I saw a bee on the woodpile. The house isn't so torturously cold. Soon it will be summer. There will be grapes.

August 4, 2000

Letter from Imaginary Tahiti
Rachel Corrie
à la Anaïs Nin

We exist here, where even the rain is warm. When we need to bathe, we smear bits of soap over each other's bodies as the zephyrs gather into oozing tentacles. As the first voices of raindrops begin to chuckle against the sand, we drag each other to our feet and begin to twirl. This is the way we remove stowaway burrs of sand or dried salt entangled in our hair. We dance the tango together until the soap falls away.

We amuse ourselves with the search for the perfect mango, and each is more juicy, and each is a finer weave of pinks and oranges. With each bite we take we congratulate ourselves on having finished the search, and with each next bite we discover the new perfect mango. We amuse ourselves with disdainful laughter at the innocuous advances of scorpions.

Our home rests on a northward peninsula where both dawn and sundown are visible over the ocean. We do not have to sacrifice one for the other. We drink umbrella drinks from clear pregnant vessels with froth in their bellies, all the colors of wildflowers. We sip them some evenings until the stars make their exit, but they never intoxicate us to the point of toppling a glass or tripping on the threshold. This is the cabana in the absence of desire. Each sunset surpasses the last in its precision of plums and pomegranates.

Above all, understand that this Tahiti exists. Just as my particular Colin exists. As traffic exists. As the mountain exists. As your breath exists when it appears as a nebula in the morning in October. I have been there. I am there. I am sending you a missive. An invitation. It is written on a lotus petal I have pressed for you into paper. I perfume it with moisture slyly extorted from coconuts. Notice that Colin has left his thumbprint in squid ink on the third fold. You will agree it is an exquisite maze. I spent a year once wandering inside Colin's thumbprint. I know its every abalone sluice. Every gray gauze wall. Can you smell the sea salt in the ink?

We have good company. The reefs are full of miniature squid the color of insect wings. Wild red iron fish sometimes venture out to flirt with us. There is a society here but never so many buildings that they overpower the palm trees.

Once I was terrified of losing my memory—not just of forgetting things, but of losing the intensity of a shade of green preserved in my

mind. Dust also falls inside the brain, a dim layer across everything past. I was terrified of the fading. Of forgetting the shape of a friend's hand, the taste of a certain soup in a certain country, the smell of my grandmother. Can you imagine?

Do you know who I discovered upon arriving here? Three clues: She is old as the ocean. She travels at night. She has everything past preserved in jars and dangling from the rafters. Do you give up?

I discovered the Tooth Fairy. She is the curator of memory. I wander down the path to her hut when I want to look over old colors and taste old soups. She unlatches the jewelry box of my baby teeth. She lifts back my hair for me while I trade a baby tooth for one of the aged teeth in my mouth. I slip in the very first tooth that ever emerged from my gums, and I can isolate the memory of apricot baby food. Or the memory of a certain lullaby on a certain night in a rocking chair under a crocheted white blanket with a million tiny holes. I can isolate the memory of my mother when some of her hair remained brown.

Don't you wish that you could be here, now that you are beginning to get a sense of my Imaginary Tahiti? Imagine having all your old sensations laid out for you like a chest of costume jewelry. Sometimes, I strike a delicious bargain with the Tooth Fairy. I let her know a very sweet secret or snip for her a shred of my hair, and she will bring out one of Colin's baby teeth. Sometimes if I tell her a beautiful lie (lies are the only things she hasn't memorized, and they are her favorite currency), she will hold back my hair while I slip a tiny tooth in between my large ones, and taste Colin's memories.

Red and lavender and peridot. I don't have words to describe this ecstasy to you. Can you imagine squeezing inside the moment when Colin first understood what trilliums were? Can you imagine sunbathing with a miniature Colin in the winter on his parents' roof? It is the sort of fluttering orgasm that flowers must have when they are pollinated by honeybees. It is approximately fifty-seven times the pleasure of floating on my back in the gentle green roller-coaster of my warm green sea. She only lets me have one tooth at a time, a fledgling piece of ivory. And after a few moments she holds back my hair while I remove it again and allow her to take it back between translucent fingers. She hides it again in a copper green box which I cannot look inside. Of course I am not perturbed by this. She administers each time the precisely right dose. She removes the burden of measuring out my own ecstasy as if she is sliding a very heavy overcoat off my shoulders. I have exactly as much of Colin's memory as I need. And she will have undiscovered memories waiting for me for the rest of my life.

This is how I convinced Colin to quit drowning out my life. Do you remember how I used to let myself disappear under the weight of Colin's stories, back in places where the rain is cold? Our proportions were incorrect. The topography of his life consisted of emergency adrenaline shots, jail, sometimes perverse bliss, near-death experiences. The topography of my life consisted of making up names for the neighborhood cats, on some days a small new poem, observing the changes in the dandelions outside, the gossip among my friends. The proportions were incorrect. My life took place on a much smaller scale. It was the dandelions. His life was skyscrapers. You remember how I disappeared. That is done now. Buried beneath gold-fabric boxes and canisters of other people's baby teeth.

I led Colin down through valerian grass and giant ferns to the Tooth Fairy's threshold. There, in the amphitheater of light created by her doorway, I kissed once lightly his lovely half-laughing lips against the *hush-sift* of the surf. We froze there as if for a photograph, and then she drew us inside. There amid the history of jewelry boxes she held back his hair while I tugged away Colin's left front tooth. I chose the smallest and dullest of my baby teeth, and with my pinkie-finger inserted it into the oversized gap. I stared at his eyelids as they dropped shut, those wide pink eyelids which I used to envy for their proximity to Colin's secrets. We performed a shimmering surgery, the Tooth Fairy and I, one by one setting each of my baby teeth into that gap—removing them, replacing them.

I led him back down the path to our home in the center of the day and the center of the night, and held him away from me in the fronds of sunset. For the first time, I saw his eyes twinkle. Never again my expression reflected in doll's eyes. It is not that he changed after tasting my memories. It is that he has empathy for me. He understands now how there is triumph in my small poems, the epic drama of the neighborhood cats. He understands how the changes in dandelions can be like the swaying of giant trees. His skyscrapers do not drown them. We are proportionate.

In our cabana in the absence of desire, Colin never sleeps with his back to me. We sleep entangled. Sometimes I wake up after him and discover he is watching me. I imagine he is taking inventory of my sleep-features. Memorizing my eyelids. I wake up and make fun of his knees.

Colin is at last safe here. We have emerged from underneath the church pews to an eternity of mild umbrella drinks and contentment.

This is your invitation laced up with dried sea fans. I have written it in the first moments of dawn and the last moments of daylight, when the sun sprays the sky without revealing itself over the horizon. I have not been distracted by the fishing pelicans. Remember to put your face close to Colin's thumbprint and see what you smell. Sea salt. Lemon soap. Camel Filters.

Will you come to stay with us in our Tahiti? There is infinite room. Do not be afraid of loneliness. Paul Gauguin is still here, you know. He left Paris and his wife and children to come here. So you can imagine what a paradise it is. All the square-armed women from his paintings are here, dark and fierce and keen-eyed. The Tooth Fairy. A few strangers. Many artists whose names you have heard.

There is a proliferation of stars. Nothing you can imagine in the North. Every night we watch the meteors hail down, echoed in the trails of phosphorescence in the surf. There are so many meteors, we don't have to be mindful of them. They mean everything and they are meaningless. They are steadier than rain. We are in good company.

It is easy to make the journey. You will know when the time comes. You will fall in love with someone who is perpetually leaving you. Someone who beats you at Scrabble and talks with big words and tells all stories as if they are blues songs. You will memorize the features of someone whose eyes are perpetually bored and whose lips are per-petually amused. One day your someone will try to escape through his armpit to Tahiti. Then it is up to you to realize that you are there.

To see it. To smell it. To be sure of it even as your head shatters the windshield and your nose breaks and bleeds. You are in the green salt water when your eyes swell shut, when he sleeps with his back to you, when he spits out bees, when he tells you in dreams that he's killing himself. You are in green salt water. You are in green salt water. You are in green salt water when he leaves on an airplane. When he gets well and gets sick again when he goes to jail when your head hits the windshield when he finally really does die.

None of that is real. It is easier than buying a plane ticket. Just realize that you are here. All the pain and the drowning out of your life is just a decoy to keep you from missing your flight. You are already here at our cabana in the absence of desire.

When you come, will you tell me something? There are baby teeth the Tooth Fairy has forgotten. Some unfamiliar places in my memory. In the places where the rain remains cold, what do people hang on their walls? What do you fill your shelves with?

It's a joke.

I laugh now. You see, in my Tahiti with its coconuts and butterfly stampedes, the walls are covered only with shells. They are arranged in no particular order. Those artists I mentioned whose names you

have heard. Paul Gauguin. They did not bring their paintbrushes here when they arrived. The few who brought a canvas or two have turned them over and built them into lawn chairs. I do not read novels here. Colin and I have abandoned our haiku fights. The locals play no steel drums. No one would listen to them. To try to add to the *hush-sift* of the surf would be superfluous. We do not look at pictures. We look at the ocean and each other.

Understand: we live in the cabana in the absence of desire.

The essential thing is to understand that this Tahiti exists.

And my particular Colin exists.

They do exist.

We float forever in green salt water.

August 27, 2000

Five people I wish I'd met who are dead:

1. Salvador Dalí

2. Karl Jung

3. MLK

4. JFK

5. Josephine

Five people to hang out with in eternity:

1. Rainier M. Rilke

2. Jesus

3. E. E. Cummings

4. Gertrude Stein

5. Zelda Fitzgerald . . .

6. Charlie Chaplin

Fall 2000

Today I spent the day being sick bleeding endlessly and reading Salvador Dalí. Then I paused for a moment and read *The Unbearable Lightness of Being*. I borrowed it when I found it in the backseat of Matt's car on the way to buy wine. He said I couldn't borrow it if I wouldn't read it, if it would only stay on my shelf or sit in my house. And I insisted that I would read it, but I meant it as a lie just to get it into my possession. I knew I was too busy to read it. I just wanted it voraciously to be in my possession.

But today I picked it up and read from cover to cover, pausing only to go and bleed some more and shove more paper towels into my underwear because I ran out of tampons. I realized that I knew a few years ago what the unbearable lightness was, before I read the book. I remember staring at the eerie poster, with the two hands and the levitating hat, that looked like an invisible head and face was cupped in the hands and under the bowler. I remember staring at the poster and wondering what the lightness was, maybe during my freshman year. And then I remember staring at the poster sometime after Russia, after Chad . . . and knowing what it was. I think Russia explained it to me—the proportions of suffering.

So it just happened that I read the first book that could make me cry in years. And it just happened that I opened my teen-angst journal to write about all the boys who have interrupted me today and realized that the last thing I wrote about was the lightness. I was certainly bound to read this book.

The Lightness. Between life and death, there are no dimensions at all. There are no rulers or mile markers. It's just a shrug. The difference between Hitler and my mother, the difference between Whitney Houston and a Russian mother watching her son fall through the sidewalk and boil to death. There are no rules. There is no fairness. There are no guarantees. No warrantees on anything. It's all just a shrug. The difference between ecstasy and misery is just a shrug. And with that enormous shrug there, the shrug between me being and me not being—how could I be a poet? How could I believe in a truth?

And I knew, back then, that the shrug would happen at the end of my life. I knew. And I thought, so who cares? If my whole life is going to amount to one shrug and a shake of the head, who cares if it comes in eighty years or at 8 p.m.? Who cares?

Now, I know who cares. I know if I die at 11:15 p.m. or at ninety-seven years. I know. And I know it's me. That's my job.

Righteousness hardly exists. I devote myself to the pursuit of beauty. It's hard to keep participating in society, caring what happens in the world around me, when it will all eventually be folded up and shrugged away. But I love the Olympics and the pain in my chest. I love my mom's voice, worried on the answering machine. I love writing it all down and playing with it. Forgetting is the part that hurts.

A few months ago, Sarah and I sat at a table and had a conversation about whether Grandpa Mesenbrink was dead. We couldn't remember. We didn't know if he was dead or not. I still don't remember when he died, or where he died, or whether my mom cried or went to his funeral. He must have been about ninety-five. That old man who turned translucent. Whose enormous pale hands I stared at when I visited him one summer. The oldest hands. Ninety-five, and his own great-grandchild couldn't remember if he died. Ninety-five years to that. The unbearable lightness of being.

September 26, 2000

Imaginary Lives:

I would be a supermodel. I would look gorgeous and smell good all the time and have interesting hair and flamboyant clothes.

I would be a shaman/healer. I would always be doing mysterious things in the woods. I would do marvelous symbolic rituals that would change the course of events.

I would be a beat poet, hitchhiker, and dharma bum. I would be a dharma bum.

I would be a UN translator. I would be fluent in six languages.

I would be a Ph.D. scholar. I would know everything there is to know about some old German guy who no one else had heard of. I would wear a funny hat.

I would be that lady on National Public Radio who interviews all the really cool people in the world and never seems nervous and always asks insightful questions and has read everything ever.

I would be an activist who works side by side with people diagnosed with mental illness to make things better for them.

2000

He said I'll fill your cup if you vote for Nader
She said what about the Supreme Court
abortion rights and that . . .
He pumped the keg and said
democrats in a panic, scare tactics
propaganda try to trick the little guy
and gave her a button of Ralph Nader's face
all tinted green like *Close Encounters*
then he gulped out of his cup
which he'd picked up off the ground earlier and
she said I'm glad I'm getting political advice

from a guy drinking out of an empty cup
and he said I'm not drunk at all, okay? listen—
and she said no—your cup's empty
and he said
I can see you're smart and I like that
and she said
I can see you've got all your fingers and
that's a-okay

it was very romantic.

December 20, 2000

Values:

Don't judge other people. Have compassion. Understand that I have limited experience and limited perspective and be grateful for people who challenge that perspective.

Try to act out of love, not anger or ego—especially with political stuff.

Respect the earth and always work to improve my relationship to the earth.

Try to be honest.

Try to act in solidarity with people who are marginalized.

Try not to profit from injustices. Do not accept personal victory in a competition with people in which I am given unfair advantages.

Depend on myself as much as possible.

Talk openly with my parents about who I am, realistically.

1997–2002

Graveyard shift out the window looking west:

When everybody goes to sleep and I have some time between Data Tracking forms and mopping, I get to peer out at the town and discover more secrets. Olympia is a town of many secret identities. One of the interventionists told me that more people per capita are diagnosed with Disassociative Identity Disorder in Thurston County than anywhere else in the entire country. All that means is that somewhere in town there's a slap-happy psychiatrist diagnosing extra personalities left and right—but it's a fun fact to romanticize. Tonight, looking southwest, I can diagnose Olympia's secret Saturday night identity.

Tonight you would never know that there are salmon still running underneath all that. Big droopy sarcophagi state buildings. The Ramada. Tonight this town has cast aside its oyster-bed roots. Olympia is a whole new woman on Saturday night after midnight. She's a sparkly lady—decked out in streams of blinking traffic signals. She's wearing a full-body jumpsuit. Sequins from here to the Black Hills. Cubic zirconium along what by day is State Street, and emerald earrings gleaming out of the neighborhoods of the west side. I work near the fire station so I know whenever there's an emergency. I can also watch the siren lights downtown. But tonight Olympia has tossed off her civic duties and the siren lights aren't the signals of emergencies. They are costume jewelry.

On weeknights all the suicidal people get out of bed at set times throughout the night, and we wheel out the bleachers in front of the west window and root for emergencies. From here we can see all the cars ramming into each other, and the ambulances arriving, and the good cars chasing the bad cars—which always eventually ram into innocent cars along the sidewalk. All the suicidal people and I sit in a big crowd on the bleachers and the guy the regional support network hired to vend to us yells, "Ice cold beer!" and gives us all corn dogs. We root for emergencies and cheer when the cars ram into each other, but when the bad cars wimp out and pull over for the cop cars without ramming any innocent cars—then we grumble and throw our corn dogs at the west window.

It's important for suicidal people to see at least three cars ram into each other a night. It's good for morale. People come here generally because they might be a danger to themselves or others. When people—or certain voices inside people—have urges to do certain things that might be a danger to themselves or others, they have to go to hospital diversion houses or the hospital or rehab until they forget about those certain urges and develop other urges—urges to practice their activities of daily living.

But cars—cars are a different story. Cars can do whatever they want. Cars are employed as athletic stars in an extreme sport that demands that they endanger themselves and others as much as possible. Cars never have to practice their activities of daily living. They get to just run around smashing themselves and others to smithereens.

Cars are the cultural heroes of suicidal people. We all sit on the bleachers and throw our corn dogs and place bets and stamp our feet and cheer for our champions, the cars, like some people cheer for Jesse Ventura. Like some people cheered for Neil Armstrong. Like some people cheered for Jackie Robinson.

Then we have to roll back the bleachers and all the suicidal people go back to their respective numbered beds and practice their activities of nightly sleeping and some people have nightmares and some people crave cigarettes but everybody feels a little prouder to be a danger to self or others because we know our brothers the cars are out there, on our side, fighting the good fight.

But that is on weeknights.

On Saturday nights after midnight there are no emergencies. There is only another town. Blinking ruby things and emerald things and electric blue things. Spangled as a showgirl. No sign of an oyster anywhere. Vegas.

1997–2002

Morning Sweet Morning

On the bus after graveyard shift—I walk down to the stop on State to meet it. I have my snacks from last night in a paper bag. I can feel how pale I am on the bus. I make eye contact with a cute boy in the back who looks back balefully.

I become enraptured. Everyone on the bus is chatty today. Two women with sculpted hair and lipstick talk across the aisle to each other about their plans for getting health: "And I'm going to walk more, to work on the weight problem."

"And diet. Diet is really important."

I begin to grin as we pass the auto-glass shop. I can see what the guy across from me is reading and try to guess if he is an old man or an old woman. Behind the ladies, a black man with longish hair tells the woman next to him, "People here don't know what poor is. They're making seventy thousand dollars a year and they think they're poor."

"Because money makes you spend more money. You get stuff and then you have to take care of your stuff," the woman agrees.

She's young. Maybe my age. In the back of the bus someone is talking about some band and they're trading headphones around.

All these people are awake and chatty and I'm tired from grave-yard shift. I really do love them. I love us, riding the bus together. And I know it's a privilege to love riding the bus after having a car, but you know—I don't really care. Fuck that car. Fuck all of that. I love us, riding the bus together. I love the transit center.

February 2001

Qualities I find attractive in others:

Bravery: ability to risk failure. Not afraid to look stupid.

Honesty: ability to admit to deficiencies. Ability to tell people when they're uncomfortable, pissed, confused.

Talent: persistence and skill at some specialty—especially something unusual. People who always have guitars/sketchbooks with them. Metalworkers.

Energy: people who run around a lot/take initiative, keep busy. People who always have something interesting to do.

Independence: people who value alone time and take it. People who have their own agenda. People who are their own best friends.

Wildness without self-destructiveness.

Being in control—understanding what is going on in any given situation—being savvy.

February 21, 2001

Work Was Profound

"M" said she was worried about staying at HDH while she waits on her case manager to get her an apartment because the census is high and she doesn't want to take a bed that someone else "who's suicidal or having a lot of voices" might need. Fuck. Who the hell else thinks like that when they just got out of psychiatric hospitalization and they're homeless? I was touched by that woman when I first met her. I remember the sense that she was speaking a different language. And I remember such awful fear and pain. Now she's lucid as day. And wise. My God. I feel guilty. That's a kind of strength—altruism—I truly do not believe I have. I was humbled.

2001

When I get off the bus at 8:30 to go home and go to bed there is motion in the grass. The grass is tall now and lop-eared in places. After graveyard shift Capitol Way zips and grunts like a speedway. Dangerous. The cars are incomprehensible and careless. I expect several of them to sideswipe each other—skip the track—and flip over the fences into people's yards—just in the time it takes me to cross the street, pick up the newspaper, and enter the house. The grass ruffles and I look to see why. A small brown seal fumbles in a meandering line. A little brown hairy man twitches and hesitates and crawls along with small nude hands and feet, feels its way and nuzzles. Mole—in the open by the speedway. I've never seen one aboveground before.

Colin and I walk to school together in the morning and finally it rains. The gully at his driveway is full of ferns and skunk cabbage. It really rains, enough to wash the pavement smell out of the air and wake up the moss smell: epiphytes and bryophytes. I don't want to go to school. I want to climb over the slick guardrail and head up into the gully amongst the ferns. By the time we reach Overhulse my sweatshirt is soaked. Colin wants me to walk faster. I uproot one long sword-fern plume and try to attach it into my ponytail like a peacock feather. Now my hair smells like soil and the decay of pine needles.

Colin always wants to walk faster and I always want to trudge and identify ferns. Today rain seems like a call to play. When we walk through the S-curve shortcut the mud is saturated again and we have to pick our way on tiptoes in order to save our shoes. I want to take my shoes off.

I shake my hood off so that the rain slides down my hair and into my eyelashes, a glacial slide across my cheekbones and chin. This seems like the first real rain in forever.

It was an eerie, dry winter. Months without rain is like weeks without sleep—your eyes begin to burn. It was a strung-out winter. Stabbed through the eye and brained with bald sunlight. During droughts here, the forest squirms with thirst. Writhing and parched it begins to reach out beneath the surface of the town and express itself through the behavior of people. Puppets. We begin to bump into things, dance arrhythmically, scream at each other in the bathroom, crush cars, drink too much, lay awake at night, twitch. I blame everything that happened this winter on the absence of rain.

Now there are leaves on the trees, miraculously. Despite the absence of rain. And at long last the real rain comes, and starts the leaves in nonsense conversation.

I try to piece together fragments of conversation from the leaves, and the long last rain whispers: *kitty cat lick nip. flint ship. kitty cat. kitty cat. buttercup. knickknack. knickknack. hint nit flip top. shataqua. shetaqua. limp lap. kitty cat. posh.*

Everywhere there are secrets.

1997–2002

We trudge on a road that we paint as we go
paint our face with the red dust that gathers on our toes
sometimes intent on the logic of feet
each in front of the next—sneaker to sneaker
eating a straight chain methodically
and so on and so forth like a balance beam
I forget to look up sometimes.

Inventory of items passed on walk to Batdorf from work after grave-yard shift:

- One lilac tree
- One disembodied adapter cord—looks like the hookup for head-phones or speakers—has one of those male metal drill things on the end but the connecting wires are torn off. Black cord.
- One extinguished cigar
- One penny in the grate around a tree for protecting roots from pedestrians
- One AOL promotional CD-ROM in the gutter that looks like all the colors of Tokyo
- One overturned Big Mac box like a discarded clam shell
- A fleet of cigarette butts at the transit center: lights, regulars, wides
- Two plastic bags
- One fragment of torn yellow CAUTION: DO NOT ENTER tape
- One motorcycle
- One ugly picture of a lion in a goldish frame on sale at the furniture store which is always, as long as I can remember, having a sale
- One handsome gentleman in an orange hard hat who wants to know what I'm writing about
- Several purple clovers
- One graffiti statement in large letters on a beige wall: RAPE EVOL (particularly mysterious)
- One unending mass of gray clouds

This is an important job I have—inventory. Someone needs to take stock of things after graveyard shift. After graveyard shift the town is listless and nascent. The cars have yet to wake up en masse, so each noise is distinct and dramatic. Some bird somewhere screeches. Brakes whine. A guy in flipflops crosses the street and the soles make the smacking noise of someone chewing gum loudly. Between these things a drawn hiatus from noise—and in the silence it's evident that there is no silence, only subtle noises. The ripples in the bay. The rumble of an engine warming on a side street somewhere behind me.

There is a wasteland quality in the air after graveyard shifts. This is the time when everyone who was out in the night has finally extinguished the last cigarette into an empty beer can and rolled over into drunken sleep on a couch or a floor somewhere. There is leftover shrapnel—bags fluttering around, candy wrappers, bottles. It's the time when goods liberate themselves and meander, to the best of their abilities, through the street. After the people who purchased them evacuate and before the people who keep the street clean in the daytime arrive to gather things up. A window of maybe a few hours. The litter is also more exposed in the absence of traffic. An important time to assess things. One disembodied fuchsia blossom. One plastic dessert container. One M&M's bag. A Band-Aid.

I am tired and jittery and my mind is blank and shocked from sleep deprivation. In the absence of internal dialogue, my senses begin to clamor. Color of sky. Color of windshield. Shine of dew on marble bricks. Rattle of takeout fast food bag. Keen of seagull. Musk of the inlet, always the musk of the inlet.

Other beings moving around, like the city. I am wordless and resonant. Uncommunicative. Other beings moving around on parallel crosswalks with their mandible shoe noises and their eyes that watch things. They dart sometimes, lurk in running cars, move in strange, jabbing ways, seem to have plans, seem to be on their way somewhere.

The town and I, we are listless, echoey. A white bus lumbers through my consciousness. A sparrow. Rhododendron. All these things, disjointed. Asteroids. The city and I, we form no opinions. We are witnesses.

Other beings with eyes that see and brains that rested last night must be rapidly forming theorems. Opinions. Strategies. I'll keep my distance. If one strikes up a conversation, I can't engage. I forgot language in the night. I turned into an alien. They might catch me and perform experiments.

Or they might be as panicked and instinctual as I am. We might peck each other's faces off.

April 11, 2001

Old School Pizzeria

Johnny Cash—sun far in the west over King Solomon's Reef now. Teenage heartthrob in an orange sweater almost the color of wild salmon—he steals my chair. I tell him so. He apologizes. "I don't really care," I say. I remember we all lusted after him in high school. Middle school. Weird Formica with varicose veins. Looks like halibut flesh. Some men outside standing inches apart—I think they are going to fight—one is making big arm gestures—a big wounded stork. Then I notice the other guy is laughing beneath his mustache. They are still inches apart. Mustache guy starts gently boxing the other guy. Both laughing—they step in, shoulder to shoulder, to survey something across the street—more air-boxing. It appears that they are engaged in the legendary wounded-stork courtship ritual. Airboxing. They hug. Wander off across the street together. I imagine their nest will be made of rusty truck bumpers, hair, rhododendron branches. There will be a bundle of chin-shaped orange-speckled eggs. Some of the young will be eaten by hawks and muskrats, but the others will grow strong and play rugby and air-box outside of Old School Pizza.

Teenage heartthrob. He still has the exact same body. I remember ogling it in high school. He still wears shirts with collars. The same exact body, except now it's not something to lust after. It is scary—the kind of thing you don't want to get too close to. Like a wood chipper or a jeep. It is admirable from a safe distance, but I would not know how to operate it up close, and it seems like it might shatter a femur or somehow otherwise crush or mangle me.

I wonder if that teenage heartthrob is the loneliest person alive, wandering from restaurant to restaurant stealing people's chairs in order to garnish a bit of contact. I wonder if he has sex with girls at all or if, like me, every female hastily scans for exits whenever he gets close. Solid doorways, structural walls, something to duck under in case that big, football-player body topples over on us. Like a dubiously preserved Ionic column. Someone might lose an eye.

He walks out and I think his spine is very straight and he doesn't get jitters very often. I think it would be easy to stand up straight and avoid jitters if I had all those layers of stuff around me. Big stacks of man-bones and man-muscle—like particleboard. Neck as thick as a telephone pole—thicker. Imagine having big head-sized shoulders and thigh-sized wrists. It would be like having a ten-mile barrier of forest between you and the guy in the neighboring booth. If you cut one of those big head-shoulders, I bet it wouldn't bleed, at least not for a long time. Like wearing a full-body boxing glove.

The inside of my mouth is full of tight skin and knots from hot-cheese burns. Pacing guy with a mullet smokes—glances around—smokes. Yellow hat—blue brim—blue puff ball on top. Gets on a bicycle. Good for him. The sun out of sight now. No sleep tonight. I'm not at the library.

My God—why does food do this to me? The lady loads the extra slices into a box and they dangle there from her palms for a minute, flapping. Cheese flaps. Labia. Old-lady breasts. Dumb, flaccid slabs of pizza. I cannot think of anything more disturbing than this image.

September 26, 2001

Very important map of known world as of 9/26/01

I have already made upwards of ten very important maps of the Olympia area/known world since March. My ideas about maps have less to do with representing a community than they do with representing the interface between internal and external, an individual's relationship with an area at a particular period of time. My understanding of Olympia and my sense of its geography changes drastically depending on my perspective. When I spent a lot of time with a junkie, the landmarks shifted to certain benches and pay phones,

Sylvester Park, a particular pharmacy, a specific orange building, the locus of police officers, places to buy beer. When I was growing up, landmarks were playgrounds, monkey tail trees, a certain traffic flagger who always waved, clear-cuts, key climbing trees in the back-yard, sources of ice cream, Village Mart, Brigid's house, the creek. When I worked for the Conservation Corps, parts of Mount Rainier became landmarks: salmon streams, sources of coffee, ATMs that didn't charge service fees, the roots and mouth of the Nisqually, mit-igation sites. Now, after going to people's houses and driving people around as a respite provider, I have a whole different road map: routes home for paranoid days that cross Olympia and Lacey and Tumwater without using the freeway or any four-lane streets, bus schedules, clinics, St. Pete's ER, pharmacies, places that tend to be crowded and overwhelming, convenience stores run by people who are friendly even if you are a little disoriented, cigarettes cheaper, Frank's Landing, the glass floats that washed up on the coast from Japanese ships, the area around Evergreen Christian Center that used to be where all the runaways camped. I never cease to be amazed by the multiplicity of maps of this area—unmade maps—and the way some geographies completely obscure others from view.

Fall 2001

In Centralia there is a mural of a lynched syndicalist agitator with black "sabcats" raining out of the skies and a fat capitalist pig with timber stacked behind him. That's pretty great. What is more great is that it's within sight of the 1920s erected memorial to the American Legionnaires who died in the same "battle." Just an enormously visual representation of the subjectivity of history. And of the repression of history.

I am still struck by the Centralia Mural Project and the whole idea of visual reminders of repressed history—and I am thinking about how we don't have this in Olympia.

Reading *Log Towns*, I found the name of the Squiaitl of Eld Inlet—the Stehchas of Budd Inlet—I'm quite sure I have never heard the name

Squiaitl before. I knew about Squaxin Island and Nisqually. I went to a relatively progressive elementary school and we had speakers from the tribes and ate traditional food and built Popsicle-stick longhouses. But I grew up in Eld Inlet. Literally in it, in the creek, in the mud, amongst the salmon. Did I hear that name at any point? Squiaitl. I need to know whose creek that is. You know, we don't have that.

We have a lot of murals of whales. And that's fine. Whales are just fine. We are into the environment here. It's an accessory. But there's a big difference between whale murals and the mural in Centralia. Acknowledgment of repression. Acknowledgment of conflicted histories. Whale murals are pretty benign.

Downtown there is a map that shows how Olympia is built on a bowl of Jell-O and is all infill and how the native people called that valley *Valley of the Bear*. It says, "You are here," with an arrow pointing to Swantown Marina. It has images of what was going on at Swantown Marina a hundred years ago. Two hundred years ago. People who were here. It makes it look like this has been some sort of natural evolutionary progression instead of a bloody holocaust. Instead of theft. It doesn't say, "You are here because some people thought they were God's chosen people and forced some other people off the land they had lived on since the beginning of history so that they could dump shit in the estuary and build a radio station where the oysters used to be." And that little sign is a small pale thing. Not so big as the statue of John Rogers. Not big enough to be a routine part of public consciousness.

How to make visual, public reminders of regional history? What visual icons do we have in Olympia and how do they support a certain perspective on history and exclude others?

Map as narrative. Historical map as tall tale. Map as propaganda.

October 19, 2001

Finally got the bravery up to ask my boss if I can make videos with Drop-ins Group and she seems to have less concern about the ethics of it than I do. I thought she was going to think I was mad for making the suggestion of bringing a video camera into that setting.

Someone asked me, "Do you think people with mental disabilities have the intellectual capacity to work with the equipment?"

Well, I really wouldn't know, because I don't work with people with mental disabilities, and if you are referring to the people I work with—yes, I do think they can understand the concept of a fucking video camera.

I hate being in the position of trying to explain the people I work with to other people. It's good for people to understand that just because you hear voices doesn't mean you're "retarded." But I don't think I'm the person to try and explain or categorize people who are diagnosed with mental illness. I don't like it. In my work I have to maintain confidentiality. I can't start explaining what individual people do or say. By default, that leaves me explaining the work I do and the people I work with as a category. Which is marginalizing and objectifying.

Maybe I can talk to people at Drop-ins about what they think I should say and have them script me or something. How do I do this ethically?

I think it's likely that there will always be people who hear voices, who get suicidal on a regular basis, who experience an inner reality that is difficult to communicate to consensual reality. And maybe these people will always need some sort of system in place to support them through rough moments. We are all people who experience an inner reality that is difficult to communicate to consensual reality. Don't we all hear voices?

I have a rough time trying to articulate what I know about the work I do. We are all of us humans who need help, and we are all of us sometimes isolated by the things we perceive. So what's the big fucking deal? Why diagnose people? Why marginalize people or put them in a special category when really we are all just a hairs-breadth-of-distance from each other? And most of that hair, just circumstance.

On the other hand, some people just do have it harder.

How to speak the truth about this—and do I even have authority to speak my truth about it at all?

I can't imagine what I possibly could have done in some unknown past life to be deserving of Drop-Ins Group. I can't imagine what I could possibly do to convey my gratitude. I am afraid to start talking to my clients about this gratitude.

October 25, 2001

I get the sense that the high school guys and I in those OMJP meetings (Olympia Movement for Justice and Peace) are the only people who are from Olympia. Pete and Larry have both raised families here. Then a lot of very recent newcomers. This seems how peace movements have been in Olympia. I don't think the Olympia TESC campus has the same sort of rootedness as the Tacoma campus. Olympia Evergreen is often pretty messianic in its relationship with Olympia. I feel sort of out of place at OMJP because of that sense of all these academics in a room together trying to figure out how to spread the word to the common folk.

A lot of the people (ex-military guys, Oly locals, moms) who I think would be most valuable to bring into dialogue with OMJP, I am afraid to invite, because I don't get the sense that the people in those meetings are interested in understanding where the others are coming from. Maybe I am a little overly idealistic about everybody just getting along and finding common ground—but I do find a lot of common ground with most everybody. I just don't think that comes out in large, traditionally activist settings.

On the Internet, I found some ad hoc organizations that started as a response to Sept. 11th and our attack on Afghanistan. One was International ANSWER (Act Now to Stop War and End Racism). On their web site, there's a letter from the San Francisco labor council urging people to stand against racism, recognizing that "militarization of our society inevitably leads to erosion of our rights" and stating that the WTC and Pentagon attacks were "a heinous crime rather than an act of war."

ANSWER appears to be a huge coalition of labor leaders, academics, religious leaders, activists. It seems like a good model! The statements published on the web site and that of the IAC (International Action Center) reflect the backgrounds of the people writing them (labor/religious/etc.). There are pamphlets published by NYC labor groups in protest of the war.

OMJP does not reflect a background—only an opposition to the war. I think this is a weakness—ideology without roots in a community.

November 6, 2001

Tools for Reading the News

Themes noticed in media coverage of the war:

- Focus on "Beards and Burkas"—emblematic, stereotypical, and "Western" concepts of increased freedom with fall of Kandahar, etc.

- Polarization around dissent and obfuscation:
  dissenters presented as "do nothing"
  only alternatives are "do nothing" or current situation

- Concern about duration of war/ground war portrayed as "hand-wringing" (Thomas Friedman, *NYT* "Give War a Chance" Op-Ed), neurotic, soft. Ex-military dudes as "Experts." *NYT* article picturing Phil Donahue states TV features no anti-war people, because they can't find anyone "credible" who opposes war.

- Academia portrayed as oppressive place where normal folks who are pro-war can't voice opinions. Academia as weak link (*The Olympian* cartoons). Academics as so lost in theory that they espouse totalitarianism (*Wall Street Journal*—also equation of Marxism with totalitarianism).

- Free trade as solution to terrorism

- Donald Rumsfeld as charming, rugged, Roosevelt character

- Human interest stories on immigrants who love the U.S.

- *NYT*—continuing stories on Islam in the U.S., Ramadan (what is the intent?)

- Bounds of acceptable debate: Military Tribunals or No Military Tribunals? Invade Iraq now or later? Who should we prop up as leader of Afghanistan? Torture or no torture?

I would like to have a better system for ferreting out information. In that interest—a list of media analysis/info-gathering tactics.

- Try to get historical background before attempting to decipher current press. (Not much time for this now but maybe over break I can read some history of U.S. foreign policy in the Mideast and Central Asia.)
- Reference lefty sources, ACLU (American Civil Liberties Union), NLG (National Lawyers Guild), Common Dreams for help decoding mainstream press.
- Remember names of journalists and look at their old stuff to get an idea of their biases (Judith Miller, Thomas Friedman, George Will, William Safire).
- Watch the letters to the editor following more dissenting Op-Eds for signs of a political economy.
- Read articles and images in their context within a page layout.

Questions to ask myself as I'm reading:

- How does an article/publication/writer apply constraints or challenge the constraints of the range of acceptable debate?
- What is presented as objective/credible information?
- What buzzwords are used in an article and how do they link various issues and groups in the eyes of the public (militant, extremist, radical, freedom, free trade)?
- What historical background is included or excluded from coverage of a particular event?

• What assumptions are accepted a priori as fact?

I need to find a better method of note-taking with media stuff in order to be more literate about what is going on in Afghanistan.

Write down points I can't debate/don't understand/assumptions I distrust, so I can follow up on them.

November 20, 2001

Approaching the aftermath of September 11th from a civil liberties and ethnic equality perspective might ease some of the polarizing of issues around the war—the narrow "attack Afghanistan and Iraq" vs. "do nothing" dialogue. Our local media really promote a pretty narrow view of what war is.

I think historical background also gives a lot of perspective. The similarity of rhetoric between 1798 and now is striking—as is rhetoric used against the IWW (Industrial Workers of the World). Drawing attention to the fact that "you're either for us or against us" and the suggestion that deserters should be deported were used to undercut Jeffersonian democracy. This might make it necessary, at least for people writing to *The Olympian*, to be a little more creative about the structure of their debate.

I don't think it's the greatest thing to rely on rich-white-male history as your source of historical argument. It just promotes the idea that it's the real history. But looking at this in conjunction with Japanese internment and what happened in Centralia and Everett might make it more clear why we should know by now that anytime your executive engages in a "cold war" or a "half war" or a war on anybody that is kind of hazy and not based on a preponderance of publicized evidence—and then simultaneously starts rounding up immigrants and passing legislation which makes peaceful membership in a group illegal—particularly in times when a ruling elite is showing signs of being threatened by broad-based grassroots

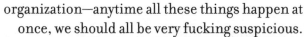

organization—anytime all these things happen at once, we should all be very fucking suspicious. Another thing about civil liberties and the ethnic/racial profiling thing—as far as local organizing goes, this has the potential for a lot more coalition-building and could make criticism of the war seem less radical and add more detail than just "peace."

Going to the City Council might not work—but it is a chance to get your cause seen on TV without going through the filters of *The Olympian* editing staff. I'm kind of interested in the response that might happen if people were shown on public television saying "Fuck John Ashcroft, Fuck the Patriot Act, Fuck Military Tribunals, and here is the historical evidence of why . . . here is how it's affected us in the past, here—locally."

2001—2002

Significant difficulties in the peace movement: lack of new tactics in public protest. Lack of cohesion and accessible networks for interorganizational communication. Lack of visible immediacy of the issue. Lack of widespread and clearly stated alternatives. Difficulty in dissenting following Sept. 11th. Difficulty integrating "peace" message into social justice, human rights, and economic justice movements. Difficulty accessing information. Lack of media coverage/support.

What part of this can government documentation/citizen muckraking address?

What local information needs to be uncovered?

How can I be of use?

What does this peace movement need to look like?

What resources do I need to analyze the local peace movement better?

What are the historical parallels between this and past crises?

What do I need to look at about myself?

What groups are already doing this work?

What are existing networks—local, international, national, for organizing around peace issues?

What can the peace movement do to be of service to this community?

How do we educate?

How do I make this into academic work?

How do I use TESC to do something of benefit for my community?

How can I use/build my own creativity while doing this work?

How does a peace movement in Olympia need to be different from a peace movement somewhere else?

What organizing is happening as organic outgrowth of the community's needs and desires?

Relationship between TESC and the community.

2001—2002

How do we catalyze ourselves and our community to respond to problems that don't seem immediate and may be invisible to us in our daily lives?

One thing we are noticing in OMJP is that the war itself hasn't particularly interfered with people's day-to-day routine in the community.

I have also thought about this with environmental issues in the Olympia area. Salmon. Things that are underwater. Shellfish.

A whole bunch of sewage leaked into the sound out of LOTT this year and all I saw about it was a small article in *The Olympian*. A small one. Have we just given up on Budd Bay? I remember sitting down by the Fourth Avenue bridge and looking at the water and thinking about how I used to put my feet in there. I have this weird memory that I am not sure is real, of being down on the railroad trestle across from Bayview Thriftway at night and walking across the bridge with all these men down there. It seems like they must have been fishing. I definitely remember swimming in Capitol Lake.

It seems like very slowly we have allowed things to get nasty. I always think about how we allow atrocious things to occur as long as they elapse over a period of time. The same way we allow something like twelve million children to die every year from malnutrition, from chronic problems, but when there was famine in Ethiopia and Somalia we paid attention. When three thousand people die suddenly in New York, we pay attention.

Fifteen or twenty years ago if someone came along and dumped a bunch of raw sewage and lead into Capitol Lake and the next day there were signs that said, "Sorry, no more swimming, kids" —well, it seems like there would have been a lawsuit or something.

It's bizarre what we allow to happen over time.

I think the way we deal with the environment as a society is very much like an addiction. When I think about catalysts, I think about a culture that is based on ever-increasing consumption—that *must* increase its consumption in order to continue operating in its economic system. How can a culture like this alter itself before it destroys itself and its environment? I think about how people get out of their addictions.

Marx presupposed a fundamental revolution in human consciousness in order for communism to work. I'm not a Marxist or a scholar of Marx, but I think about this stuff. The transformation that happens in an individual who goes from being selfish, insatiable, and ruthless into a person who is generally satisfied with the day-to-day and concerned with the well-being of other people is pretty revolutionary. And it seems to some degree analogous to what we will have to do as a society at some point to avoid being killed by our consumptive habits.

The trouble with the addiction analogy is that the general consensus on addiction is that you have to hit rock bottom before you can stop. If you apply that to environmental degradation on a sociological level, then children are dying of leukemia before you can catalyze a change in the practice of dumping toxic waste.

What helps people take action before there is irreversible damage?

I tend to see it as a flaw in my cognitive abilities that deaths of people who live across the ocean and poison in the water in Woburn, Massachusetts, seem distant to me. I don't think I am alone in this at all. Actually, I am probably different from some people in that I actively seek to personalize suffering that is distant from me. And if I am not using that to make brave, radical steps toward environmental and social change every day, what are the people who actively try to distance themselves from other people's suffering doing? What is going to act as a catalyst for them?

I think a lot in this world depends right now on the middle class in the United States. People who, while not directly manipulating the present system for their own profit, are still benefiting from it, are certainly sheltered by it, and, at this point, are still able to avoid the most dire consequences of it. Things could go pretty well if all the soccer moms in the country suddenly decided they were not going to buy from, vote for, or otherwise support anybody who dumps waste in the water or exploits moms in other places or their children.

Eventually the middle class in this country is going to come face to face with the environmental degradation and economic polarization we have been pushing elsewhere. It would be nice if we could effect some change before things had to get that much worse for everybody.

2001–2002

I'm given to making very important lists when describing scenery:

1. black phone with white transfer pads, gray buttons, red hold button

2. coiled phone cord like skin shed from a black snake
3. eerie *clack-clack* of blinds moving in living room—sometimes violently loud
4. rhythm of teapot reaching a boil
5. candy dish with mismatched lid because I broke the right one 6 months ago
6. dry-erase board with blue messages from Shirley
7. tape dispenser with fortunes taped to it: "Willing compromise is the key to gaining unity." "Our first and last love is self-love."
8. looming brick hearth (woodstove we have never used)
9. Suave antibacterial hand sanitizer (creepy clear gel)
10. *Physicians' Desk Reference—PDR* (colossal physicians' desk reference)
11. row of binders with crisis plans and respite appointments
12. chalk pastel rendition of pupil-less bunnies touching noses in greeting
13. phantom shadows that hint at ghosts in the doorway to the kitchen
14. playing cards poking out of pink ceramic dish
15. hardwood floor with its bubbles and uneven sections from bad soap
16. lurking paper shredder
17. wall clock on military time which I sometimes accidentally unplug
18. dolphins puzzle decoupaged into a solid poster (from a Christmas here years back)
19. crank-shaped brass doorknobs
20. Sharpie for writing names on charts
21. coughing from bedrooms
22. backpack discarded with my cigarettes peeking out from the front pocket

23. stack of silver charts

24. team mission statement at corner between wall and ceiling

25. Employee of the Quarter plaque with my name on it, spelled correctly

26. provider license in black frame

27. jade plant in terra-cotta pot, leans westward as if yearning for the Orient

28. file cabinets

29. biohazard box: "No Depends or disposable undergarments"

30. blue and green translucent beads hung from lamp

31. giant desk calendar with everyone's collaborative doodles

What is important about all this scenery?

Fourteen months of mopping and med-monitoring. But that's just what you can talk about. Things emerge from the floorboards and the brick hearth and then return there to lie dormant. The shadows in the doorway to the kitchen seem to move when I'm here alone. Of course there are ghosts in this house. This confidential house. Someone has to watch it all and record it. Someone has to be the audience. These are necessary ghosts.

What does a purple and teal dolphins poster mean? I wasn't working here that Christmas, but I understand about the dolphins puzzle. What does it mean to be here on Christmas? Something like being "The Little Match Girl" maybe.

That church up the street with the life-size wise men and painted donkeys all inside the fence under the huge cross with the music playing louder than anything. That church was lit up like Vegas. It was nice. Everybody said it was nice. The clients could walk up the street and look at the lights.

I look at things the wrong way. I know I do. I sat on the front porch, flicking ash into the coffee cans, watching that theme-park Nativity scene up and across the street and thinking, *Those are the popular kids.*

I was walking downtown on a cold evening, trying to thumb a ride, and a car pulled over to the curb beside me. I walked up and stood outside the passenger's side, waited for the young wife to roll down her window and ask where I was headed. I stood there for maybe a full minute. The lady and her husband simultaneously turned and looked at me and then looked in the other direction and talked amongst themselves. I waited for them to finish their private husband-and-wife conversation so they could let me into that big empty backseat, or even in the hatchback. *I'm kind of damp*, I thought. *Maybe they're deciding I should ride in the hatchback*.

But they just kept on looking in the other direction, and it got kind of weird, shivering and standing there, waiting one foot from that lady's head to tell her, *I live up towards Tumwater but you can just drop me downtown if you want thank you soooo much*. And then I followed their gaze to baby Jesus. Straight to theme-park baby Jesus and the life-size donkeys and painted wise men.

Shit. Was I embarrassed. Here I am standing one foot from the back of this lady's head thinking she and her husband pulled over to give a shivering young social service worker a ride home, and these poor people are just minding their own business and pulling over to look at Jesus. Probably scared half to death by me peering in at them like some nut. I even barked at the back of the wife's head, "Ha-ha— hey, you're looking at Jesus. Sorry, I thought . . ." at the back of the wife's head.

But I was just digging myself in deeper talking to the back of that head on Jesus' time. I puttered away.

Christmas is hard. It's cold. And there are lights on everything. My neighbors even strung lights across their lawn like yard lines on a football field. What if you don't have any lights? What if you don't have a lawn? It's those lights that make the little match girls. If people didn't spend so much time stringing those lights all over everything, maybe they'd consider investing in some matches.

I can imagine that other Christmas night when they decoupaged the dolphins puzzle.

Somebody somewhere donated a Christmas tree. Somebody somewhere donated a turkey. Maybe three or four or five people were here and there were stockings on the mantel underneath the Employee of the Quarter plaque, facing the whiteboard and the note-books with all the crisis plans and the gigantic *PDR*. And there were two staff.

What do you do? What do you do if you're having voices? What do you do after the turkey? I don't know how it feels to have voices or to sleep here in these beds with the white knitted blankets. I know how it feels not to be normal, though. Those times when you just know the whole world is out there chugging down nog inside tiers and tiers of icicle lights, patting their stomachs and saying, "God bless us every one." And you're in here with the box of blue plastic gloves for cook-ing and the no-self-harm contracts and the antibacterial hand cleanser. And we confiscated all your lighters and matches when you checked in, so you don't have the option of lighting small flames all through the night until you freeze to death.

That's why this house necessitates ghosts in the kitchen doorway, shifting past the refrigerator, over the sterilized counters, around the corner of the locked sharps cabinet with its blank Formica door. People come here for their not-normal times. When you are isolated amongst people—in a strange, anonymous house with toilet seat cov-ers and monoculture blankets, while the rest of the world has nog and "Jingle Bell Rock." When you are isolated amongst people, you have the ghosts to keep you company.

When you are in a place that does not exist, especially on Christ-mas, you have to do something quickly. You stand still too long on the strip of hardwood floor and consider your nonexistence, and then the grating on the smoke detectors threatens to shrink you and suck you up. You might shrivel and drain away into a tiny spark on the white blanket. After one person goes that way—then the whole ship. You have to do something quickly.

Threatening to spontaneously evaporate, I can imagine what they did, quickly, that other Christmas. Someone poured a fountain of purple and turquoise puzzle pieces all over the table. A few stray ones fell onto the floor and rested under the stereo. Staff brought out the two cordless phones so that they wouldn't miss any crisis calls. Someone turned on Pachelbel's *Canon* or something other than

"Jingle Bell Rock." There was a bowl of pretzels on the table and maybe some plates with pie and ice cream in the common area outside the kitchen with the ghosts. And they sat there and talked and assembled this puzzle. Everyone in the house. Maybe told jokes. Maybe staff got up and did the dishes at ten o'clock and wiped down the counters with a paper towel.

Nobody lit small flames like the little match girl and froze to death. They assembled the dolphins puzzle, and at the end stood around and admired it for a minute, and slathered it with decoupage so it could be hung on the wall like a totem:

How you survive in a nonexistent place.

November 23, 2000

I took the clients out
in the company car
for insurance reasons today
to Dairy Queen

and purchased them all dip cones and French fries
with company cash
not my own
for ethical reasons

and when they offered me a fry
I did not accept it
also for ethical reasons
but instead ate only
ketchup and fire sauce with my finger

and they confessed
one by one that their voices were accusing me of hypocrisy
so I initiated a long talk about their trust issues
and they each cried a little
and Jim lost his appetite

so we processed that while the butterscotch shell
wilted off his dip cone
and he cried some more
and called me a hairy little bitch sabotaging his ice cream day
so I refocused him
on his own anxiety

and asked if he wanted to go back to the hospital
and he said
fucking hell
no
I do not

and I said I hear that you're feeling angry
but you'll have to use appropriate social skills and language
or there won't be any more Dairy Queen

and then the clients got very escalated
and asked me just what exactly I was threatening to do
to Dairy Queen
you power-drunk little
overeducated slut

and I put everyone on time-out
to practice their deep breathing
and then everybody's dip cones melted
and the cones got all soggy
and I think April tried to kick me in the shin beneath the table.

By the time time-out was over
the surface of our table was completely decompensated
and Jim was whispering to himself
between deep breaths
and I gently asked if he was responding
to internal stimuli

and he made an obscene gesture with his right hand
and spit in my reservoir of ketchup and fire sauce
and then the Dairy Queen guy saw our table and
asked us to leave.

On the ride back in the company car
the clients asked me

how can we maintain a healthy and goal-directed outlook
on our lives
when the very people who are paid to empower
and advocate for us
allow our dip cones to melt

and make veiled threats against Dairy Queen

and sometimes appear to intentionally make us cry?

and I said
have you noticed those lovely clouds over there
on the horizon all rosy and backlit by the sun?
why don't we all focus on the rosy clouds
and practice our relaxation skills?

and they said, yes, we have
noticed
back in the Dairy Queen
when you made us breathe
and please desist from using the word *we*
as a transparent and superficial attempt
to transcend the client/counselor relationship and
persuade us to
trust your
bony ass

and I said
what's that like for you
and they said
shut it—okay
hippie?
our voices are telling us you
suck ass
and really need to get laid

and I bracketed my personal feelings and pulled over
and said
you are never going to eat at Dairy Queen again
I swear it on my mother's grave.
And we drove on
in silence.

Hey
they said
since
you are obviously cracking and made an atrocious
breach of professionalism
do you think
today can be
Mexico Day?

and I said
what?

and they said
what?

and I said
what did you just ask me?

and they all stared at me in the rearview mirror
and that's when I realized

nobody
said
anything
at all
but April winked
before I flicked my eyes back to the road
and Kelly said
we've got the car

and I said
yeah.
I got the gas card too.

And Jim said
sorry your mom's dead
and I said
that's okay Jim
we all deal with loss throughout our lives
and
he said
don't push it

and we sang a lot of Beatles songs
in Oregon
and Goodbye Ruby Tuesday
728 times in California
and the Dead
on the border
and all the voices joined in
on the harmony
for Bobby and Phil.

———————————————

March 12, 2002

Okay all.

For those of you who don't know, I'm working with other peace-and-justice-niks to put together a collaborative art project for Arts Walk and a big troupe of doves in the Procession of the Species. If anyone wants to participate in the planning of these projects, we're having meetings Fridays at 12 at Traditions. Starting March 14th we're having work sessions (for doves) at the Procession Studio. Come to any or all of these events.

As things pick up, I'd like to organize some big work party days, so that we could all come as a class. Let me know if you are interested and dates that might work. What I need right now are supplies and creative talent.

If anyone has any nontoxic art supplies, white sheets, fabric pens, red, white, or blue fabric 12″ x 12″ or larger (flowered, patterned, not completely monochromatic fabric is fine), feathers, good ideas/directions for mask-making, bird costumes, flag-making, wings, photographs/images of doves . . . please bring them with you to class on Thursday, or if that is inconvenient, call me at home.

Also, can anyone think of a species that represents justice (think economic justice/democracy/solidarity, not the arm of the law)?

All my love forever and ever to all y'all.

Rachel

March 28, 2002

This week I quit smoking. Became violent. Developed a huge school-girl crush. Resumed flossing. Feel anxious. I hoped the anxiety would go away. Anger. Intense anger. Snapping out.

Colin doesn't take this quitting as seriously as I do. Or he doesn't show it in a way I can recognize.

Tomorrow will be five days and I will deserve a CD. Even Phil from the Blue Heron Bakery is happy for me. Quitting for him sounds like a spiritual experience not unlike quitting drinking was for me.

I am treated well and welcomed at the Procession Studio. I feel content there. I need to have a community to be creative in—then I am very satisfied. I don't know if the Procession is exactly the community I imagine for myself. It is a beautiful thing. Seems to me to have a very privileged and predominantly white feeling. Possibly even some cultural appropriation. But nonetheless, on the whole, very much, irrepressibly, beautiful. In my ideal community art space, people would not have to self-censor out "political" implications—censorship is an *extremely* political act.

Dreams about living in the Procession Studio. I live in an old house that reminds me of Iowa. Inside my house all kinds of people are working on art projects, probably making things for the Procession of the Species. Josh is standing at a big table right inside the door. He is working on something. I am very concerned about all the people in my house. I am surprised and happy to see Josh again. I tell them that I have only slept a little. I tell them I have been awake for sixteen hours. I don't think I actually kick them out—I just want them to be quiet.

I am so happy to see Josh and am full of tenderness. I ask him some questions—he stares at me. A little distant or reluctant to speak. I just want to touch him. I kneel down on the ground and put my head in his lap and consider telling him that I don't drink anymore. Other people are around so I don't cuddle with Josh.

March 2002

Going crazy, having digestive trauma, and being the biggest bossiest mother-hen dove.

Worrying about the Procession. What if this goes off miserably? What if it goes off huge and a bunch of people storm the procession in ugly dove costumes and nobody can see the lizard or the rain forest or the snail?

S went away for treatment.
Prayer for S.
He's probably shaking.
Prayer for S.

Tomorrow
Review Conference Plans
Reserve time Friday in linear suite—ask about barrel
Call Wes 9:30
Call Nancy and Maureen
Fill in cue cards
Set goals for Procession
Check I-net, Mark's #

1997–2002

after you lean across me
to flick out the lamp
when your belly fits against the small of my back
and your arm returns
to curl around my shoulder
when you whisper hot
goodnight against the hair
on my neck
simultaneously
your belly button tells my spine
that the electric bill
will be paid
the primroses will not die of thirst
the moon will not explode in the stress of clouds
and there will be coffee and bagels to eat in the morning.

March 2002

R	C
28	36
14	20
12	38
35	12
12	13
18	14
32	29
22	62
39	—
212	224

DISSENT IS PATRIOTIC!
BRING FABRIC ASAP
Please donate red, white, and blue fabric (patterns okay)
12″x 12″ or larger
for a collaborative community art project
in opposition to the war
to be displayed at Arts Walk.
CRITICAL THINKING IS PATRIOTIC
BRING FABRIC ASAP!

1997–2002

I imagine an eternal unwitting procession of poets. Each one sits down to write the bit that will stop the cars on the freeways and turn Budweiser-stained eyes on speedboats up and across toward the mountains. Each pen scrabbling to get down that one true thing that will stop the evolution of this picture—of this, my home, my heart— my winding, weary Puget Sound and Strait of Juan de Fuca. I imagine all the ink we have wasted, loose at the peak of one of these mountains, could maybe break a small dam somewhere. As we each cease to be poets, turn nasal and didactic, trying to write down the one true thing that might freeze the incessant human remodeling of this long wet natural architecture.

And you, Colin, you my five-colored kite, my too quickly disappearing lover, you know from my letters the results of a sentimental poet who abandons images of shorebirds and pleads for time to slow down. I whine the same whine for you as I do for the mammoth cedar stumps and the fleeing trilliums and the ever-changing patchwork of clear-cuts and second-growth Doug firs behind my mama's house.

1997–2002

Is this my hangman or yours?
We unwittingly misplace and
trade them like Bic lighters.

garbanzo security

Spring–Summer 2002

I was encouraged to believe in Santa Claus, in the Tooth Fairy, and in the Easter Bunny, but not in God. I don't know how much we talked about God when I was small. I remember I knew about Jesus. I think we made some pretense about being Christian. We went to church on holidays. I think my mom explained that we were Christian but we didn't have to believe anything about Jesus or anything we heard at church.

Maybe my mom never told me we were Christian. I vaguely remember being asked by classmates. I think I told people we were Christian. I got confused when they would ask what church I went to. I thought we were Christian because we were white people who weren't Jewish. Those were the only options I was aware of. I just don't remember understanding much about religion at a young age.

When I was a little older I asked her if we were atheists. I think it made her sad that I thought we were atheists.

My dad's side of the family are all insane rationalists. People who believe themselves to be objective. "The great agnostic Mackamans," as my cousin Beth described it. After she finished seminary and became a minister, one of my great-uncles said, "They didn't make a Christian out of you, did they?"

I think of my mom as being extremely moralistic. Not religious. Not dogmatic. My mom held us to extraordinarily high moral standards—maybe impossibly high. Sometimes I've looked back on that and thought it's pretty much the only way I had a lot of direct pressure from my folks. Not in such a bad way. Just there were things that nobody did—playing some jokes on people, lying, teasing, taking things, just being rude to people.

I know a woman who's pregnant and she's decided not to assign a gender to her baby until it chooses its own. I think that's a little nuts. Male is a word we use for people with penises. I think it would be confusing to grow up without references to this part you have.

Anyway, I think my mom had a similar attitude toward my spirituality. She was determined I would define it for myself. My mom is a pretty healthy parent. I remember her telling me in the car one day that even though I'm not a religious person, I am a spiritual person. Sometimes my mom wondered if we would be healthier, better children if she had taken us to church. This may have been a scare tactic of hers.

June 4, 2002

Thurston County by Trivia
Self in Context

LOCAL KNOWLEDGE

Olympia sits at the southern tip of Puget Sound on Budd Inlet, cradled between Lacey and Tumwater. A glacier dug the inlets during the most recent ice age. They were the last words of that glacier—spit out at California—before it receded back up into Canada and into humps on the backs of the mountains.

To the left of Olympia is Eld Inlet, hooked like a claw into the Black Hills. The people who lived here first were the Squiaitl. There are trees all over the hills, but they are new trees. The biggest are only a hundred years old—maybe. McLane Creek flows into Mud Bay, and Perry Creek empties into the inlet just beyond Mud Bay. Salmon still make it up both creeks to spawn.

After so many awkward starts focused on myself, I'm gong to write about context for a while—about locale. I've been here my whole life. There's an overlap between self and context. Writing about creeks feels much like writing about where I've come from. Perry Creek winds its way out of forest roads and lookouts near Rock Candy. In the winter the salmon come back, purpling, and fight upstream.

I didn't intend to become deeply involved in activism this year. I'm not sure what compelled me to sign up for a program with such a big degree of community involvement. I'm phobic of community. I'm scared of people, particularly people in the Greater Olympia area.

I think my plan was to study Mason County all year and hopefully not talk much to anybody. I imagined myself sifting through archives in Shelton. It was going to be a break from Olympia. Almost like being an exchange student. I don't think my intention was to be of any particular use to the communities we studied. I was looking for curious factoids to flesh out an authentic setting. Trivia.

Years ago I did a bull trout survey in the Skokomish at night. You put on a dry suit and snorkel downstream with a waterproof headlamp searching for the fish. All we found was a single pink egg, tremulous under the flashlight, like a lost pomegranate seed. Then we drifted until the current began to pick up dangerous speed and Larry Ogg had to pull me to the shore by my arms. Later, when I read *Shelton's Boom*, I discovered that Larry was descended from a long line of Mason County Socialists. On the ride home he gave us bite-size Milky Way and Snickers bars, and I fell asleep before we were out of the forest roads in the Olympics.

When I worked at Mount Rainier we followed a woman into the woods. She had become part owl. Her job was to entice them out. Our job was to carry the live mice. Somehow, after years of doing spotted owl survey, this woman's larynx changed. She croaked in a language that was articulated somewhere deeper than tonsils. Her tongue must have changed shape. We followed her through the woods on the northwest side of the mountain all day and we saw no owls. And no owls croaked back at her.

Pockets of loss lurk like volcanic gas all over the terrain here. As it gets hot this year I notice how the air seems visibly brown. The mountains are blurry. Our memories are blurry about what has happened here. The wildflowers have been raked off Mount Rainier by foot traffic and low-level ozone. Jobs are gone. I think about how many of us doing any kind of progressive work in this region are out on bull trout survey: We swim beneath the surface combing for what was here before, and taking inventory of what is now. There's the chance that you will be changed by what you're looking for. Your tongue could change shape like the woman at Rainier.

Almost everyone I know and have known in Olympia came from somewhere else. There is a lot of new growth here. A very few people's grandmothers live here. I am a local only in the sense of people who could be born anywhere. Nobody in my family needed the water, timber, fish, or for that matter the brewery. My dad got a job at an insurance company that closed a few years ago. Most of us around here are that way. This is, at times, a town of particularly short memory.

This is another place where progressive white people escaped a few decades ago, like Eugene and the Islands. Where kids come for the music and hippie kids alight after touring with jam bands. College town. Even the legislature imparts a degree of transience. It's as seasonal as ski chalets, as raspberries. My friend Frank says if you've been here less than thirty years you're a tourist. Olympia is overrun.

This area is known for its endangered species, for its water, for its beer, for its music scene and its scenery. You can live for years here passing Northwest Coastal Art on street corners and sending your relatives smoked salmon on holidays. You can live here for years and believe you understand and yet not understand what it is you are living in. This is the difference between knowledge and trivia, between trivia and history. Facts can be arranged in a way that invites participation or they can be dispensed loosely and without correlation.

At the same time, a historical society formed this year and there are these little local histories popping up in the bookstore. There's a collective reach back. People look for what was here before. Maybe in an attempt to connect more completely, to put down roots.

I like reading about the IWW, criminal syndicalism, Woody Guthrie working for the Bonneville Power Administration. I'm glad I know about the people who lived on Eld Inlet. I'm glad I know about the internment of Nisqually people on Fox Island. We're traditionally presented with history as a thing that happened somewhere else—certainly nothing to intervene in—trivia.

During fall quarter the meat of my work was really around local history. We worked on video and I followed the news. I went to OMJP meetings. But a lot of my work was reading about criminal syndicalism and the Loyal League of Loggers and Legionnaires. Studying the history of this area roots me. It makes me more conscious of the land and more conscious of myself and of the people around me as actors in history. Studying local history is motivating. We've certainly waded in the same water and wandered on the same beaches as very brave people. It makes bravery seem more possible. Something that can occur on the forest roads around the Skokomish.

Maybe all places are this way and everyone is startled when, dredging through a tedious history, they stumble upon a massacre a little to the south, internment camps amongst the islands, genocide stretched wide and sore across the surface of everything. We are startled to discover that the places where we live are important.

This area is contested. And chock-full of progressive white people who moved from somewhere. We can believe somehow that we gave birth to this place, that we have some measure of responsibility for its beauty, that it's somehow a testament to our own ingenuity that we wound up here. We can exist here a very long time without noticing that our location is dynamic, settled in the midst of the continuum of a brutal history.

Shortly before school started I walked with Colin to Puget Pantry to get cigarettes and a few last-minute prizes for a bingo game I was coordinating at work. It was late morning. We were having a bingo party because it was my last day as "drop-ins coordinator." I had been "drop-ins coordinator" for a year. I drove people around in the company car. We went for walks in the woods and watched them pile-drive bridge-posts into the muck beneath Fourth Ave. We always joked about stealing the company car and going to Mexico. I convinced Colin to walk with me because Puget Pantry had "The Who's Tommy Pinball."

I picked out various pastel gel pens in complementary color combinations while Colin tried to figure out how to plug in the pinball machine and the man behind the counter searched for my brand of cigarettes. On the radio the announcers were talking about giving blood. It was hard to hear. They were talking about giving a lot of blood . . . fast. It was the quantity of blood that made me pay attention—like something out of that *Hellraiser* movie. What would make the radio announcers ask the whole country for blood, a surreal amount of blood?

I asked the man behind the counter what happened. I had trouble understanding what he said. "Two towers. Someone bomb."

"Someone bombed the World Trade Center?"

"Airplanes," he gestured with his hands.

"Someone crashed airplanes into the World Trade Center?"

He nodded at me. I asked him for matches. The people on the radio continued to talk about all that blood. Colin and I sat on the sidewalk beneath the pay phone and smoked cigarettes. We thought it might be World War III. We went home and set my boom box up in the living room and listened to the radio. I was supposed to fly to Boston to see my parents the next day. I called my dad. Then I walked to work. I still thought it might be World War III.

On the way to work I had, for maybe the third or fourth time in my life, no doubts about whether I was in the right place doing the right thing. I figured if it was World War III, being "drop-ins coordinator" was a damn fine situation to go out in. I liked the people I drove around in the company car. I couldn't think of something I'd rather be doing. I felt overwhelmed with joy and gratitude all the way to work, where we decided not to play bingo. A right moment.

Around the time I stopped being drop-ins coordinator, I made a map. The salmon beneath downtown Olympia were on the map. Perry Creek was on the map. Coffee and Anxiety were on the map. The busiest place on the map was around work: Staff Office was big. My boss was on the map. St. Peter's Hospital Crisis Services was on the map. This is how I know things have changed. My job is no longer the axis of my map. I trust myself to do other things. For a long time I stuck with my job because I had some modicum of success there. It was what I had. It was a big risk and a big sacrifice when I stopped being drop-ins coordinator. I cried about it sometimes during fall quarter.

Part of the last nine months has been trying to find other right moments. Trying to put myself in their trajectory. Trying to be useful and trying to be fulfilled by my work. This year I also dealt, albeit distantly, with some of the aftermath of those planes flying into buildings.

The Patriot Act passed. Over a thousand people are still, as far as I can tell, being held somewhere in the United States, and it's unclear why. They arrest the "Dirty Bomber," someone apparently "in the very early stages" of planning an attack on the U.S., and this is big news. What does this say about the other thousand people held somewhere? That they weren't in the early stages of planning anything.

Things like this send you scurrying into history for what has occurred before: the Smith Act, the Espionage Act, the Criminal Syndicalism Acts, the Alien and Sedition Acts, years of internment, centuries of slavery and genocide, the Chinese Exclusion Act, the Palmer Raids, HUAC, the Canwell Committee, COINTELPRO.

Working in OMJP, and trying to decode escalating fascist policy changes, gave me a rabbit hole to follow into history. I tried to use my study of local history early in the year and later my study of media history to inform my response to the current war and the current level of domestic repression.

Drawing links between historic repression, racism, propaganda campaigns and xenophobia to our present situation has been very empowering for me. It took two quarters before I really felt ready to immerse myself in community work, but I think these quarters helped me have a better understanding of what this particular war means in this particular place. Labor history in the Pacific Northwest has been particularly impacted by war, and the West has been deeply marked by racism. The brutal history drives home the importance of resistance and it makes national and international events relevant on a local level. So much of this has happened before. We can look at that history and then choose which side we want to be on now, and how willing we are to fight.

I still looked for my trivia factoid history. Things that might make good asides in a novel someday. I bought the book about the Wild Man of the Wynoochie. I don't remember ever paying a lot of attention to regional history in the past. I have an introduction now.

In a lot of ways the Pacific Northwest is a place that has been continuously colonized, first by white people and then by waves of more affluent white people. Land begins to shrink. There is less and less access to the water. Histories get buried in sediment, because we feel attached to this place and we want to believe it is ours.

It's important to search for what was here before. And to remember the racism, class repression, genocide. This process has been happening for me off and on for a while, but I searched with more intensity this year. I spent an insane degree of time with *Shelton's Boom*. My seminar thought I was crazy, but I was able to step outside of packaged history and form my own conclusions by comparing various texts. This was an empowering experience for me—the sense that something new could be accomplished with history. The sense of something dynamic.

Looking for where I fit into all this forced me out into the community. I think if someone told me last year at academic fair that I was going to spend spring quarter of this year at meetings, asking large groups of people to dress up as doves, and putting my phone number on flyers, I would have signed up for FOVA. There have been times this year when my fear of nonlinear editing and my agoraphobia have been engaged in a fight to the death. Sometimes I think my fear of technology just won. It's that shocking to me—where I've come as far as my involvement in community.

At some point in the past, I stopped really observing Olympia and started preparing to leave. I began escaping. It's tiring to pay attention to a place your whole life. At some point it becomes very enticing to just assume you know. In many ways the last year has been about seeing my home.

You come to take for granted where you belong in a town. Like in bad relationships where one partner is always in the parent/caretaker role. If you are bored, you begin to rearrange facts out of the front pages of the phone book until they sound mythological. If you have an overactive fantasy life, you just start making things up. You try your lies out on newcomers. You can remember just enough unrelated pieces of trivia to hold up coffee table conversation and never have to think about anything disturbing or demanding of action.

They call Olympia the gateway to the peninsula. Highway 101 begins, spontaneously, between Capitol Lake and Tumwater Historical Park. Highway 101, the real gateway to the peninsula, occurs in the sky above the broken parkway. It splinters away from I-5 in the midst of an overpass, gargantuan and disconnected from the earth. I-5 was bent to pass within sight of the Olympia Brewery. The Brewery belches effluent into the river. The river we floated in inner tubes, screeching Buddy Holly and the Supremes.

Most of my knowledge of this area trickles out in a random smattering of unrelated facts. A trivia collection and a set of unspoken superstitions. I used to tell people there was something in the water: once you drink it you won't be able to stay away for long. The trees have ears. Everybody believes there is something special about the people they know and the place they are in when they're nineteen. Superstition and factoid.

Trying to understand history as something situated firmly on the streets, all down the inlets and amongst the trees, is in many ways a blind search. I think the process of learning to see what's around me has been just as much that night snorkel trip down the Skokomish.

I'm still pretty shell-shocked by this quarter. I spoke to a room of about forty international students. I collected hundreds of linens. I've helped in the planning of two conferences, facilitated meetings, danced down the street with forty people from the ages of seven to seventy dressed as doves. I'm comfortable with the dynamics of the Olympia area and I've done a lot of the elements of it. I've designed templates that became headdresses and worked with costumers and mask-makers. I've facilitated a lot of people's artwork. I've had the pleasure of working on art in a place where there was a community supporting artwork. I've designed or facilitated three games. I've gathered a lot of food donations.

Who is this person who likes to put on conferences? How did I get here?

At no point did I choose to be active in OMJP. This is just something that occurred. I think one of the truths about the learning style of Rachel Corrie, which has been firmly established this quarter, is that I Work Well in Groups. I will not leave the house if it's to turn in my own work or complete some other act of self-preservation. I will never leave my bed. This is how I was hoping to study the archival material I gathered in Shelton: from bed. I have a strong sense of responsibility to groups. I just imagine Larry sitting alone in The Olympia Center and I get on the bus.

I'm not sure how relevant my work has been to this area. I think peace doves and cranes will happen again next year, and hopefully they'll be a Procession institution. So that's slightly more of a venue for the expression of anti-war values. It's a community-building opportunity for people who do peace work. It's intergenerational. It gives people in the Evergreen community a chance to work with people in the broader progressive community. In a lot of ways I think the Procession is a values statement. I'm happy to see a peace message included in that. I think it's important for people who oppose war and repression to speak about who we are as a community in addition to speaking about war and racism and injustice. We are not outside. I think it's important that human rights and resistance to oppression be included in the way we define ourselves as a community.

There were some moments: a couple of girls from a local high school saw the announcement in Oly-Network and came by to help make batiks, even though they weren't going to be in town on the day of the Procession. I listened to a longtime activist Ramona Hinkle explain to one of my mom's friends about the role of the United States in the overthrow of the Allende government. *No, we haven't been "helping" down there for all these years.*

Those moments made me think that creating a space for people to interact is as valuable as anything else. I think a number of people who wouldn't march in a protest showed up for doves. I hope those people will be slightly more likely to march in a protest from now on.

I think our conference in April was certainly a good networking opportunity. The event we're planning for the 29th is an attempt to continue to build an activist network in the region. We have contacts in Seattle and in Portland, as well as in more remote places like Eatonville and McCleary.

The unexpected thing that happened for me this quarter was the Procession Studio. I have misgivings about that place. It ate up a lot of my time being there. People were offering themselves as human shields in Palestine and I was spending all of my time making dove costumes and giant puppets. Having that place is such an immense privilege. There's something uncomfortable for me about having a lot of privilege and using it to make art. I think it relates to a similar wariness of espousing radical politics and having big hair on a college campus. Maybe there's something escapist about it.

At the same time it felt right to be there. Ignoring all other factors, I would choose to spend eight hours a day for the rest of my life making things in a giant room full of other people, of various skill levels. On a personal level, I would like to find that somewhere else. Collectivity around art. Support for it. A roomful of people helping each other make things. I was startled by how much I felt at home, and I was a little conflicted about it. I'm glad I had the experience of being in a crowded place where everyone believed that the thing in my head needed to be made. I'm not entirely sure I've had that feeling before.

The other unexpected thing was that I cried on the bus after the last day of class. I remember once at the beginning of fall quarter we broke into groups and talked about community-building within the context of our program. I told Lindsay and Jamie that I didn't really care about getting to know people in the class. I think I said, "I don't need you to be my friends." It was some kind of preemptive strike.

I would not have figured out how to be as active as I am without the other people in Local Knowledge. I spent a lot of time with the homeless group. I went with them to the City Council. I went to the community conversation. I slept out overnight on May Day. I go to events at SPSCC and in Olympia and on campus. I'm much better informed about my community because of the time people have spent studying it. I also faithfully attended video screenings without ever producing anything of my own. The screenings were a great way to invest myself more in supporting other people's work.

I've never been in a yearlong program. I'm glad that I did it. It forced me to be a lot more accountable than I have been in the past, and to be more honest about my process. It took me most of the year to feel at all comfortable letting people see my process and asking for feedback. I need to take more risks with people in the future, I think, in order to get support for my work. It's good to know that I *can* work with people for a long time and let them know what I'm up to without anything terrible happening. I'm not sure how the work I did in Local Knowledge will look on a résumé. I learned a lot about what to do when you aren't at work (assuming you're not lucky enough to work at a progressive nonprofit). How to engage in civic discourse. How to create civic space. How to be in community.

I remember reading a description of Evergreen in a college guide about schools you could go to if you *weren't* valedictorian of your high school. It said, "Evergreen is the kind of school that transforms students' lives." I've always kind of waited for that religious experience to happen. I'm not sure that I'm ever going to get a job making dove costumes or gathering food donations for conferences. Certainly not teaching economics. I developed a whole different modus operandi through the work I did in this program. I think giving up comforting habits and behavior patterns is one of the most radical things that can happen. Think what would happen if we all gave up oranges in the winter and driving cars? So it's a radical change that I abandoned the Shelton archive-bed education plan. I think this program will have more of a long-term impact on my day-to-day life than anything else I've done at Evergreen.

Perry Creek bleeds out into an estuary as it empties into the inlet. In the beginning of winter, the smell of the carcasses rises all the way up into the hills. In the summer the fry dart around in the pools beneath logs. Waterflies live in strange earthenware cocoons beneath the water, clinging to rocks. Sometimes morays piggyback in salmon redds. That way they don't have to dig to spawn. They aren't something you want to run into wading up a creek: little wiggling eel creatures with disproportionate mouths.

In the summer the rushes grow so tall you can hide in them and be completely invisible. This is where I came from: tunnels through rushes. I could spend all the light hours of all the days in tunnels through rushes in the middle of the estuary at the mouth of Perry Creek. This is where I came from and this is where I would have liked to stay: sunburned and hidden and close to water, making up whole pretend histories about shipwrecks and Swiss Family Robinson.

At some point signs went up in the middle of my estuary. Two red metal signs. Once I peeked out of the reeds and saw a kid I went to middle school with walking up one of the channels on the rocks. I slithered away through the reeds like a snake. These are the ways that places cease to be utterly intimate, childishly private. I took care not to read those signs. To this day I don't know whether they were warnings about the water quality or about the pipes buried beneath the stream or about private property. The signs were uncomfortable company. I disliked them. They did not belong.

It's difficult to relinquish our sureness of the places we live. It's difficult to look at warning signs, to seek out history, to confront the pieces that aren't idyllic. There's a lot in Olympia that wants to be idyllic in one way or another.

There have been so many times over the last several years when I've wanted to be anywhere except Olympia. I think I'll be gone within the next year. It's hard to explain it, to explain me in it, to explain how many different ways there are to see it.

The salmon talked me into a lifestyle change. The salmon beneath downtown Olympia are church. Years ago a group of us doing salmon restoration work rode a bus down to the East Bay Marina and observed the hole in the bulkhead. Salmon swim into that hole. Salmon have to make it all the way up Plum Street in that hole. That hole is Moxlie Creek.

Once you know that there are salmon down there it's hard to forget. You imagine their moony eyes while you walk home from the bar in your slutty boots. You're aware of them down there when you ride around in somebody's car—fanning their gills. It's hard to be extraordinarily vacuous when you always have the salmon in the back of your mind: in that pipe down there—on their way to daylight at Watershed Park. Salmon are the history that isn't trivia, the history that is now. They are what was here before.

I can picture the estuary at the mouth of Perry Creek in my head as it looks at this moment from the Perry Creek Bridge. The sun is starting to go down on the right side of the creek and the rushes are turning golden-green. Every blade moves. Rocks the size of my fist line the edges of the channels. Shade creeps in from upstream between the alder. The tide creeps in from the opposite direction and prepares to make all the detail disappear beneath a layer of brackish water and floating weeds. From the bridge you can hear the chuckling of the water and the noise of the grass.

At times I have been so angry at this place. I've been ashamed of this place. Suffocated in it. I look at this place now with no overwhelming desire to escape. No dissociation into factoids and trivia. No agoraphobia. Certainly no bored invention of mythologies to pass the time. I look at this place now and I just want to do right by it. The salmon beneath down town and the people who came to Drop-ins Group and the creeks and the inlets and the people who were here first and my elementary school teachers and my mom.

August 2002

My mother.

My mother walked with me to the bottom of the hill to wait for the carpool—I was nervous that I would do it wrong. My mother walked with me to be picked up and carried away by the cars—VW vans with heavy doors and crank door handles that took too many tries to open and close. Vans with seats in back that faced each other. Vans full of plastic cars and old garbage. I remember, or maybe I invent, that occasionally we walked down to the bridge and decided on the way that I wasn't going to school. Some days, I believe, my mother and I decided we couldn't part with each other—and we stood, holding hands on the bridge—explaining to the carpool driver that—thank you, we would stay.

We stole time that way. My mother taught me about skipping school. She took me to lunch. She drove me in the car to the Nisqually Delta and on the way we played the ABC game—and I won by finding the J's and Q's off of license plates. My mother wore no lipstick and we found minks in the alder saplings at the edge of the water.

We went to look for books in the bookstores in Seattle—two-story bookstores with complimentary cookies and castles inside. My mom bought me books on love and delinquency and, although she never said it straight out, I'm sure she was hoping I'd become a bank robber. My mother would never admit it, but she wanted me exactly how I turned out. Scattered and deviant and too loud.

I hallucinate that on those days when we turned away the carpool, we spent hours on the bridge—gazing back at the estuary I grew up in—counting herons. I hallucinate that this was the time when she taught me to spit and shout off that bridge and into the estuary.

My mother held me in her lap. She held my hand and she told me stories about fine things. I hallucinate that on this particular day my mother leaned down as we trudged back home from the bridge and whispered a truth to me.

She said, "You are my favorite. More favorite than either of your siblings and even more favorite than your father—more favorite than anyone who ever lived in Iowa and more favorite than ice cream." She whispered this in my ear and then she pulled back to look at my face to be sure I understood. She kissed my forehead, and she left little bits of the kiss there for the rest of my life—so she could spy on me through them when I became a teenager.

My mother also taught me how to see mystery: some people can't see mystery at all and this is tragedy. My mother—she is simple and smiles a lot. She is riddled with mystery. It's in the creases of her hands. My mother's hands glow. They have an ivory about them. My mother's hands. They are folded and curled in the blankets flayed out near her blunt shoulder. My mother has enchanted hands.

I am heartbroken when I search in my mother's drawers. I am heartbroken by the way she arranges jewelry. I am heartbroken at the thought of her, standing in her big bra and her pantyhose stretched over her underwear—standing and dabbing on lipstick. She takes good care of her lipstick. I can't describe her drawers: bracelets. Treasure of my mother. I know she returns her earrings to their little boxes when she finishes with them. My mother and lipstick—my mother moving pink powder across the bones of her cheeks—rubbing it into her pores until it hangs on. My mother ages and puts on makeup—slides bracelets across her wrists—where the skin is loose.

Sometimes my mother is up there, bobbing in the sky like Macy's parade balloons. Sometimes my mother is so big she looms over everything.

Summer 2002

Today—the 25th or 26th? I hear from Chris in Gaza. I am being invited there. I need to go. This is what I need to do: Reorder my passport. Make lists. Send Tuesday's minutes out over the Internet. Go to the protest tomorrow. Write an article for Monday's staff newsletter. Call Tom again—find out about county L&I mtg. Find out when Bush is coming to PDX. Order transcript. Make a list of things hanging over my head.

Hey everybody, some of our local leaders have come up with a great idea to make our jobs a little easier. Imagine this: If all of us donate a small portion of our paycheck every month (or even if only those of us who own homes donate), we can afford to build a giant warehouse in which to store many of our clients. They will have one big roof over their heads, and very little access to sunlight, and they might even get to come off their meds suddenly and with very little supervision. This will be an especially good option for our folks who don't have adequate shelter: the warehouse will be a place that accepts everyone—regardless of rental history! Sound good to you? Studies show it's only a little more expensive than building adequate low-income housing in the county and providing good support to people dealing with mental illness!

You may be asking yourself—who is writing this, and what happened to the real Rachel? Actually this warehouse idea isn't mine, but it's pretty similar to a phenomenon that's happening in our local government. Many of us have read in local papers about the "Downtown Safety" or "Anti-homeless" ordinances that arose this spring in the Olympia City Council. The most notorious of these, an ordinance making it illegal to car-camp, was defeated in the council in late June. There has been strong criticism of the series of ordinances as treating the symptoms of a problem without looking for a cure.

As these ordinances have been making their way through study sessions at the city level, the county has been doing a study of crowding at the jail. They have come up with a plan to build a new "Regional Justice Center" (read: mega-jail) as a solution to jail overcrowding. In the last month they have opened the issue for public comment, but they are only asking the public to comment on where we think they should put the mega-jail. They did not bother to ask us whether we think this is the most realistic solution to jail overcrowding. The county is pushing to float a bond to fund the jail in late fall.

Let's take a minute here and consider how this relates to us. How many clients have we seen who de-compensated to the point of doing "criminal acts" such as panhandling, urinating in public, or shouting obscenities because they did not have access to adequate shelter? How many clients have we seen leave HDH, most likely to return to drug use and imminent homelessness, because there were no available treatment beds for them—even though they wanted to get clean? What is the significance of closing beds at the hospitals and opening them in a big jail? What does this say about the value our elected officials place on the work that we do, on the welfare of our clients, on our jobs?

The county has scheduled a hearing on this issue for September 4th at 6 p.m., location TBA. Keep your eyes out for an announcement of the location.

September 2002

Hi everybody,

This is a reminder and a plea. I am going to be spending 14 hours at Percival Landing helping to facilitate the "Convergence for Peace" on Wednesday, September 11th. It starts with a candlelight vigil at 5:30 a.m. There will be a "bread-breaking" at 11 a.m. (bring your own loaf) and an open mic at 5:30 p.m. Between times we are inviting people to come gather around Percival Landing—particularly in the field across from The Olympia Center—and create a space for critical thinking, hope for peace, commitment to social justice, and resistance to racism and militarism. You can read a description of the event at www.omjp.org. We are also going to have a "wall of reflection" throughout the day, where people can draw/write/post reflections on September 11th and the past year. Era and I have both been working hard on this, as have several others. This day is going to be really dependent on people coming with their own contributions to the space—be that art, music, stories, leading meditation, shared food, literature, education, participatory activities, etc. If you can, please come by for a while, and please bring a contribution of some kind. Lawn chairs and such are welcome. Also, if anyone has a truck they like to lend out—or wants to get up at 5 a.m. and drive a "wall of reflection" downtown—we need some help.

Thanks,

Rachel

8/5/02 c 2350 :

Colin Reese sheds one tear.

(subsequently said tear to be eaten by the author herself)

September 17, 2002

The experiment of living with Colin comes to an end with mixed results. I stop wanting to kiss him on the mouth. We still want to talk ceaselessly to each other. I stare at him. He tells me we should sell short on crude oil. He tells me we could have made some money this year if we just filled my art nook with some barrels.

Tonight, I went to hear the ISM returnees from Freedom Summer. I can't imagine Palestine. They say we are invited there. I can't believe this can be true. Even me? I feel a strong need for more education.

September 19, 2002

I am pretty much gone from my home with Colin now.

Today I went out into the world a little. It makes me feel a little better. Went to the library and lost Sarah's coffee mug. My honeymoon with Sarah and Kelly is over and now we enter the period when I break and lose things.

September 25, 2002

Hi Gustavo!

Thank you for that article. I've been wondering about the potential for the U.S. government and U.S. companies to try to subvert democracy in Brazil because of fears that Lula may win and jeopardize FTAA (Free Trade Area of the Americas). Particularly with increased U.S. financial and military presence in Colombia and the Venezuelan coup. I am really shamefully ignorant about Latin American geopolitics. Do you know of online resources that talk about the U.S. role in Colombia, Andean Regional Initiative, Chávez coup? I have heard a lot of people say that the coup in Venezuela was CIA-backed and that it was easy to see it coming. Given the Bush administration's reactions to the coup, and given that half his advisors are carryovers from the Reagan administration, and given the history of my government's involvement in Central and South America, it seems very likely that the coup was CIA-backed. But I haven't seen any actual documentation of evidence of this. Do you know more about it?

Write back and tell me how you're doing. I don't have a lot of time to write at the moment. I'm just getting ready to start school again. We are also gearing up protests and letter-writing to try to stop war in Iraq. I think the U.S. public is against this war. I haven't talked to a single person (veterans, American Legion members, people with family in the military) who thinks we should go bomb the people of Iraq. A lot of people just don't understand why this is happening. I just think that the very small group of people who are in power right now are desperate to maintain that power and will manufacture excuses to do it. I think we will probably see another gulf war, but I really don't think it's what the public in the United States wants.

I hope you're well.

Beijos,

Rachel

Fall 2002

the rules

1. be subject to change

2. like blues brothers, be on a mission from god—yours is a search

3. be mindful of clues

4. respect

5. follow nose, stars, and old man with cool glasses

6. lose things/molt

7. do not tell yourself the story until you get home

8. always be planning rise to political power

9. do not make fun of candy ravers making out on the couch or you will morph into them before dawn

10. best to have a mental condition at all times but never to find a clinical name for it

11. above all things: beware of summer-camp love

12. leave no part of you behind

13. if you are bored, it's because you're too big and overgrown

14. it's best not to give too much power to the girl who lives in your room

15. every painting that anyone ever made was at least partly about grief

16. bees and meteors are clues

17. never forget that you were blessed with a lucky soul

18. all islands are the symbol of unenlightened desire

19. there's no time like the present but there's no lover like a former lover

20. there are worse things than spending a lifetime missing something you once had and lost

21. the working class and the employing class have nothing in common

22. cultivate keen eye for perverts and gated communities

    Rule 22 clause a: substitution of the phrase "in the buff" for "naked," "butt nekkid," "three sheets to the wind," "nude," "bare-ass," or "pert-nippled and pink flappies flying" is proof of pervert status

    Rule 22 clause b: gates are made of all kinds of things

23. as stated by Colin Reese 9/10/02 at 2300 hrs: "Peace is not supposed to make you cry late at night in front of your computer."

24. there is very little in this world you can count on

Fall 2002

Colin is missing his wallet and has two days' worth of messages on the phone. And either hadn't left or been to the house since the *New York Times* came last night.

How recent is the terror that he might be dead—that he might be dead in the apartment. No. Colin is not dead. Colin is visiting his friends in Seattle.

I worry about Colin. I know it must drive him crazy to come home to a litany of messages from people trying to subtly ascertain that

 he's still alive. This is unhealthy, unfair, and a vestigial way of living. Still, I am fearful for him. When you constantly think someone is about to die, you wear out after a while and just wish they would make up their mind one way or another. When out of the blue you are struck again by how temporary the people you love are, then it drives home their preciousness.

Colin, precious Colin. My terrible fear of losing him from this world. This belief that people are so easily disappeared in this country. A terror out of my childhood—that there is a world of nightmares waiting to snatch my loved ones from me.

Fall 2002

Colin is in jail and may get out on home monitoring. How is this better? He could die of an overdose in home monitoring and I am sure his manacle would never know the difference.

We are about to go to war. None of the churches want it. Nobody in Olympia wants it. Maybe someone in Idaho.

Fall 2002

Colin:

I know exactly how this works because I have done it before. Now I invent pictures of you because you have perpetually just left. In a few months I will look at these made-up pictures with a sick feeling in my stomach and wonder what sort of meticulous invention this is: like Orientalism. In a month or two I will realize that you never existed.

Who will I ask about diminishing marginal returns?

The tomatoes of our love finally turned red. Your mom ate them.

I dream about tomato plants.

The jail phone says, "Thank you for using US West" after I agree to letting my phone be tapped. As if I had a choice.

I am so sick of this.

Fall 2002

gray heron love

one gray heron stalks
corner to corner the shadow laced bedroom
tremors of heron legs like jointed straws
lined in digital clock light

the scattered heron march:
slowly one leg, then the other knee raised up
heron pacing projected on venetian blinds
hooking them with a heron claw
to cast stray dog eyes across parking lots
at the orange building
where junkie john's light lingers

you see them from a distance skating on the mudflats
origami bodies, wire necks and tissue paper wings
always singular, these gray herons past the subaru windowpane

you notice—touch your index finger to the glass
so your mom looks too but
her eyes sweep automatic back to the persistence of the highway
immune to the petrified distraction of the heron dance

anonymous gray herons:
their forms slip into your dream vocabulary
your eyes save them in deep linty pockets and amber jars
but their beaks are needles and they don't notice you pass
eyes with no pupils in constant dialogue: heron with itself
they send messages with their outlines
then glide into the horizon while you're forming your reply

tonight up close
it's not so graceful
heron heels rattling on unkind floor
and your eyes parched for a highway they can sweep back to
get stuck on brittle arms clasping brittle rib cage
one gray heron twitching
you are not immune
to heron wings: elaborate maps of
collapsing charred vein rivers, tiny pinprick cities
track mark freeways

things happen
a skinny boy perches on the split pea soup couch
stares under your eyeballs across his camel filter
he shows you thumbholes in his sweatshirt
smells like lemon soap, takes a piece of your hair
things happen
old ladies with blue perms find winning lottery tickets
on the ground
kids step in dog shit running barefoot along the waterfront
a stranger with thumbholes takes your hand
and jumps out the window
you enter the dance of one gray heron

retrace no steps
pucker lips around no question
flick your eyes back to no persistent highway

you hang your need on each other's foreheads
like older sisters practice lipstick and curling irons
on their toddler brothers

you hang your need on him at the door
kiss him too quickly to conceal your bared-teeth smile
search his eyes praying for pupils
look for signs of the monotonous gray heron stare

you kneel down in his mother's need
she appears above the mirror as you brush your teeth
in her white nightgown
she leans forward letting her book close in her lap
and she and you kneel down in recognition
of the need and hope you pin like ribbons
on each other's foreheads

his need is like smog in los angeles
it only shows up at the horizons, shades the hills
but invisible it lurks everywhere.

the gutterpunks outside the coffee shop squeak at you for change
you don't stop to dig through your pockets anymore
their pupils look small but it might just be the sunshine
every outstretched hand becomes potential heron beak
snapping up your quarters and inserting them
into the undersides
of shrinking elbows

you dream about peeling the gray heron out of him
extracting feather after feather from cheekbones and neck
until you can lay palms flat on his skin

and kiss the glow of eyelids
you dream about waking up
next to an empty black sweatshirt with thumbholes
you wake up and he's next to you unknotting into sleep
sweat creeps across the sheets and breathes against your arms
when you run a thumb across the ridge of his shoulder blade
he flinches, twists away into the covers

your hand scampers back to the shelter of your chest
the other curls around it, knuckles keep each other company
you curl around yourself
outside the starlings wake and complain amongst themselves
about the eyesores around their choice of nests
it's a choice, you know, everything's
a choice and you can shake
the heron feathers off your sheets in the morning
and share your bed with the stray cat that sneaks in for leftovers
it's a choice, you know, but
fatalism makes better poetry and
you never did learn how to drive, so the highway gives
no persistent immunity to anything
it's a choice, you choose
what you witness from the cushion of your pillow but
before you jumped out the window what was it
you were looking at?
the gray heron waxes corpulent on need
but nobody injected you with anything
you can always change your mind and tomorrow
he can take his sweatshirt and go and the heron will go too
it's his. it's not yours
but things happen
and your sheets will always tempt you
with vestigial lemon soap and camel filters
it's a choice. you choose

your left eye opens in daylight
at a soft smile across the pillows

the long-fingered hand snatches gently
a piece of your hair
big ripe pupils and a kiss and your awkward jokes
and he hugs himself to keep from being dismantled
by his laughter
only a shred of heron down in the venetian blinds
certainly no flinch at your touch

the need hangs back in the morning
allows you time for dancing in your socks
and sly kisses searching behind your lips
in daylight the whole bed shakes when your boy giggles
making fun of each other's feet

you can be done witnessing
thumbholes in his sweatshirt
the grin as he makes up stories
about all the people in all the cars
the kiss he sneaks on your ear
you can lift his hand off your belly and send him away now
and never worry again when a spoon disappears
after he finishes kissing the tip of your nose three times
and conversing affectionately with your big toe
you can turn your eyes away from the heron dance
retrace no steps. pray for no pupils
blame no imaginary bird
it's a choice. you choose.

Fall 2002

Colin. The only person who understands why Colin and I made it so long is Colin. Colin also could have it much worse. Colin could be dead. Which to him would be neither here nor there. Colin.

I told him he's a loose cannon and I don't know if I want him in the apartment anymore. He is staying the night at his parents' house. I imagine them eating dinner and talking quietly about the Mariners and making puns. I imagine them eerily quiet. Everyone in my family would yell disastrously if I did these things.

What am I to make of Colin. It is no longer, at last, my concern. Oh colin colin colin. Somebody gap-toothed with girl lips.

Fall 2002

We are all born and someday we'll all die. Most likely to some degree alone. Our aloneness in this world is, maybe not anymore, a thing to mourn. Maybe it has to do with freedom.

What if our aloneness isn't a tragedy? Tragic passing of love affairs and causes and communities and peer groups. What if our aloneness is what allows us to speak the truth without being afraid? What if our aloneness is what allows us to adventure—to experience the world as a dynamic presence—as a changeable, interactive thing?

Fall 2002

Thinking about privilege—going to Gaza.

What is privilege? It is the thing that is uncomfortable to say. Your secret kinship with Sam Walton. Any advantage you enjoy based on your position in a society—anything unearned—arbitrary.

What is white-skin privilege. White-skin privilege is the giant iceberg looming beneath the tip that is security checks at the airport.

Fall 2002

ISM Connection—what would difference be

Reading—*Drinking the Sea at Gaza*—Amira Hass

The Gaza Strip: The Political Economy of De-Development—Sara Roy

What will happen in case of war in Iraq?

How do we link with Israeli activists?

Do you know anybody in Rafah?

Do reports on U.S. policy—what would interest people in Gaza?

ISM—act in ISM name with ISM control

Building a longer-term connection—keep institutional link

Gaza—reoccupation of Gaza

Sharon—long-term, low-intensity warfare—create clashes, go further, create more space between Egyptian border and Rafah—wall

Itinerary—spend a few weeks in West Bank

Joe—going to West Bank in January

Graham Usher—best journalist on West Bank—*Palestine in Crisis*

Al-Ahram Weekly—Cairo

Gaza Community Mental Health Programme

Fall 2002

Identifying Baby Steps

- continuing ed finished
- Major Pieces—get CPR
- List Baby Steps each day
- immediate things I can do/get out of the way
- watch a bunch of videos
- do training/contact with people from ISM
- figure my budget

- get traveler's checks
- price plane ticket/buy plane ticket
- check travel advisory for immunizations
- organize group of people to go
- meet with Jean E—call to set up interview re sister cities
- get flags to Fellowship of Reconciliation
- take out an ad—sell stuff—my stuff
- box stuff up
- contact *Olympian*
- make *Olympian* contact happen
- make master list
- list at bedtime for next day
- personal calls
- clean room
- Plan A—finish continuing ed
- Arrest support
- ISM training
- hang out with ISM for a while
- then go to Gaza
- CPT—Christian Peacemaker Teams
- adopt a refugee camp
- UN support
- Cultural Centers—Refugee Camps
- Ibdaa Dancers

Fall 2002

I am in love with my new coworker Isaac. I laugh so hard around Isaac. Like I laugh with Colin. Like Jacob makes me laugh.

Lately I am so in love with laughing. That's one of the things I noticed walking around with Jacob at Burning Man. I think maybe I picked it up from Jacob. Jacob is in anticipation of a good laugh. Jacob nurses the laughter out of things and then just gives in to it. A really willing-to-laugh person. He clearly appreciates laughter and he knows it. He knows he likes laughing with other people. I think he seeks it.

This made me conscious of laughter as something to seek. Coax it out. Laughter with people. Laughter with people is a turn-on. I remember Jacob saying that when people really know about something you are passionate about—like for him spiritual practice—it's a turn-on.

That's why I've fallen in love with my married coworker Isaac.

I love to laugh and I love to be creative and I love to make other people laugh and I love to be creative with other people and have other people feel the joy of making things.

Fall 2002

More to Do:
   Report-backs:
   Call programmers at KAOS
   Set up web-based report-backs
   Record, translate, get radio spots
   Call Glen
   Program Schedule 12–2 spot
   Cell phone, computer, P.O. Box
   Check computer for modem port
   Fund-raise

Fall 2002

Contact ISM—people doing stuff in Rafah

People in West Bank

People in Seattle

Get for Will—*One Land, Two Peoples*

Set up meeting with Simona

Make list of questions for Simona

Send out letter

Go over notes from Jean

Go over notes from Steve

Make itinerary for arrival in Israel

Write a mission statement—intention

Dinner together

All write down individual reasons we're going

Read books, seminar—read different things and compare

Packing—things to bring/not to bring

Contacts in Israel

Formalize contacts with Sesame—contacts in Olympia

All of us make lists of folks to call in case we get arrested

Local media contacts, media strategy

Make connections with schools—pen pals

Get ideas about sister-city community in Israel

Winter 2002

What did I do fall quarter—

created resource sheets

workshop proficiency

acted as networker

facilitated discussions

applied for and got a grant

participated in the organization of two protests

designed group activities

did background research on budget issues

wrote a bibliography, read, surfed the web

How does this fit into my academic career?

Developing an understanding of local politics in the age of globalization and using limited resources to organize on a local level

Moving from observation to experimentation to participation in local organizing efforts

Learning by sharing information with others

Looking at ways to make information more accessible

December 2002

Goals

Why do I want to go?
I've been organizing in Olympia for a little over a year on anti-war/global justice issues and at some point it started to feel like this work is missing a solid connection to the people who are most immediately impacted by U.S. foreign policy. I feel pretty isolated from the world in some ways because of living in Olympia my whole

life. So I've had this underlying need to go to a place and meet people who are on the other end of the portion of my tax money that goes to fund the U.S. and other militaries.

This is an extension of the work I've already been doing for the last year and a half or so. It's also an opportunity to get the learning that comes from traveling while hopefully having my trip have some use to the people I'm going to see.

My activism at this point has been extremely tied to Olympia. The way I work comes out of living in Olympia my whole life. Thinking about the ways in which U.S. foreign policy impacts people in this area—and how that relates to the impact of neoliberal economic policy in this area—trying to experiment with forms and methodologies of social change work that are appropriate to this community—using contacts and resources that I've developed through living in this community. Trying to be local and be respectful of the local is a big part of my ethic, I guess.

January 2003

Call Michi

Barbara: Options class—pen pals

Joe F.

Get guitar

Call TESC (paycheck)

Get Sarah note about paycheck

Call Israeli woman

Call San Francisco ISM

E-mail Adam Shapiro

Return library books

Garage

E-mail AIC

Hey Mom, I'll call you tonight, but you could e-mail to me with anyone you know who it would be good to contact if I get in trouble—
though I'm not planning on it—friends or family who would call their
congresspeople, etc.—also, friends who might be interested in getting info or at least knowing that I'm going. The emergency contact
people should probably be sympathetic to the cause, otherwise it
could cause a lot of problems for me. Also, the media has enough
contact with people who are not supportive of Palestinian self-
determination. I don't need to put them in touch with more. But for
the other list, people who might be interested in hearing that I'm
going . . . that could be pretty much anyone who wouldn't mind getting a letter or an e-mail.

I'm going to give *The Olympian* your number. Please think about
your language when you talk to them. For instance, if you talk about
the "cycle of violence," or "an eye for an eye," or "no side is right,"
you could be perpetuating the idea that the Israeli-Palestinian conflict is a balanced conflict, instead of the national liberation struggle
of a largely unarmed people against the fourth most powerful military in the world. These are the kinds of things it's important to think
about before talking to reporters.

Also the word *peace* . . . the word *nonviolent* . . . I think it's
important to spend a lot of time on what *peace* means. Especially in
the context of Oslo. *Peace* meant a tiny fraction of what was once
Palestinian land, an actual increase in settlements on that remaining land, a network of Jewish-only roads crisscrossing that land, and
no guarantee that a Palestinian state would ever exist. *Peace* meant
the continuation of an economic stranglehold on Palestinians, and
Israel's veto power over any laws passed by the Palestinian Authority. *Peace* for the Palestinians has also frequently meant being
attacked, as Israel has a history of violating cease-fires. I don't know
if you saw Steve Niva's article on *Counterpunch*, but Sharon has, I
think, pretty much admitted that suicide bombings are a way of getting more land under the guise of security. *Peace* for Sharon means
not having an excuse for land grabs.

I think it was smart that you're wary of using the word *terrorism*.

It's important to realize that state policies that lead to deaths by malnutrition, destruction of housing, "accidental shootings," assassinations, economic strangulation, and imprisonment without trial ("administrative detention") are all acts of state terrorism—if we define terrorism as acts of violence directed at civilians for political purposes. In terms of the suffering of innocent people, it's a little ugly to try to quantify that suffering with numbers, but it is true that many more Palestinian children have been killed since the outbreak of the first intifada. The London *Independent* apparently doesn't even allow journalists to use the term *terrorism* because it's obfuscatory and it gets in the way of reporting.

The scariest thing for non-Jewish Americans in talking about Palestinian self-determination is the fear of being or sounding anti-Semitic. Reading Chomsky's book and talking to my non-Zionist Jewish friends has helped me think about this. Mostly, I just think we all have the right to be critical of government policies . . . any government policies . . . particularly government policies which we are funding. It is important to recognize that the people of Israel are suffering and that Jewish people have a long history of oppression, which I think we, as U.S. citizens and as non-Jews, still have some responsibility for—at least for understanding the role of anti-Semitism, U.S. foreign policy, and the slaughter of Jewish people in Europe (which the U.S. did not intervene to stop immediately, and some of which we might have prevented had we allowed Jewish refugees to come here in greater numbers).

I think white people sometimes suffer in the United States from a system that still privileges us over people of color; men suffer from the system that privileges them over women; and Jewish Israelis suffer (much more than white people and men in the U.S.) from a system in Israel that privileges them over Palestinian-Israelis and Palestinians in the Occupied Territories. Nevertheless, the system remains a racist one.

I also think it's extraordinarily important to draw a firm distinction between the policies of Israel as a state, and Jewish people. That's kind of a no-brainer, but there is very strong pressure to conflate the two. Thus, the pro-Israel lobby becomes the "Jewish Lobby" and criticism of Israel becomes anti-Semitic. I try to ask myself—whose interests does it serve to identify Israeli policy with all Jewish people? All I can think of is that it serves people who want to stifle all critique of Israeli policy, people who want to execute various foreign policy goals under the guise of doing something humanitarian for Jewish people (i.e. U.S.), and neo-Nazis who want to use Israel's policy as a way to justify their hate. Anyway, I just wanted to encourage you to think about these things when you talk to the press.

This kind of stuff I just think about all the time and my ideas evolve. I'm really new to talking about Israel-Palestine, so I don't always know the political implications of my words.

Rachel

Winter 2002

What you might not realize is that for me, this is *the end of life as we know it*. Life has always been based here, in Olympia. There has never been a me that did not live here. I have never had a home that was not here.

What does this mean about leaving? And what does it mean about going to a place where there are people who have never seen their homes?

December 2002–January 2003

My values. My values. My values.

I value respect for other human beings.

Responsibility for myself—accountability

Love

Trust other people.

Believe others are doing the best they can with the resources they have.

Independence/Autonomy

Creativity

Ethical—inside

Forgiveness

Honesty

Humor

Integrity

Courage

Loyalty

Critical thinking

Curiosity

Celebrating people

Community

Family

Keep myself safe/protect my core

Equity/Justice/Fairness

January 25, 2003

Very little problem at the airport. My tight jeans and cropped bunny-hair sweater seem to have made all the difference—and of course the use of my Israeli friend's address. The only question was, "Where did you meet her?" The woman behind the glass appeared not to notice my shaking hands. Took a sherut into Jerusalem. Noticed that the Holy Land is full of rocks and it seems like driving, you could fall off these hills. Just before we leave the airport, I read in the *Let's Go Israel* book Will got from Barnes & Noble that more Israelis have been killed in car accidents than in all of Israel's wars combined. I am still trying to decide what to make of this tidbit of information a day later.

The servis/sherut was expensive—eighty shekels—because I arrived around 4:30 Friday—at the beginning of Shabbat. A man from France helped me talk the price down from one hundred shekels. The driver said to tell anyone who asked that we paid forty shekels, because they would make him go back if we said we paid eighty. I didn't understand at first, but then, sure enough, an Israeli airport security person leaned into the taxi . . .

- buy Israeli phone card
- buy phone
- e-mail Michael
- call Joe
- print Will's contact
- call Gili
- change $
- call Mom with cell #
- call Beaver

January 25, 2003

My introduction to curfew is gentle: a rush out into the street in the midst of our training to buy lunch before the shops close in Beit Sahour. When we enter the street to buy shawarma and falafel there is music—singing in Arabic—pouring into the street from somewhere. A hidden loudspeaker. By the time the whole group of us have food, the noise is the bleat of military jeep horns and a voice shouting through a bullhorn—the squeal of a car pulling backward down the narrow streets after it comes face to face with the first jeep— border police or IOF—I don't remember which. The jeep backs them down and I think they might crash—with people still in the streets and walking fast and shops closing and the voice in the jeep yelling— I understand on a shallow, surreal level, why people call the Israeli military fascist/Nazi, etc., because the only experience most kids my age living in relative comfort in the U.S. have that involves squealing jeep tires and megaphones and yelling (Susan translates: "Go home—Get inside") is watching World War Two movies based in Nazi Germany or occupied Poland. As we go on with the training there is noise and flashing lights outside and then more loudspeakers—but it is not real for me because somehow I am inside this building with these people—mostly young people—and it is like one of those Crisis Clinic trainings at Cispus camp. Everyone extending theories into the air—elaborating—everyone precisely revolutionary.

Demos—call everyone in-country

Talking—no hearsay. Call hospitals, official sources. Quote. Don't appear to judge rightness or wrongness.

Nonviolence—Don't touch those we're confronting. Don't run. Nothing that could be used as a weapon. No self-initiating actions.

Border Police—blue, gray/black jeeps, "Police"
- have the right to arrest me
- sometimes are "Druze"—marginalized in Israeli society

Soldiers/military—olive green, APC—small tank, jeeps—no lights/ yellow orange
- right to detain but not to arrest

DCO/DLO—white jeeps with yellow lights (District Coordination Office, District Legal Office)
- at checkpoints you can ask to speak to DCO
- DCO—permission

Drone—very low hum 1–2 hours many pictures taken

F-16, Apaches

Hummer
- sometimes carries special forces or units
- every jeep has 4 soldiers—2 places free

White 4x4 (someone in senior military position)

Tanzeem—armed Palestinian vigilante groups

January 26, 2003

Travel Beit Sahour—Jerusalem. Meet Paul and Hugh. Reports of checkpoint closing due to election. Meet Eden. Spend evening with Hatem and friends.

January 27, 2003

There was an attack in Gaza the night before last that killed fourteen and injured around thirty. Also, I think, in Nablus several were killed and many were injured. Some people seem to think this is Sharon's tactic to prevent the various Palestinian parties from negotiating amongst each other to have a cease-fire. I have not been reading as much as I want to be; but as I understand, representatives from Hamas, PFLP, Fatah, and others have been in Cairo this week negotiating. An attack on Gaza while "Hamas is in Egypt" seems obviously likely to provoke retaliation during the Israeli elections tomorrow. This is good for Sharon's chances of reelection, and also, according to some analysis, the "assassination—suicide attack—land grab" progression appears to be a conscious tool of Sharon's to slowly take over the remaining areas of Gaza and the West Bank that are not colonized under the guise of security. I don't have time to go into this much further, but Steve Niva had a very good analysis of Sharon's fingerprints on the recent Tel Aviv attack on *Counterpunch* several weeks ago. Chomsky, also, details the strategy of sabotaging cease-fires in order to justify land grabs.

The West Bank and Gaza are under extremely strict curfew for the next few days—until after the election tomorrow. Most people I have talked to believe that there will be an attack within the green line in the next few days, and that then many more people will be killed and the attacks much worse in Palestine. Remember that curfew also means you are not allowed to leave your house at all. Not for food. Nothing. I am still in Jerusalem today, and trying to get to Rafah tomorrow to join other internationals there trying to prevent the demolition of civilian homes. I don't know if we'll be able to get there.

I am still relatively sheltered by being in annexed Jerusalem. There is evidence here of the occupation—very disturbing things. Walking around with Palestinians, I wait while they are stopped for no reason to show ID. There are donation boxes in the Old City that say things like "Old City Reclamation Fund." I think this is much the same Orwellian word use as the "freedom foundation" in the U.S. I am most disturbed, in some ways, by the blue Stars of David spray-painted on doors in the Arab section of the Old City. I have never seen that symbol used in quite that way. I know that this is something I can't really understand right now. I am used to seeing the cross used in a colonialist way. I can't really explain that sight. The reality of curfew, of the checkpoints—the few brief tips of the iceberg of occupation that I have witnessed so far—is not quite real to me yet. I'm sort of embarrassed about how long it takes me to really realize in my gut that people live this way.

The blank e-mail I sent to you was asking for help with media contacts—particularly fax numbers, of people at *The Olympian*, at KGY, KAOS, Co-op newsletter, KPLU, and MIXX 96 (Oly main-stream radio—but I think secretly leftists). Also, anywhere else you think I could get info to. I can't remember what else.

Love you. Colin will probably send you the e-mail list I started. Let me know when you have it.

January 27, 2003

Travel to Rafah. Pass soldiers at bus stations—bombed market in Gaza City. Jehan greets cab. Children grab my ass, throw garbage at my head, scream, "What's your name?" Sleep in tent. Gunshot through tent. Start smoking.

January 29, 2003

Thanks for looking out for me, Anne. I would like to be doing a better job of communicating back to Oly, but right now I have only extremely limited access to slow Internet and a bad keyboard. The three original delegates of the Rafah–Olympia sister-city association have all arrived in Rafah, a border town—mostly built of refugee camps from 1948–in the southernmost Gaza Strip. Olympia's newest sister city has already received some ambassadorship from the United States, and Washington State in particular. Someone showed me a bomb casing dropped from a helicopter when I first arrived here and said, "Made in America."

The United States, perhaps one of the most racist countries in the world, loves to make-believe that all sorts of other people are full of blind hatred and racism—at least when it's politically expedient. But people here are more discerning. Regularly they tell me that governments are different from people or that I come from a beautiful country . . . and when I give them the disbelieving look, "Well. I saw the nature on TV."

I don't have time to write, but we need more people here. This is a jail that the jailkeepers decided was too big, so now they are squeezing it smaller. The people here live within smell of the ocean but they can't go see it anymore.

"What is there beautiful? We could go see the ocean. One thing beautiful. Now I cannot see the ocean. What is for the children that is beautiful?"

An eight-year-old named Ali died the day before I came.

"He just wanted to look at the tank—see the tank—and they explode his head."

The surreal thing is that we are safe. White-skinned people stand up in front of the tanks and they open their weird tank lids and wave at us. Children play behind us and we yell, "La! La!" when they try to wander out into the rubble to play with us—because somehow even though you are born in a cage and you have never lived without shooting all night, you are still able to play.

I couldn't even believe that a place like this existed. But even more—can you believe there are children here? Forget the fear. They tell me that at night. Forget the fear. I am ashamed that I am scared for my own body and dying anonymously inside a house in one of the most populous places on earth, where children die as martyrs of the occupation, which we pay for quietly without ever knowing their names. We need more people.

I love all of you.

Rachel

January 31, 2003

Today I decide to follow Joe's lead and write in every spare crack of time in every day. I always regret the blank space in my journal from Russia. Here it is different. I am older and the world does not revolve around me. We are in Jehan's brother's apartment in Khan Younis. In the corner is a pedestal, much like my brass one, and on it is a framed shaheed poster. I believe this man, with a thin face superimposed onto an image of a gold-domed mosque, maybe Dome of the Rock, is Jehan's father. Killed in his car on her wedding day.

There is some visible class difference between this building in Khan Younis and say—Brazil or Block J. There are toys for the children. A table. But this apartment—with blank walls and wide windows and birds weaving in through this shortcut of rooms and out through windows on the other side of the building—would be symptomatic of nearly crushing poverty in the United States.

There is greenery in Khan Younis. Some trees and grassy places. Maybe it is shielded a little by Rafah—razed and bullet-riddled and bare, for the most part, of greenery. Jehan's uncle comes to meet us, sits with us. He is wearing what looks like a very drab dress, but he says he is wearing his pajamas. He tells us that there was a peaceful time in the late seventies and early eighties—when many Palestinians went from the Gaza Strip to work in Israel. "We build their buildings. We work in the factory." He says he built buildings in Israel. He says it is the leaders that make war. He says that things were better before Sharon.

Visits
- Gaza: Nursing
- UN
- Bank Action
- Khan Younis
- Children's Parliament 10–15-year-olds
- Women's group
- Teachers

Needs
- 1 beautiful banner—Arabic/English
- Many other supplies
- Use $ for banner fabric

Decisions Made—Jan. 31st Khan Younis Mtg.
- Take down tents, put up banners
- Put up banners in multiple areas, specifically Brazil & Block J

January–February 2003

Anise's House

11:30 p.m. two people in house. "Dangerous when tanks came to Brazil. Didn't see. Too dangerous. Stayed in bathroom." Sixteen meters between him and explosion. Israelis blew him up into air. Injured ankle and leg and back. "There is no work now." Wife pregnant—left house.

January–February 2003

Dr. Samir's house/garden: deflated soccer ball, hose into sapling lemon tree, bicycle, barbecue, handball paddles, blanket drying on a line. Trellises with vining trees. Tea on brown plastic wicker table. Rosebush with pink rose, water tanks with concrete, brick wall, long shadows.

Garden—dill, lettuce, garlic

onion in small hole

plastic bucket with crayon-colored clothespins

fig tree with small green fig buds

white plastic chairs

patchy lawn

apples

Dr. Samir's House

2 bulldozers, tanks

Went to kitchen. Stayed 2 hours. Tank stayed (no work, no school)

Most houses [in neighborhood] destroyed

Families escaped 1–2 months before

Usually 10 o'clock, suddenly tank shots

"We also afraid—no other place to go—three hours they destroy house. Before—no tanks, no bulldozers, no gunshots. Quiet. Good weather. No noise. After Intifada, daily. Gunshots daily. They will destroy fifty houses. No gun in my house, nothing. I trust in my God—so no problem."

$ = life—thirty years collecting money for house

Two families living in one house

1st time IDF came—11 p.m. to 4 a.m. brother's family and Samir's family in one room

Women and children—patted down first

They put heavy machine in brother's floor of house—gun turret thing—took windows and shot from upstairs

Play with children to distract

2nd time—10 o'clock—20 cm from door—tank stepped right into house

Another time 5 a.m.—destroy two houses

Soldiers—one came with sledgehammer on outside of house

Tank started firing—family started watching TV in kitchen—Tom & Jerry

"I go outside and look at my garden—lemon tree—some other trees— I ask myself, 'Okay, Samir, this year will you eat from these trees like other years?'"

Other houses empty and still standing

February 1, 2003

Eternally unprepared. We are at the head soldier's office drinking Fanta inside Usama's gated community of Rafah. This is my very poor drawing of the dead body we just carried, Tamer Khadeer, age nineteen. DFLP took responsibility for his attack on soldiers at Rafah checkpoint into Egypt around 2–2:30 a.m. last night. He had a big white hand poised in the air off the stretcher as if doing the crawl stroke or throwing a baseball. He was shot in the head and abdomen. We think. After we helped the water people do more repairs, we went to look for banner fabric. Jehan found Will and me waiting to pay the man for thirty meters of white cotton—told us there was a shaheed at the Rafah–Egypt border that ambulances couldn't get to. We met up at the apartment and rode in a strangely Californian SUV past the cemetery to the Palestinian side of the border crossing into Egypt. A swarm of people waited there—we were given a stretcher and ushered into an office—people talked for a while and then we went out—each of us with a handle.

We started into the field: five internationals plus Jehan. Jenny spoke over the bullhorn saying, "Do not shoot," "We are unarmed civilians," "We are internationals," naming the countries we came from and letting the IOF know our intention to retrieve this man's body.

The first response we noticed from the IOF was shouting. "Go back." At approximately midway between the buildings from which

we entered the field and the area of the body, the IOF shot in front of us about twenty meters.

As we continued to walk in the approximate direction of the body—the IOF shots shifted in direction—hitting the ground two to four meters in front of us. We also heard one to two high-pitched, whistling shots in the air above our heads. At this point we stopped and Jenny continued to talk to the IOF and requested to talk to the commanding officer. Initially, the individuals in the IOF building stated that we would not be allowed to speak to the commanding officer.

A white truck with a blue light rolled up and the person in the truck spoke over the loudspeaker. Told us to leave. Stated, "You'll get the body later," or "We'll talk to you later."

White truck cruised away and a tank and a bulldozer emerged from the IOF side of the checkpoint and proceeded toward the olive grove. They began moving dirt between us and olive grove. Smoke blew.

Created mound of dirt.

Shot repeatedly into dirt.

February 1, 2003

Subject: Re: much love

Holy shit, Todd—come here, come here! It's so important . . . and I think it could be particularly important to continue to have people come from Olympia. The e-mail I sent out to LK was pretty distraught—limited sleep and still getting settled in. Now I'm a lot more calm. I feel like the work we do is important and has the potential to be much more important, and also needs people who have a strong sense of how to support the people in this community in their struggle—rather than just starting our own separate glamorous "international solidarity show." The people here are incredible. Come here come here come here come here come here come here come here come here come here come here.

February 2003

oh rafah. aching rafah.
aching of refugees
aching of tumbled houses
bicycles severed from tank-warped tires
and aching of bullet-riddled homes
all homes worm-eaten by bullets and then
impregnated through bullet holes by birds.

oh rafah. aching fingers of rafah.
children born without fingers
and fathers unable to travel the twenty or thirty miles
to Gaza to repair their children's fingers.
clawed knuckles from old gunshots
bandaged fingers
and slimy small poking fingers between puffy lips of children
slobbery and wondering and blinking like all children
    but fingers patting and tapping at strange big
    hands
     amidst the music of shelling
      and the constant anonymous night-vision
       telescope of murder
        above and beyond and around and
        even inside.
       fingers
       cracked crusts of spackle concrete
      fingers
         of the endless rebuilding of
          things crashed:
           home.

         home.
          oh rafah. aching homes
            of rafah.

home of the rafah camp
rafah grown permanent with the names of the countries
that paid for the neighborhoods still attached.
home of rafah unleavable.
homes stickered
with glow-in-the-dark stars in teenagers' rooms.
homes constructed over a lifetime and unraveled in the night.
ache of rubble
and weedy rebar craning out of concrete boulders.
ache of ghost homes
looming without volume without mass
straddling this wall and this wasteland the wall demands.
ache of dinners
knees and haunches kneeling dinners spread over floors
in the music of gunfire the irregular heartbeat of the border
and living-dead homes waiting immobile
for bulldozers and tanks
and the shattering of tea glasses the bending of rebar
the tumbling of concrete and the ejection of people:
baby.
grandmother.
small girl curling her entire small hand around one big finger.
teenage boy with teenage boy legs and teenage boy laugh
ejected into rubble and homelessness and scattered
if not killed.

oh rafah. aching rafah.
children of rafah exploded.
children of rafah deafened:
deafened to tank wheels
deafened to explosions
gunshot music
shocking claps
drones.

———————————————————

February 6, 2003

Sitting in Ashraf's office with both Jennies and Will talking about the possible consequences for Gaza of a U.S. invasion of Iraq. Jenny's family may disown her if she doesn't go back to Britain.

Gaza may be invaded. "Transfer" is mentioned yet again. Yesterday Jenny spoke with the former colonial governor, who told her we were staging a "political protest" and that terrorists would sneak into our "political protest" and attack the settlements. The only people with us were the same water workers we've been working with for days. Jenny asked the man if he thought Ashraf was a terrorist. The man got very angry about that but Ashraf thought it was funny.

I got to be a bulldozer cowgirl again and no doubt many sexy pictures were taken. Two bulldozers repaired the road throughout the day. Jenny and Will held a banner and spoke through the megaphone for us. A tank stayed present throughout the action. And at some point a jeep arrived. This frightened me because I know at least one person was shot by soldiers in a green jeep—and I believe more than one person.

I started to feel really angry watching that jeep drive up—imagining that this is the same jeep that has been just aimlessly cruising around shooting people going about their business. Like the "sniper" in D.C.—only for the person in this jeep there are most likely no consequences.

Some youths—maybe three—came out toward the banner, and then soldiers got out of the jeep and shot toward the internationals. Jehan found bits of shrapnel later in her shoes.

My Jobs:

• Call workers' committees

• Call journalist union

I have been in Palestine for two weeks and one hour now, and I still have very few words to describe what I see. It is most difficult for me to think about what's going on here when I sit down to write back to the United States. Something about the virtual portal into luxury. I don't know if many of the children here have ever existed without tank-shell holes in their walls and the towers of an occupying army surveying them constantly from the near horizons. I think, although I'm not entirely sure, that even the smallest of these children understand that life is not like this everywhere. An eight-year-old was shot and killed by an Israeli tank two days before I got here, and many of the children murmur his name to me: Ali—or point at the posters of him on the walls. The children also love to get me to practice my limited Arabic by asking me "Kaif Sharon?" "Kaif Bush?" and they laugh when I say "Bush majnoon" "Sharon majnoon" back in my limited Arabic. (How is Sharon? How is Bush? Bush is crazy. Sharon is crazy.) Of course this isn't quite what I believe, and some of the adults who have the English correct me: Bush mish majnoon . . . Bush is a businessman. Today I tried to learn to say "Bush is a tool," but I don't think it translated quite right. But anyway, there are eight-year-olds here much more aware of the workings of the global power structure than I was just a few years ago—at least regarding Israel.

Nevertheless, I think about the fact that no amount of reading, attendance at conferences, documentary viewing, and word of mouth could have prepared me for the reality of the situation here. You just can't imagine it unless you see it—and even then you are always well aware that your experience of it is not at all the reality: what with the difficulties the Israeli Army would face if they shot an unarmed U.S. citizen, and with the fact that I have money to buy water when the army destroys wells, and the fact, of course, that I have the option of leaving. Nobody in my family has been shot, driving in their car, by a rocket launcher from a tower at the end of a major street in my hometown. I have a home. I am allowed to go see the ocean. Ostensibly, it is still quite difficult for me to be held for months or years on end without a trial (this because I am a white U.S. citizen, as opposed to so many others). When I leave for school or work I can be relatively certain that there will not be a heavily armed soldier waiting halfway between Mud Bay and downtown Olympia at a checkpoint with the power to decide whether I can go about my business, and whether I can get home again when I'm done. So, if I feel outrage at arriving and entering briefly and incompletely into the world in which these children exist, I wonder conversely about how it would be for them to arrive in my world.

They know that children in the United States don't usually have their parents shot and sometimes get to see the ocean. But once you have seen the ocean and lived in a silent place, where water is taken for granted and not stolen in the night by bulldozers, and spent an evening when you didn't wonder if the walls of your home might suddenly fall inward waking you from your sleep, and met people who have never lost anyone—once you have experienced the reality of a world that isn't surrounded by murderous towers, tanks, armed "settlements," and now a giant metal wall, I wonder if you can forgive the world for all the years of your childhood spent existing—just existing—in resistance to the constant stranglehold of the world's fourth largest military apparatus—backed by the world's only super-power—in its attempt to erase you from your home. That is something I wonder about these children. I wonder what would happen if they really knew.

As an afterthought to all this rambling—I am in Rafah: a city of about 140,000 people, approximately sixty percent of whom are refugees—many of whom are twice or three times refugees. Rafah existed prior to 1948, but most of the people here are people—or descendants of people—who were relocated here from their homes in historic Palestine—now Israel. Rafah was split in half when the Sinai returned to Egypt. Currently, the Israeli Army is building a fourteen-meter-high wall between Rafah, Palestine, and the border, and carving a no-man's-land from the houses along the border. 602 homes have been completely bulldozed according to the Rafah Popular Refugee Committee. The number of homes that have been partially destroyed is greater.

Today as I walked on top of the rubble where homes once stood, Egyptian soldiers called to me from the other side of the border: "Go! Go!" because a tank was coming. And then waving and "What's your name?" Something disturbing about this friendly curiosity. It reminded me of how much, to some degree, we are all kids curious about other kids. Egyptian kids shouting at strange women wandering into the path of tanks. Palestinian kids shot from the tanks when they peek out from behind walls to see what's going on. International kids standing in front of tanks with banners. Israeli kids in the tanks anonymously—occasionally shouting—and also occasionally waving—many forced to be here, many just aggressive—shooting into the houses as we wander away.

In addition to the constant presence of tanks along the border and in the western region between Rafah and settlements along the coast, there are more IDF towers here than I can count. Along the horizon—at the end of streets. Some just army green metal—others these strange spiral staircases draped in some kind of netting to make the activity within anonymous. Some hidden just beneath the horizon of buildings. A new one went up the other day in the time it took us to do laundry and cross town twice to hang banners. Despite the fact that some of the areas nearest the border are the original Rafah—families who have lived on this land for at least a century—only the 1948 camps in the center of the city are Palestinian-controlled areas under Oslo. But as far as I can tell, there are few, if any, places that are not within the sights of some tower or another. Certainly nowhere invulnerable to Apache helicopters or the cameras of invisible drones we hear buzzing over the city for hours at a time.

I've been having trouble accessing news about the outside world here, but I hear an escalation of war on Iraq is inevitable. There is a great deal of concern here about the "reoccupation of Gaza." Gaza is reoccupied every day to various extents—but I think the fear is that the tanks will enter all the streets and remain here—instead of entering some of the streets and then withdrawing after some hours or days to observe and shoot from the edges of the communities. I went to a rally a few days ago in Khan Younis in solidarity with the people of Iraq. Many analogies were made about the continuing suffering of the Palestinian people under Israeli occupation and the upcoming occupation of Iraq by the United States—not the war itself—but the certain aftermath of the war. If people aren't already thinking about the consequences of this war for the people of the entire region, then I hope they will start.

I also hope you'll come here. We've been wavering between five and six internationals. The neighborhoods that have asked us for some form of presence are Yibna, Tel al-Sultan, Hi Salaam, Brazil, Block J, Zorob, and Block O, as well as the need for constant night-time presence at a well on the outskirts of Rafah after the Israeli Army destroyed the two largest wells (providing half of the water for Rafah, according to the municipal water office) last week. Many of these places have requested internationals to be present at night to attempt to shield houses from further demolition. After about ten p.m. it is very difficult to move at night, because the Israeli Army treats anyone in the streets as resistance and shoots at them. So clearly we are too few.

I continue to believe that my home, Olympia, could gain a lot and offer a lot by deciding to make a commitment to Rafah in the form of a sister-community relationship. Some teachers and children's groups have expressed interest in e-mail exchanges, but this is only

Rasha

the tip of the iceberg of solidarity work that could be done. Many people want their voices to be heard, and I think we need to use some of our privilege as internationals to get those voices heard directly in the U.S., rather than through the filter of well-meaning internationals such as myself. I am just beginning to learn from what I expect to be a very intense tutelage in the ability of people to organize against all odds, and to resist against all odds.

Thanks for the news I've been getting from friends in the U.S. I just read a report-back from a friend who organized a peace group in Shelton, Washington, and was able to be part of a delegation to the large January 18th protest in Washington D.C. People here watch the media, and they told me again today that there have been large protests in the United States and "problems for the government" in the UK. So thanks for allowing me to not feel like a complete Pollyanna when I tentatively tell people here that many people in the United States do not support the policies of our government, and that we are learning from global examples how to resist.

My love to everyone. My love to my mom. My love to the cult formerly known as Local Knowledge program. My love to smooch. My love to FG and Barnhair and Sesamees and Lincoln School. My love to Olympia.

Rachel

February 7, 2003

Hi friends and family and others,

I know some of you may be surprised to hear from me—let alone from me in the Gaza Strip . . . so feel free to e-mail questions if you have them, although I have very limited access to e-mail right now—mostly due to limited time. I am asking people who care about me—or just have some passing interest in me—to use my presence in occupied Palestine as a reason to actively search for information about the Israeli-Palestinian conflict, and of course particularly about the role of the United States in perpetuating it. I am here because I recognize that as a citizen of the United States I have some responsibility for what is happening here. I'm also here because I need to see for myself. I want to suggest a few resources for people who may be new to the issue—or who are solely reliant on the U.S. media—everything always of course through the lens of critical thought:

www.palsolidarity.org—This is the web site of the International Solidarity Movement, which I am working with here. There are two others—soon to be three—in Rafah from Olympia, so if you check out the reports section you can hear from them.

www.ahram.org—*Al-Ahram Daily* is a newspaper produced in Egypt—English-language. Graham Usher has been suggested to me as one of the best reporters on Palestine.

Ha'aretz—a mainstream Israeli daily—available in English free online—but I don't remember the address.

www.merip.org—*Middle East Report*

www.electronicintifada.org—This Palestinian-produced web site provides thorough accounting of the impact of occupation on the people of Palestine.

Also, if you don't know any of the history, I suggest the book *One Land, Two Peoples* as a starting point . . . but again . . . I can't remember who wrote it. I also have an annotated bibliography of things I read before I left if anyone is interested.

February 8, 2003

Al Wafa Outreach Center—Al Wafa Medical Rehab Center

• health and disability statistics for Rafah and access to health care

• starting to collect information—about rehabilitation into activities of life, vocational rehabilitation

• working at stage 2—addressing immediate physical concerns

• wants to move toward addressing quality of life issues + vocational rehabilitation

• 4 physical therapists

• 2 occupational therapists

• 2 nurses

- 2 health educators
- program concerned only about people disabled by Israeli army
- 950 sessions last month for 80 people—about 30 sessions a day
- Care International funds Rafah

GUPW—General Union of Palestinian Women—Rafah Branch

- union for all Palestinian women and women married to Palestinian men
- office with embroidery on walls—veiled computers with little posters with cameo pictures of shaheed
- picture of Arafat with sunglasses and green, white, red, and black-painted Palestinian woman holding Palestinian flag
- currently working on women working with children
- train women in crocheting and needlework
- very bad economic situation
- how to make simple things useful
- concerned about women in rural areas—communication, gender, cooking, sewing
- mental support, social support, economic support
- training
- CHF provides furniture
- five workshops—for 2 weeks: women's rights, taking care of children, women's rights in religion. Q'uran gives women many rights. Women can choose their fiancés and husband. Education about these rights. Democratic elections—right to elect whomever you want, be in council.
- no women on council

Women's associations in the U.S. that would like connections with
  GUPW Rafah :

• Women's Center at The Evergreen State College

• maybe women's groups connected to Highlander

• Dick's e-mail for Traditions Fair Trade Association

Fatima's School

• GUPW president. Was teacher since she was only thirteen years old. Also in school.

• Six years renting. Now own their own place since Fatima.

• Fatima is fronting $ for materials and paying for labor.

• pillowcases, coin purses, glasses cases, dresses, wall hangings, keffiyehs, tablecloths, all hand-stitched. Larger "money necklaces."

• sources of materials

• International Women's Day march

• exhibition, Palestinian food

• 17 kilos of cookies sold last week—made fresh in accordance with demand—anise cookies

Gaza checkpoint—Abu Holi checkpoint—shops are being destroyed

---

February 8, 2003

I got a number of very thoughtful responses to the e-mail I sent out last night, most of which I don't have time to respond to right now. Thanks, everyone, for the encouragement, questions, criticism. Daniel's response was particularly inspiring to me and deserves to be shared. The resistance of Israeli Jewish people to the occupation and the enormous risk taken by those refusing to serve in the Israeli military offers an example, especially for those of us living in the United States, of how to behave when you discover that atrocities are being committed in your name. Thank you.

From: Daniel Dworsky
To: Rachel Corrie
Subject: Thank You

My Name is Daniel Dworsky. I am a reserve First Sergeant in the IDF. ID BDRCK2297771

The military prisons are filling up with conscientious objectors. Many of them are reservists with families. These are men who have proven their courage under fire in the past. Some have been in jail for more than six months with no end in sight.

The amount of AWOLs and refusals to serve are unprecedented in our history as a nation as well as are refusals to carry out orders that

involve firing on targets where civilians may be harmed. In a time now in Israel where jobs are scarce and people are losing their homes and businesses to Sharon's vendetta, many career soldiers, among them pilots and intelligence personnel, have chosen jail and unemployment over what they could only describe as murder.

I am supposed to report to the Military Justice Department. It is my job to hunt down runaway soldiers and bring them in. I have not reported in for eighteen months. Instead, I've been using my talents and credentials to document on film and see with my own eyes what the ISMers and other internationals have claimed my boys have been up to. I love my country. I believe that Israel is under the leadership of some very bad people right now. I believe that settlers and local police are in collusion with each other and that the border police are acting disgracefully. They are an embarrassment to forty percent of the Israeli public and they would be an embarrassment to ninety percent of the population if they knew what we know.

Please document as much as you can and do not embellish anything with creative writing. The media here serves as a very convincing spin-control agent through all of this. Pass this letter on to your friends. There are many soldiers among the ranks of those serving in the occupied territories that are sickened by what they see. There is a code of honor in the IDF called Tohar Haneshek. (pronounced TOW-har Ha-NEH-shek). It's what we say to a comrade who is about to do something awful like kill an unarmed prisoner or carry out an order that violates decency. It means literally "the purity of arms." Another phrase that speaks to a soldier in his own language is Degel Shachor (DEH-gel Sha-HOR). It means "black flag." If you say, "Atah MeTachat Degel Shahor," it means "You are carrying out immoral orders." It's a big deal and a shock to hear it from the lips of "silly misguided foreigners." At all times possible, try to engage the soldiers in conversation. Do not make the mistake of objectifying them as they have objectified you. Respect is catchy, as is disrespect, whether either be deserved or not.

You are doing a good thing. I thank you for it.

Peace,

Danny

February 11, 2003

Underground explosions in Yibna and Rafah due to Israeli Army anti-tunnel bombs.

Group [ISM] monitored, photographed, and demonstrated presence with banners. Tufah visits. Internationals witness aftermath of house demolition in Block J and another large explosion in Block J-Yibna area. Abu Holi checkpoint reported closed after army killed a man there. Principal day of Eid festival.

February 11, 2003

Tufah

2:00: said checkpoint would open

2:40: open with microphone

Six old men proceeded—then IOF announced only five at a time

Five women with four children and baby-in-arms

People exit along fenced corridor to left (south) of checkpoint. Do not appear to be getting checked.

Two more women—two walk back

Yelling—man runs forward—women kneel, stand up again, return

Yelling "Hamsa"

Men, women, and children come out of checkpoint from Mawassi

Young twenty-two-y.o. woman says sister denied visa—can't go to family in Mawassi—three months living out of Mawassi

- Women above thirty-five years old OK to enter

- Men above forty years old OK to go in

- Father inside. Family inside. Roadblock in Mawassi.

No problem passing between Rafah and Khan Younis

Here since 7 a.m. trying to get through

Ten 35-year-old women enter

Must prove identity

3:00: five to six men

3:04: five more men

One group stands at yellow sign halfway between checkpoint and roadblock—when allowed to move forward another group follows them.

Large crowd—women and kids on right, men on left

Bunker to right of checkpoint

Guard barriers

People with ID passes in hand

Women with babies, buckets, baskets, all middle-aged

3:10: group of women and children turned back—then proceed

Alternating women and men

3:25: men waiting—five

February 12, 2003

Continued underground explosions [by the IDF]. Abu Holi closed several hours. Unsuccessful attempt to enter Mawassi-Tufah. Two houses demolished in Block J-Eshroot area at 6 p.m. Four tanks, two bulldozers, and backhoe returned between 9 p.m. and 10 p.m. No further demolitions reported. Eid festival continues.

February 13, 2003

My new job = Media, make sure reports get written, call Michael at outset of actions, get numbers for press contacts from Joe.

Prepare for Simona interview

Prepare paragraph for rally

Set up system for media work

Finish journal for Monday & Tuesday

Resend e-mail to Simona, Sesame

Go to Block J and investigate homestay-work tonight

Go to Hi Salaam and visit new house—set up interview time

Buy cassette tapes

Call Dr. Samir

E-mail Phan and Michi about letters—Children's Congress

Talk with Phil, Alice about Children's Parliament

Right to education

Get UN guy e-mail, #—Joe

Get Hebrew from Danny letter, Hebrew for "Internationals"

Talk with other Israelis about use of Hebrew

Call Lela—working women on settlements—Mawassi settlements

Call Imad PRC about Saturday action

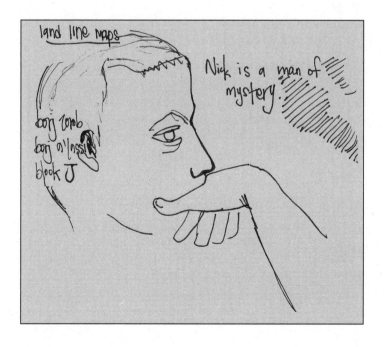

Call Mohammed

Call Jehan for Houda's details

Call Gili for talk with Alice, plan for Women's Day

E-mail pictures of products to Olympia

Tonight

Call Imad again

5 p.m. visit Ahmed

Call *Al-Ayyam*, Tagrit (*Arab Times*)

Tomorrow

E-mail out Arabic signs for Olympia

Call Imad again

E-mail Michael

Call Ahmed

Call Ashraf

Before mtg.—visit new house

Sat. a.m. mtg.—choose new house

February 13, 2003

Today's demo

Water update—tie to Rafah fifteen-year plan

At least ten greenhouses destroyed—cucumbers, peas, olives, tomatoes

300 people dependent on farms to live

No resistance in the area

Gush Katif point into Al-Hash area—asked those above age fourteen to go out—destroyed 1/2 house or house and 25 farmers' greenhouses

Arrested 150–200 men, shot around them, beat them, six people in the hospital

Quiet area—conjecturing that maybe they want to expand settlements

What are you going to do—"They don't understand what has happened"

Near road—has happened before—not here—maybe they want to see better through the greenhouses

1982—Settler road built

Before settlement, it was open to sea

When they started building road, no farms—trees and forest behind road

Before 1995 there weren't blocks on road—no block

Like 1948—transfer them away

February–March 2003

Naela,

You are a beautiful person inside and out. You have been very kind to me, and I can see that you have a good heart. I can also see that you are very intelligent. Thank you for being my friend, for helping me with Arabic, for accepting me into your home. I will never forget your generosity. You are a very talented person. Do not ever forget that you deserve all the best things in life. I hope you will follow your dreams. I believe that you will be good at whatever you do. Whether you are a teacher, a chemist, a translator, a diplomat, or anything else, the world will be better because of your work. Life is difficult for people here in Rafah. The world should be ashamed of this. But also, we should be inspired by people like you who show human beings can be kind, brave, generous, beautiful, strong—even in the most difficult of circumstances. Thank you for existing, for helping me see how good people can be, despite great hardship. I will be thinking of you. Follow your dreams. Believe in yourself. Don't give up. Much love and respect, Rachel Corrie from Olympia, WA, USA

February 2003

Intensive care unit—12-year-old girl

Houda Nain Darwish—shot in school
    near Nasser Hospital

11 p.m.

1st time IDF came in 2–3 km—housing
    project

    Nam Sowi—Austrian Housing

Behind West Camp

Shooting

Came from settlement & from Tufah
    into main market

2–3 Apaches

Evacuated apartment building—8 families—with microphone

8 houses that went down with 1 building

Destroyed wall

Shot inside hospital—3 injured—nurses

Tower—in the way of view

6 a.m. houses demolished

41 injured

Who will go with Mohammed tomorrow?

25–30 houses partially damaged

Palestinian lawyers with Israeli ID

February 2003

Children killed here, Ali Gris, date killed? How the children feel when . . .

Azza—when the Israelis shooting very afraid and cried at first—when she hears the shooting in the house she went alone to see if the door is open or closed—she thinks if the door is open the Israelis may come to cut her up or take her—so she went alone to close the door. When she sees the people go to Ali's house she doesn't know why. She sees the people come to take him but she doesn't know what it means that he died. That he will not come back.

We are here for human rights leaflets.

battery-charged striplights

megaphone

lamps

fabric

envelopes

February 14, 2003

Reports received of two men trapped or killed in tunnels. Internationals respond to house demolition in Block O. Bulldozer partially demolishes house with internationals inside.

February 14, 2003

Okay guys. I'm going to send you all a series of jpegs of the signs we thought up in Arabic and English for the demo tomorrow. Some of the messages may not be totally appropriate for Olympia—like "Israeli Occupation Forces: You Are Killing Unarmed Civilians." I think the connotation of the one that says "Olympia: Stop War on Rafah and Iraq" is that this is the message coming from Oly. Let me know if you get them and are interested in using them. Also, I've been having a terrible problem with hotmail so please confirm that you got today's and yesterday's messages if you get a chance. Love to all. I will send a paragraph from Rafah to be read at the rally in Olympia tonight. If you get blank attachments tell me as soon as you get them and I'll try to resend.

PRESS REPORT/ARTICLE:
PALESTINIANS FACING HUNGER AND HOUSE
DEMOLITION DEMONSTRATE WITH INTERNATIONALS
AGAINST WAR ON IRAQ

For further information contact Rachel at . . .
Pictures of protest signs mentioning Rafah are welcome.
The full texts of UNRWA press briefings are available at
www.unrwa.org.

Names have been omitted from this article in order to protect the safety of Palestinians involved and the ability of the internationals to continue to do human rights work in the occupied Palestinian territories. The use of full names and biographical information may be available on an individual basis for use in local press.

Internationals and Palestinians Demonstrate in Rafah, Gaza
Saturday, February 15, 2003

At 11 a.m. on Saturday the 15th of February, 100–150 Palestinians were joined in Rafah by nine internationals in a march for peace for the people of Iraq, in protest of U.S. government policies towards the people of Iraq and Palestine, and in support of the political rights of protesters in New York City. This demonstration occurred in conjunction with protests around the world.

Messages from Communities Around the Globe

Palestinians and international friends from the United States, the UK, and the Netherlands marched along Sea Street, Sharia al-Baha, one of the central streets in Rafah Camp. As they approached the center of town they began to shout through bullhorns in Arabic, "Hurriyah la Falesteen! Hurriyah la al-Iraq! Hurriyah la Rafah! Hurriyah la Baghdad!" and in English "Freedom for Palestine! Freedom for Iraq! Freedom for Rafah! Freedom for Baghdad!"

Internationals carried handwritten signs: "Amsterdam says no to War on Iraq and Rafah! Olympia USA says no war on Rafah and Iraq! City of Chicago Stop War on Iraq! South London for Peace in the Middle East. Malvern Against the War. Dingle for Peace in the Middle East." Palestinians carried signs saying "Stop Repression in New York," a nod to the illegalization of marches scheduled for New York City today. Some internationals reported that friends at home marched with identical signs mentioning the situation in Rafah.

"Freedom for Palestine. Freedom for Iraq."

At about 11:10 this crowd converged in Al-Awda Square with a group of children from the Children's Parliament, youth from the Fatah youth organization, as well as adults from Fatah and various community organizations. Children joined in chanting "Hurriyah la Falesteen wa Hurriyah la al-Iraq"—and passed forward crayoned United States flags to the center of the demonstration. A U.S. national burned these flags, while the children waved peace signs and continued to chant. A few of the children burned crayoned Israeli flags.

As rain began to pour on the streets of Rafah at about 11:30, Palestinians and internationals walked through traffic. The bullhorns went off, and the chanting dissipated to child voices and adult voices yelling "Hurriyah la Falesteen! Hurriyah la Falesteen! Hurriyah la Falesteen!" Freedom for Palestine. Freedom for Palestine. Freedom for Palestine.

The Situation in Rafah

Rafah is a city and refugee camp of about 140,000 people in the southern Gaza Strip immediately adjacent to the Egyptian border. Currently, the Israeli Military (IDF) is constructing a wall approximately ten meters high paralleling the border.

The Rafah Popular Refugee Committee estimates that over six hundred houses have been destroyed on the Rafah side of this wall. Seventy-nine houses were destroyed in Rafah in January alone, according to a United Nations Relief Works Agency (UNRWA) press release Tuesday. UNRWA Commissioner General Peter Hansen urged the international community not to ignore the situation in the West Bank and Gaza as focus intensifies on Iraq.

Internationals engaged in human rights work in Rafah report daily demolitions of civilian homes and "ceaseless shelling" from tanks stationed along the outskirts of Rafah. Palestinians living on the "front line"—those houses immediately facing the now-open area where other homes once stood—refer to the shelling and larger bomb blasts as "music."

An international from the United States pointed out that the children involved in this demonstration rarely have direct contact with the outside world. "They have never seen Israelis except inside of tanks and sniper towers."

What Does This War Mean for Rafah?

When asked what war in Iraq means for people in Rafah, one of the Palestinian organizers of the demonstration remembered his experiences as a child during the first Gulf War:

"During 1991 in the first Gulf War Israel had bunkers and Israelis had gas masks. We had no masks. Israel is a technological country and knows how to deal with these things. But in the camps—no one cares what happens to us in the camps."

He described the uncertainty of wondering whether Iraqi missiles aimed at Israel would hit Gaza and the difficulty of living under twenty-four-hour curfew imposed by the IOF.

"We made some things, the best we could. We shut all the doors and nailed nylon over the windows. We knocked a hole in our wall to move between rooms."

UNRWA alludes to further consequences of an Iraq war for Palestinians. According to Tuesday's press release, UNRWA's emergency programs—"including the feeding of 1.1 million people"—will run out of resources and come to an end in mid-March unless donations are received immediately.

As of Tuesday, no funds had been received by UNRWA in response to a December call for U.S. $94 million in emergency aid. UNRWA mentions Rafah in particular as an area of need—"Supplies of food, tents and cash to those made homeless cannot continue unless donations are forthcoming."

Hansen makes the connection between the international community's inaction and the potential for war: "The paradox is that our emergency funding for the year may be threatened because donors are holding back to see what is needed in Iraq."

When asked what the IDF might do in Gaza in the event of an Iraq war, one Palestinian from Rafah replied, "We cannot know what they will do. We just wait." No one made mention of the potential for mass famine.

"We know what this is like and we do not want this for the people of Iraq."
A shopkeeper in the vicinity of the demonstration described the sentiment of many in Rafah that U.S. aggression towards Iraq in the midst of continuous support for Israel demonstrates abject disregard for the value of Palestinian lives. He mentioned the IDF's possession of weapons of mass destruction and killing of Palestinian civilians:

"This is something we cannot understand. We know the government is not the people, but why America wants to attack Iraq so much? Just the oil? They have all the oil. The Middle East is already as a base for America—army everywhere. Why do they want Iraq? What is the difference between Iraq and Israel? Why do they want these things for us?"

Another Palestinian organizer expressed doubt that the demonstration in Rafah would matter in the international community. "There were demonstrations before but the media doesn't come here from Gaza. No one will see our demonstration." Others in Rafah echo this sense of invisibility:

"We make protest here for Iraq, but we need to think about ourselves. Things are bad enough here. Nobody here likes Saddam Hussein. We make protest for Iraq because we know what this is like and we do not want this for the people of Iraq. Saddam Hussein is a king. He will not die. He will not be hungry. He will not suffer. We make a protest for Iraq. Because we have experienced this. Who makes protest for us?"

February 15, 2003

Gustavo,

Here is a picture from our Rafah protest against U.S. Policy in Iraq and Palestine. Although it appears that I am trying to open my mouth wide enough to swallow a small child—I am in fact chanting with these children, "Hurriyah la Falesteen! Hurriyah la al-Iraq! Hurriyah la Rafah! Hurriyah la Baghdad!" Freedom for Palestine. Freedom for Iraq. Freedom for Rafah. Freedom for Baghdad.

Good to hear from you indirectly. Here is a funny piece of info—Before I came to Palestine I debated a little about trying to go to Brazil to learn more about popular education and of course see you and your family. Now that I am here I am staying in a refugee camp called Brazil—I think either because Brazilian money paid for its construction or because Brazilian soldiers were once stationed here (I never knew Brazilian soldiers were stationed in other parts of the world, though, so maybe you can fill me in on the likelihood of this).

264

And also one of the internationals I've been working with is a teacher in a Swedish folk school—sort of running on a popular education model. So anyway—whenever I go to Brazil at night I think of you and look forward to coming to see you. How's work? Your studies? I also never wrote to you to congratulate you on Lula's victory—but I did watch the election—and Lula's statements after the election. Many of us are watching Brazil as an example for the rest of the world—and hoping that Lula sticks to his roots and resists neoliberal policies.

E-mail when you have time. Beijos.

Rachel

February 17, 2003

Palestinian ISM activist witnesses assassination by military plain-clothes commandos and two tanks on road between Abu Holi and Gaza. Man killed is later confirmed by international media to be Riyad Abu Zeid, a Hamas leader. Unconfirmed numbers injured. ISMers see smoke rising from settlement/Mawassi area for much of the morning. Unable to identify source.

February 19, 2003

Eleven reported killed in Gaza during night of February 18th. During day, four "Qassam" rockets reported by international media to be fired from North Gaza strip toward Sderot. Hamas claims responsibility. Water work continues.

February 20, 2003

Checkpoints closed all day.

February 20, 2003

Mama,

I'm so glad about the work you are doing in Charlotte. I think you are a really strong person, and in a lot of ways I think it takes a lot more courage to do this kind of work in a new community and a conservative community than in Olympia or here in Rafah, where it earns marriage proposals (which are also difficult).

The incursions you wrote about have been large and bloody, but all near Gaza City or in Jabalia refugee camp. One of the Palestinians in our group witnessed the assassination of at least one person (I think Hamas member) in the car in front of her on the road on the way to Gaza. She couldn't tell how many were killed or injured because the IDF took the bodies. First, plainclothes IDF commandos shot into the car, and then two tanks cut off the road on either side. Several months ago, this woman was riding in the car on one of her wedding days (there are sort of two in Muslim marriages) when her father was assassinated. So, of course it is really sad to think about her witnessing something like this again. But she is pretty tough, and just kept saying she wished she had a camera.

Now the Israeli Army has actually dug up the road to Gaza, and both of the major checkpoints are closed. This means that Palestinians who want to go register for their next quarter at university can't; people can't get to their jobs; and those who are trapped on the other side can't get home; and internationals, who have a meeting tomorrow in the West Bank, won't make it. We could probably make it through if we made serious use of our international white-person privilege, but that would also mean some risk of arrest and deportation, even though none of us have done anything illegal.

The Gaza Strip is divided in thirds now. There is some talk about "the reoccupation of Gaza," but I seriously doubt this will happen because I think it would be a geopolitically stupid move for Israel right now. I think the more likely thing is an increase in smaller below-the-international-outcry-radar incursions and possibly the oft-hinted "population transfer."

I am staying put in Rafah for now—no plans to head north. I still feel like I'm relatively safe and think that my most likely risk in case of a larger-scale incursion is arrest. Did you see my report yet about the demo? That goes a little bit into some of the more hidden outcomes for Palestinians of war in Iraq—also part of why I don't think they'll reoccupy Gaza. That would

generate a much larger outcry than Sharon's assassination-during-peace - negotiations/suicide - attack - within - the - green - line/land-grab strategy, which is working very well now to create settlements all over the Occupied Territories, slowly but surely eliminating any meaningful possibility for Palestinian self-determination. Reoccupation now would also mean Israel taking on some responsibility for the livelihoods of Gazans at the very time when UNRWA is saying that they can no longer feed people—a big, stupid step for a country that is already faltering economically, and, of course, a massive portion of the Israeli society is sick of this, and would be outraged if Sharon were to invade completely. So that's what I think. Who knows whether it will prove true.

Time to go. Meeting with the Youth Parliament. Know that I have a lot of very nice Palestinians looking after me. I have a small flu bug and got some very nice lemony drinks to cure me. Also, the woman who keeps the key for the well where we still sleep keeps asking me about you. She doesn't speak any English but I managed to convey to her in broken Arabic that you saw my picture in the paper. But she asks about my mom pretty frequently—wants to make sure I'm calling you.

Love to you and Dad and Sarah and Chris and everybody.
Rachel

February 21, 2003

One man reported killed by army at Erez checkpoint, another killed at settlement in Northern Gaza strip. Médecins Sans Frontières group report being fired upon while trying to cross Abu Holi checkpoint, despite prior permission from military. Mosque destroyed in Block J. Was abandoned previously due to earlier attacks.

February 22, 2003

Water work continues. Internationals, responding to reports of house demolition in Block J, witness further underground bombing. Reports are received that one house was demolished prior to their arrival. Heavy shooting in Block J during the night. Reports, later confirmed by various sources, that Israeli soldiers on foot entered at least one house in Hi Salaam area during the night.

February 24, 2003

All checkpoints in Gaza Strip reported closed during morning. Water work continues. Abu Holi checkpoint alternately open and closed during day. House protected Sunday is destroyed during the night of February 24th.

PRESS REPORT/ARTICLE:
HUMAN SHIELD WORK CONTINUES
WITH RAFAH MUNICIPAL WATER WORKERS

Internationals in Rafah have been continuing support work with workers from the Rafah Municipal Water Authority since Sunday, February 16th, following a break due to the Eid holiday. ISM-Rafah continues to send internationals to sleep at a third well in the immediate vicinity in order to protect it from destruction. The workers are currently building a barrier surrounding the Canada Well (#P-144), in the Canada-Tel al-Sultan area of Rafah. This well, along with the Al-Iskan Well (#P-152) was destroyed by Israeli military bulldozers on January 30th. On several occasions, the internationals have witnessed shooting from military vehicles on the settler road, which passes along the northwestern edge of the sand dunes and agricultural areas on the outskirts of Rafah. Bullets have not hit the ground or objects in the immediate vicinity of the workers or internationals, a change from previous human shield actions with the water workers.

According to the Rafah Municipal Water Authority, the Canada Well had a capacity of 180 cubic meters of water per hour, thirty-five percent of Rafah's total water supply. The two wells destroyed were the largest of six in Rafah, providing about sixty percent of Rafah's total municipal water supply.

The Municipal Water office has made attempts to compensate somewhat for the emergency, by connecting the municipal wells with a private agricultural well which is owned by local farmers. The municipality also redistributed the remaining water according to districts, implementing a strict program in which each district has access to water for six hours a day.

The Canada Well cost $250,000 at the time of its construction in 1990. Its construction was funded by the Rafah municipality. The Al-Iskan Well was implemented by the Canadian International Development Agency at a cost of $205,000 in 1999. The municipality reports receiving $40,000 from the World Bank through the Local Affairs Ministry to repair the two wells. All of this money was used in the construction of fences and protective structures surrounding the well site. The municipality estimates that $300,000 will be needed to repair the Canada Well, and $100,000 is needed to repair the Al-Iskan Well. The municipality is waiting for money promised by the Japanese, Canadian, and Norwegian governments in order to restore the wells to capacity.

For information on the above report please contact Rachel.

February 27, 2003

Mama,

Love you. Really miss you. I have bad nightmares about tanks and bulldozers outside our house and you and me inside. Sometimes the adrenaline acts as an anesthetic for weeks—and then in the evening or at night it just hits me again—a little bit of the reality of the situation. I am really scared for the people here. Yesterday I watched a father lead his two tiny children, holding his hands, out into the sight of tanks and a sniper tower and bulldozers and jeeps because he thought his house was going to be exploded. Jenny and I stayed in the house with several women and two small babies. It was our mistake in translation that caused him to think it was his house that was being exploded—although it abuts the settler road immediately next to the Gush Katif settlement, so I think it is only a matter of time. In fact, the Israeli Army was in the process of detonating an explosive in the ground nearby. One that appears to have been planted by Palestinian resistance. This is in the area where Sunday about 150 men were rounded up and contained outside the settlement with gunfire over their heads and around them, while tanks and bulldozers destroyed twenty-five greenhouses—the livelihoods of three hundred people. The explosive was right in front of the greenhouses—right in the point of entry for tanks that might come back again. I was terrified to think that this man felt it was less of a risk to walk out in view of the tanks with his kids than to stay in his house. I was really scared that they were all going to be shot, and I tried to stand between them and the tank. This happens every day, but this father walking out with his two little kids just looking very sad happened to get my attention more at this particular moment, probably because I felt like it was our translation problems that made him leave.

I thought a lot about what you said on the phone about Palestinian violence not helping the situation. Sixty thousand workers from Rafah worked in Israel two years ago. Now only six hundred can go to Israel for jobs. Of these six hundred, many have moved because the three checkpoints between here and Ashkelon (the closest city in Israel) make what used to be a forty-minute drive, now a twelve-hour or impassable journey.

In addition, what Rafah identified in 1999 as sources of economic growth are all completely destroyed—the Gaza international airport (runways demolished, totally closed); the border for trade with Egypt (now with a giant Israeli sniper tower in the middle of the crossing); access to the ocean (completely cut off in the last two years by a checkpoint and the Gush Katif settlement); Mawassi village, closed for entry and exit for people between the ages of about fourteen and thirty-five. The wells in the settlement are deeper than the wells here; and the settlements in the Gaza Strip are located in the west, above the freshwater aquifers. And then the IDF destroyed the two wells I told you about before.

The count of homes destroyed since the beginning of this Intifada is up around six hundred, by and large people with no connection to the resistance but who happen to live along the border. Most of these are refugee homes, people who landed here in 1948 when their homes in Israel/historic Palestine became unlivable. Rafah was three large families and about six hundred total people in 1948. Many of these families have already been relocated since their arrival in Rafah—most notably in the Canada and Brazil camps, which were moved back into the Gaza Strip when Israel withdrew from the Sinai. This in addition to the killings every several days. I think it is maybe official now that Rafah is the poorest place in the world.

There used to be a middle class here—recently. I imagine you're reading about that in the Amira Hass book. We also get reports that, in the past, Gazan flower shipments to Europe were delayed for two weeks at the Erez crossing for security inspections. You can imagine the value of two-week-old cut flowers in the European market, so that market dried up. And then the bulldozers come and take out people's vegetable farms and gardens. What is left for people? Tell me if you can think of anything. I can't.

So when someone says that any act of Palestinian violence justifies Israel's actions—not only do I question that logic in light of international law, which recognizes the right of people to legitimate armed struggle in defense of their land and their families; not only do I question that logic in light of the Fourth Geneva Convention, which prohibits collective punishment, prohibits the transfer of an occupying country's population into an occupied area, prohibits the expropriation of water resources and the destruction of civilian infrastructure such as farms; not only do I question that logic in light of the sheer ridiculousness of the notion that fifty-year-old Russian guns and homemade explosives can have any impact on the activities of one of the world's largest militaries backed by the world's only superpower, I also question that logic on the basis of common sense.

If any of us had our lives and welfare completely strangled, lived with children in a shrinking place where we knew (because of previous experience) that soldiers and tanks and bulldozers could come for us at any moment (which would perhaps be a somewhat less cruel death than starvation, chronic malnutrition, and nitrite poisoning caused from increasing reliance on wells located at a distance from settlements, eastward, where the water quality is poor), with no means of economic survival and our houses destroyed; if they came and destroyed all the greenhouses that we'd been cultivating for the last however long, and did this while some of us were beaten and held captive with 149 other people for several hours, do you think we might try to use somewhat violent means to protect the edge of the greenhouses, to protect whatever fragments remained? A bomb buried in the ground, after all, can't be detonated unless a large piece of machinery rolls over the top of it. I think about this especially when I see orchards and greenhouses and fruit trees destroyed—just years of care and cultivation. I think about you and how long it takes to make things grow and what a labor of love it is. I really think, in a similar situation, most people would defend themselves as best they could. I think Uncle Craig would. I think probably Grandma would. I think I would.

I really don't think it was the farmers who placed the explosive, so please don't interpret this that way. They report no previous resistance activity in their area. We interviewed them Monday, and it was clear from their faces that they were absolutely in shock. Most of them just kept repeating over and over again that they had no idea why their livelihoods were destroyed. I have no idea who planted the thing. For all I know, it was the Israeli army just messing around; but from its location, it seemed like common sense why it would be there.

You asked me about nonviolent resistance, and I mentioned the first Intifada. Much of the leadership of more moderate resistance during the first Intifada has been assassinated, deported, or held indefinitely. Settlement activity, in fact, increased in the years following Oslo. As I said before, in the early 1990s Israel and the United States did not prevent the development of Hamas. I think it was seen as less a threat to the power balance than secular resistance. But anyway, yes, there was Gandhian nonviolent resistance during the first Intifada. And, of course, there still is staunch nonviolent resistance. The vast majority of Palestinians right now, as far as I can tell, are engaging in Gandhian nonviolent resistance. Who do you think I'm staying with, in houses that are going to be demolished amid gunfire, which often happens with absolutely no response whatsoever from Kalashnikovs—resistance weapons—ringing all around? Who do you think are staffing the human rights centers? Who do you think are still trying to maintain their farms every day directly in sight of sniper towers? Who do you think engage in protest with us? What do you think this Palestinian-led movement is that I joined—that engages in nonviolent direct action? Who do you think continues to walk down Salah el-Din Street where children are shot? Who do you think these families are that I tell you about, who won't take any money from us even though they are very, very poor—and who say to us, "We are not a hotel. We help you because we think maybe you will go and tell people in your country that you lived with Muslims. We think they will know that we are good people. We are quiet people. We just want peace"? Do you think I'm hanging out with Hamas fighters? These people are being shot at every day—that, on top of the complete strangulation I described above—and they continue to go about their business as best they can in the sights of machine guns and rocket launchers. Isn't that basically the epitome of nonviolent resistance—doing what you need to do even though you are shot at?

When that explosive detonated yesterday it broke all the windows in the family's house. I was in the process of being served tea and playing with the two small babies. I'm having a hard time right now. Just feel sick to my stomach a lot from being doted on all the time, very sweetly, by people who are facing doom. I know that from the United States it all sounds like hyperbole. Honestly, a lot of the time the sheer kindness of the people here, coupled with the overwhelming evidence of the willful destruction of their lives, makes it seem unreal to me. I really can't believe that something like this can happen in the world without a bigger outcry about it. It hurts me, again, like it has hurt me in the past, to witness how awful we can allow the world to be. I felt after talking to you that maybe you didn't completely believe me. I think it's actually good if you don't, because I do believe pretty much above all else in the importance of independent critical thinking. And I also realize that with you I'm much less careful than usual about trying to source every assertion that I make. A lot of the reason for that is I know that you actually do go and do your own research. But it makes me worry about the job I'm doing. All of the situation that I tried to enumerate above—and a lot of other things—constitutes a somewhat gradual—often hidden, but nevertheless massive—removal and destruction of the ability of a particular group of people to survive. This is what I am seeing here. The assassinations, rocket attacks, and shooting of children are atrocities—but in focusing on them, I'm terrified of missing their context. The vast majority of people here—even if they had the economic means to escape, even if they actually wanted to give up resisting on their land and just leave (which appears to be maybe the less nefarious of Sharon's possible goals), can't leave. Because they can't even get into Israel to apply for visas, and because their destination countries won't let them in (both our country and Arab countries). So I think when all means of survival is cut off in a pen (Gaza) which people can't get out of—I think that qualifies as genocide. Even if they could get out I think it would still qualify as genocide. Maybe you could look up the definition of genocide according to international law. I don't remember it right now. I'm going to get better at illustrating this, hopefully. I don't like to use those charged words. I think you know this about me. I really value words. I really try to illustrate and let people draw their own conclusions. I'm just thinking about that. If I'm really honest I won't talk about the power imbalance when people ask about Palestinian violence. I will talk about resisting genocide.

Speaking of words—I absolutely abhor the use of polarities like "good" and "evil"—especially when applied to human beings. I think these words are the enemy of critical thinking. They are an escape from finding solutions and are an incitement to further violence. For a long time I've been operating from a certain core assumption which only recently I started to articulate as such. Just the belief that we are all essentially the same inside, and that our differences are by and large situational. That goes for everybody—Bush, bin Laden, me, you, Sarah, Chris, Dad, Gram, Palestinians, everybody of any particular religion, Uncle Craig, Tony Blair. I know there is a good chance that this assumption actually is false. But it's convenient, because it always leads to questions, and it usually leads to analysis of power dynamics—and the way privilege shelters people from the consequences of their actions. It's also convenient because it leads to some level of forgiveness, whether justified or not. And it leads to pretty immediate rejection of analysis that rests on ethnocentric explanations for everybody's behavior.

I question this assumption sometimes. Reagan, I think, very possibly didn't really understand what he was doing to people all over Latin America. Kennedy, possibly, didn't understand what he was doing to people in Southeast Asia. I think there's a good chance that

Bush doesn't quite understand—but that's dwindling. It's with people like Kissinger, Cheney, and Ariel Sharon that I start to wonder.

And isolated here, I start to wonder, how many people out there know? I will say that I think the vast majority of us who are in some way passively supporting this genocide are unaware of what it is. I don't think that is any excuse, but sometimes at night I quibble over it. I don't think it matters much. It certainly doesn't matter for the Palestinians. It is my own selfishness and will to optimism that wants to believe that even people with a great deal of privilege don't just idly sit by and watch. What we are paying for here is truly evil. The largest evil I have witnessed directly. Maybe the general growing class imbalance in the world and consequent devastation of working people's lives is a bigger evil. Being here should make me more aware of what it might mean to be a farmer in Colombia right now, for example.

Anyway, I'm rambling. Just want to write to my mom and tell her that I'm witnessing this chronic, insidious genocide, and I'm really scared, and questioning my fundamental belief in the goodness of human nature. This has to stop. I think it is a good idea for us all to drop everything and devote our lives to making this stop. I don't think it's an extremist thing to do anymore. I still really want to dance around to Pat Benatar and have boyfriends and make comics for my coworkers. But I also want this to stop. Disbelief and horror is what I feel. Disappointment. I am disappointed that this is the base reality of our world and that we, in fact, participate in it. This is not at all what I asked for when I came into this world. This is not at all what the people here asked for when they came into this world. This is not what they are asking for now. This is not the world you and Dad wanted me to come into when you decided to have me. This is not what I meant when I was two and looked at Capitol Lake and said, "This is the wide world and I'm coming to it." I did not mean that I was coming into a world where I could live a comfortable life and possibly, with no effort at all, exist in complete unawareness of my participation in genocide. More big explosions somewhere in the distance outside.

I probably sound a little crazy, reminiscent maybe of going to Russia years ago, although that situation was not like this one. I know you wondered if going to Russia was a bad thing, because it sort of seemed to ruin me. I think the reason I went crazy was not because Russia was bad for me, but because of the initial disappointment in discovering that my government really did lie to me about the Russians, and in the massive absence of justice in the world, and again (through observing U.S. companies' investment in natural resource extraction in newly "democratized" Russia and the devastation of the Russian economy in the wake of the arms race) in discovering my participation in the subjugation of other people. When I come back from Palestine, I probably will have nightmares and constantly feel guilty for not being here, but I can channel that into more work. Coming here is one of the better things I've ever done. So when I sound crazy, or if the Israeli military should break with their racist tendency not to injure white people, please pin the reason squarely on the fact that I am in the midst of a genocide which I am also indirectly supporting, and for which my government is largely responsible.

I love you and Dad. Sorry for the diatribe.

Okay, some strange men next to me just gave me some peas, so I need to eat and thank them.

Rachel

Attachment:

P.S. Both Al-Haq and Al-Mezan are organizations that we work with some—mostly by giving them reports about what we witness. They have also offered some assistance in trying to go through Israeli courts to stop the demolition of houses that seem to be particularly targeted as acts of collective punishment—as opposed to the vast majority of houses here which are targeted because the Israeli military wants the land they stand on. You could do a web search. I think both have web sites.

Thanks, Mom, for your response to my e-mail. It really helps me to get word from you, and from other people who care about me. I'm really sad to hear that Sarah's Crohn's situation is so bad. I will send her an e-mail. Please tell her that I love her very much. She sent me some really nice e-mails a few weeks ago which I very much appreciated. I haven't heard from her since, and I imagine it is just stress and sickness, but if you talk to her, you could tell her that if she is well enough and has a little time, she can send me e-mails that aren't political—that don't have anything to do with where I am, and that are just about how things are with her and Kelly and the cats. She sounds like she has really made an effort to find out about Israel and Palestine. Politics of any sort is the hardest topic for Sarah and me, so I felt like this was just really a big deal and a real expression of love, if not political sympathy. It was hugely important to me. I don't want her to feel like communication with me needs to have any political element to it. I think I may have neglected to answer her last e-mail—so don't interpret it as me thinking she's neglecting me. Just send her my love, and I will too.

After I wrote to you, I spent the evening and this morning finishing the big report I sent out, and then had a long talk with my friend Stefan—who was here and then returned to Sweden—and then I went incommunicado from the affinity group for about ten hours which I spent with a family on the front line in Hi Salaam—who fixed me dinner—and have cable TV. The two front rooms of their house are unusable because gunshots have been fired through the walls, so the whole family—three kids and two parents—sleep in the parents' bedroom. I sleep on the floor next to the youngest daughter, Iman, and we all share blankets. I helped the son with his English homework a little, and we all watched *Pet Cemetery*, which is a horrifying movie. They all thought it was pretty funny how much trouble I had watching it. Friday is the holiday, and when I woke up they were watching *Gummy Bears* dubbed into Arabic. So I ate breakfast with them and sat there for a while and just enjoyed being in this big puddle of blankets with this family watching what for me seemed like

Saturday morning cartoons. Then I walked some way to Brazil, which is where Nidal and Mansur and Grandmother and Rafat and all the rest of the big family that has really wholeheartedly adopted me live. The other day, by the way, Grandmother gave me a pantomimed lecture in Arabic that involved a lot of blowing and pointing to her black shawl. I got Nidal to tell her that my mother would appreciate knowing that someone here was giving me a lecture about smoking turning my lungs black. Nidal's English gets better every day. He's the one who calls me "my sister" after we did human-shield work with water workers in his neighborhood. He started teaching Grandmother how to say "Hello. How are you?" in English.

You can always hear the tanks and bulldozers passing by, but all of these people are genuinely cheerful with each other, and with me. When I am with Palestinian friends I tend to be somewhat less horrified than when I am trying to act in a role of human rights observer, documenter, or direct-action resister. They are a good example of how to be in it for the long haul. I know that the situation gets to them (and may ultimately get them) on all kinds of levels, but I am nevertheless amazed at their strength in being able to defend such a large degree of their humanity—laughter, generosity, family time—against the incredible horror occurring in their lives and against the constant presence of death. I felt much better after this morning. I spent a lot of time writing about the disappointment of discovering, somewhat firsthand, the degree of evil of which we are still capable. I should at least mention that I am also discovering a degree of strength and of the basic ability for humans to remain human in the direst of circumstances—which I also haven't seen before. I think the word is dignity. I wish you could meet these people. Maybe, hopefully, someday you will.

As far as activist burnout goes, I think you are very likely in a much less supported position than I have ever been as an activist. I know that hearing about your work supports me. I know that some of the most unrelenting activists I know, who have made it for decades, do allow themselves to relax and enjoy things, and give themselves breaks. I'm thinking of Larry Mosqueda, in particular. Larry is a really amazing scholar. He has risked his life in order to enter war zones. He is a tireless activist. And he is a parent and partner. One of the things I have most appreciated about my activist work in Olympia is the opportunity to work side by side with people like Larry. I could be paying thousands of dollars to some other institution to sit in the back of an auditorium and hear him lecture. Working with him, even though I am well aware that he has an incredible career's worth of study behind him, I always feel like my opinions are valued, and I'm treated as an equal. I also like that Larry is pragmatic. In the case of the Iraq war he is the person in groups that routinely points out that professing a specific ideology is not as important as stopping the war. His politics are definitely radical—and he's definitely not religious; but he's able to work with whichever group seems to be doing the best work, and still preserve a commitment to radical change. Anyway, I really admire him. He always tells people to take it easy. He points out that the goals of this administration are not one- or two-year goals; they are fifteen- or twenty- or fifty-year goals, and that he is prepared to continue to do this work for as long as it takes. That said, it's okay to take breaks, to not be constantly in the process of planning a massive demonstration, to attend to your kids, to take nights off, to go have a beer.

Right now is a crisis time in the world. I'm not sure you and I agree on this point, but I would argue that this particular crisis time is the most obvious manifestation of a very large-scale problem with a widening disparity of wealth and power, a problem with increasing private control over matters of public interest, basically a very large-scale problem with democracy, that is becoming increasingly murderous. I don't think my work on this is going to be finished in this lifetime. It's very likely that given the existing power structure, if not Iraq it will be North Korea, or Colombia, Iran, eventually Saudi Arabia. I think we are in agreement that this is a war for oil and power. I think it's largely a war against OPEC and for control of the economies of Europe and Japan. It's pretty likely that you don't think that, but at least I think we can agree that much of the problem is massively powerful private interests which have basically taken control of public policy-making, at least in the case of Iraq. I hope to God we don't invade Iraq. But even if we don't, I do not think this sort of thing will end anytime soon. Maybe this is not encouraging at all.

I don't expect to see the world that I want to live in emerge during my lifetime. I expect things to get worse before they get better, as wealth and power continue to be concentrated in the hands of the few, and as the quality of the environment degrades exponentially every generation. I know this sounds incredibly angry, cynical, and negative. It's just the reality as I can see it, so I sort of try to operate from that. Given that, I look forward to a lot of things.

I think I could see a Palestinian state or a democratic Israeli-Palestinian state within my lifetime. Freedom for Palestine could be an incredible source of hope to people struggling all over the world. It could also be an incredible inspiration to Arab people in the Middle East, who are struggling under undemocratic regimes which the U.S. supports. I think a lot of the world is closely watching what goes on in Brazil right now. The election of Lula amidst economic blackmail from foreign investors is an incredible example of a people's demand for autonomy and democracy in the face of immense pressure.

I look forward to continuing to see creative attempts at cooperatives, intentional communities, and sustainable agriculture all over the world.

I look forward to seeing an escalating number of people willing to risk life and limb in order to resist the direction we are moving in.

I look forward to increasing numbers of middle-class privileged people like you and me becoming aware of the structures that support our privilege and beginning to support the work of those who aren't privileged to dismantle those structures.

I look forward to more moments like February 15th when civil society wakes up en masse and issues massive and resonant evidence of its conscience, its unwillingness to be repressed, and its compassion for the suffering of others.

I look forward to more teachers emerging like Matt Grant and Barbara Weaver and Dale Knuth who teach critical thinking to kids in the United States.

I look forward to the international resistance that's occurring now fertilizing analysis on all kinds of issues with dialogue between diverse groups of people.

I look forward to all of us who are new at this, developing better skills for working in democratic structures and healing our own racism and classism and sexism and heterosexism and ageism and ableism and becoming more effective.

We are particularly new at this in the United States and in the middle class. Like you said, we are all unlearning years of programming that's been imprinted on us our entire lives. We are working against massive, sophisticated, and entrenched structures of power. We are working in the midst of information systems that tend to persuade us that our personal experiences are irrelevant, that we are defective, that our communities are not important, that we are powerless, that the future is determined, and that the highest level of humanity is expressed through what we choose to buy at the mall. Lately, from hanging out with Europeans, I realize how much our time is co-opted by privatization in the United States. Our middle class is much more insecure than theirs, although theirs is increasingly more so. If we decide as individuals that it is important to devote a large portion of our lives to improving everybody's lives, and if we are financially capable of taking the time off work to do so, we face the loss of health care, loss of secure retirement, loss of access to education, loss of transportation and any number of other aspects of security.

Of course as activists, we burn out. Of course it is overwhelming. I don't know if we will be able to stop this war on Iraq. I do know that the immense amount of effort and creativity worldwide that is being expended to do so bodes well for the future.

Anyway. I didn't mean to write another diatribe. I think you know, better than I do, how to be persistent. This is actually something that I've picked up from you in the last few years, more than when I was a kid. One other thing—I think this a lot about public protest—like the one a few weeks ago here that was attended by only about 150 people. Whenever I organize or participate in public protest I get really worried that it will just suck, be really small, embarrassing, and the media will laugh at me. Oftentimes it is really small and most of the time the media laughs at us. The weekend after our 150-person protest we were invited to a maybe two-thousand-person protest. Even though we had a small protest and of course it didn't get coverage all over the world, in some places the word "Rafah" was mentioned outside of the Arab press. Colin got a sign in English and Arabic into the protest in Seattle that said "Olympia Says No to War on Rafah and Iraq." His pictures went up on the *Rafah Today* web site that a guy named Mohammed here runs. People here and elsewhere saw those pictures. I think about Glen going out every Friday for ten years with tagboard signs that addressed the number of children dead from sanctions in Iraq. Sometimes just one or two people there and everyone thought they were crazy and they got spit upon. Now there are a lot more people on Friday evenings. The juncture between Fourth and State is just lined with them, and they get a lot of honks and waves, and thumbs-ups. They created an infrastructure there for other people to do something. Getting spit upon, they made it easier for someone else to decide that they could write a letter to the editor, or stand at the back of a rally—or do something that seems slightly less ridiculous than standing at the side of the road addressing the deaths of children in Iraq and getting spit upon. Just hearing about what you are doing makes me feel less alone, less useless, less invisible. Those honks and waves help. The pictures help. Colin helps. The international media and our government are not going to tell us that we are effective, important, justified in our work,

courageous, intelligent, valuable. We have to do that for each other, and one way we can do that is by continuing our work, visibly.

It's important for people in the United States in relative privilege to realize that people without privilege will be doing this work no matter what, because they are working for their lives. We can work with them, and they know that we work with them, or we can leave them to do this work themselves and curse us for our complicity in killing them. I really don't get the sense that anyone here curses us. People here are actually more concerned in the immediate about our comfort and health than they are about us risking our lives on their behalf. At least that's the case for me. People try to give me a lot of tea and food in the midst of gunfire and explosive detonation.

I feel like I'm giving you advice, which is kind of stupid. But I do think that it's important to recognize all the zillions of small things we can do for change. I don't mean just recycling or something and then congratulating ourselves. I mean small, revolutionary things. Certainly the lengths that you go to educate yourself, your open mind, all your hard work for people over the years—all of this is exceptional and is having an impact on more people than just your daughter. I really appreciate you. I love you very much. Maybe you should try to get Dad to quit his neoliberal job and become a math teacher. That would be revolutionary. Maybe you should try to get Dad to sabotage his neoliberal job. Do you think Dad could accidentally dump a lot of dollars very cheaply into international markets?

Okay. Sorry. I love you guys. Take care of yourself.

Rachel

March 1, 2003

Hello Olympia activists,

So today the Israeli military shot very close to myself, two other internationals, and four Palestinian workers trying to repair a water well. The Palestinian standing next to me estimated the closest shot was within half a meter of him. It was fired at the ground, so we were

all showered with dust and small rubble fragments (the rubble fragments weren't dangerous, but this illustrates the proximity). The
municipal water director coordinated with the district command
officer of the military this morning to ensure everybody's safety,
because they have been shot at there before. The well (and another)
was destroyed by occupation force bulldozers on January 30th, an
attack which activists documented, as we began to do human-shield
work around water issues. The two wells combined provided over
half of Rafah's municipal drinking water supply. They are the largest
of six municipal wells. They are also located in the west, where the
groundwater quality is the best. Not by coincidence, this also places
them very close to the settlements.

The ISM media coordinator is going to try to get *The Olympian* to
publish my writing about the well attacks within the next few days.
Probably a long shot (no pun intended). I'm wondering if you guys
could exert some pressure. The water crisis in the Gaza Strip is not
going away anytime soon. This seems like an opportunity to get some
small part of it visible, though, because of the little acute crisis point
today, the local-girl connection, whatever. If they don't publish anything, I think it is good for them to know that there is someone from
Olympia here who is doing human rights work—and maybe to begin
to associate that work with water.

Thanks,

Rachel

PRESS REPORT/ARTICLE:

Today at approximately 10:30 a.m., three internationals joined four
men working for the Rafah Municipal Water Authority at the Al-
Iskan Water Well (#P-152) on the outskirts of Tel al-Sultan, Rafah.
This well is one of the two largest municipal water wells in Rafah,
both of which were destroyed by occupation tanks and bulldozers on
January 30th of this year. This well is being rehabilitated with funding from Norway and Canada. At full capacity, it provides twenty-five
percent of Rafah's water supply.

Workers at the well reported being fired upon on Thursday. Today, the Municipal Water Authority reported speaking directly with the Israeli district command officer, who expressed that he had coordinated with occupation forces in the area in order to ensure the safety of the Palestinian workers.

Despite this coordination, and the presence of banners and megaphones, the activists and workers were fired upon several times over a period of about one hour. One of the bullets came within one to two meters of three internationals and a municipal water worker, close enough to spray bits of debris in their faces as it landed at their feet.

This well is located within sight of the Rafah–Mawassi checkpoint, settlement buildings and greenhouses, bunkers in the militarized zone surrounding the checkpoint, a low sniper tower to the south and a very tall sniper tower in the distance in the north. The activists were unable to locate the precise origin of the shots amongst the various occupation-force buildings.

For information about this report or other issues related to the destruction of civilian water supplies in Rafah, please contact Rachel.

March 2003

PRESS RELEASE/ARTICLE:
INTERNATIONALS CONTINUE TO TAKE DIRECT ACTION AIMED AT HINDERING THE DEMOLITION OF CIVILIAN HOMES BY OCCUPATION FORCES

Rafah continues to witness the destruction of homes and agriculture on a daily basis. The activists confront barriers to direct action work in most of these cases. These barriers manifest themselves in several ways.

First, limited numbers of internationals are attempting to respond to demolition which occurs without warning all over the edges of Rafah. The most recent house demolitions witnessed were accompanied by the amassment of twenty tanks nearby in the border strip. There are currently seven international ISM activists working in Rafah.

Secondly, with a few exceptions, house demolitions in Rafah are carried out by bulldozers and tanks which fire into the houses or begin to demolish them as notification to the inhabitants of their arrival. Many of the homes destroyed are empty, because the inhabitants have fled with their belongings after experiencing gunfire through windows and walls and the partial bulldozing of their houses. The homes here are not targeted because of any connection with suicide bombings, but because of their existence along an area which the Israeli army finds strategically useful. Thus there is little predictability about which homes will be destroyed next, and no opportunity for direct contact with the army in order to negotiate or notify them of the presence of internationals in the homes.

Much of the destruction occurs at night. Many of the streets of Rafah are impassable in the dark due to sniper towers positioned along the perimeters of Rafah. In the dark, internationals attempting to carry out nonviolent direct action rely on battery-charged lights, banners, and the accuracy of unknown local collaborators to make the Israeli military aware of their location.

Another factor in attempting to stop the destruction of a home is a variable factor: the question of whether the driver of a particular tank cares about injuring internationals in the process of destroying the welfare of the Palestinians living here.

On the afternoon of Friday, February 14th, seven internationals responded to reports of house demolitions in the Block O area, with support from Palestinian organizers. They encountered two bulldozers and a tank, which fired shots around the internationals that seemed directed at Palestinians in nearby alleys. The internationals stood in the path of the bulldozer and were physically pushed with the shovel backwards, taking shelter in a house. The bulldozer then proceeded on its course, demolishing one side of the house with the internationals inside. The driver then dropped a sound grenade out of the cab of the bulldozer, and continued to demolish the house, at which point the activists were able to escape, amid gunfire from the tank.

The next day activists responded to reports of house demolition in the same area and approached a bulldozer while identifying themselves by megaphone and banners. They were unable to position themselves between the bulldozer and nearby structures, and were beckoned away from the front line by Palestinians in the area.

On the 11th and 12th of February and from the 21st till 23rd of February, internationals arrived on the scene of demolitions (homes, greenhouses, and a mosque) too late to respond. This is in addition to house demolitions which the internationals discovered several days after the event.

On the afternoon of February 23rd, six internationals achieved some success in interrupting the work of a bulldozer and a tank demolishing houses in the vicinity of Salah el-Din gate.

The internationals arrived in the "Sha'ar" area near Salah el-Din gate in the late afternoon, and found the bulldozer completing the demolition of a house and chicken coop near the border strip. Palestinians in the area requested the internationals to do whatever they could to try to stop further destruction. The group approached the bulldozer and tank from the side, carrying banners and announcing their presence by megaphone. Although the tank moved into their path, the internationals were able to maneuver into the path of the bulldozer, at which point it moved to a nearby house and began to demolish a garden wall.

The tank again moved between the internationals and the bulldozer. The group split briefly while one member of the group moved onto the porch of the house from the back. The remaining internationals stood within several meters of the tank, which began to fire machine guns near them, close enough that one international was pelted with small brick fragments when bullets hit the wall next to her. The international on the porch led the way for the others to climb over the wall and into the house. They then proceeded to the roof. The bulldozer moved back to its previous work destroying a chicken coop and hitting the edges of other small civilian structures.

Two internationals remained on the roof, while the remaining four proceeded back toward the bulldozer. The tank again fired a stream of bullets in their path, but desisted as the internationals continued to walk forward, reminding the tank by megaphone of the clear absence of any threat to the vehicles, of international law, and of the right of human beings to housing and livelihoods.

As the internationals positioned themselves in the bulldozer's path, the tank and the bulldozer turned eastward and withdrew behind walls into the border strip some distance away. The four internationals followed the tank and bulldozer to the edge of the border strip, fearful for the homes of friends in the direction the vehicles headed.

The internationals returned to the partially demolished house and helped the family living there carry their belongings—bedding, furniture, family portraits, dishes, vases, all the elements of a family home—into a house nearby. Four internationals remained overnight with the family in the house where the furniture was relocated.

The activists involved felt they had some success in this action, as they were at least able to delay the work of the bulldozers in demolishing houses.

On February 24th at approximately 9 p.m., on their way back to the Sha'ar area for another night, ISM activists received notification that the bulldozers had returned. Despite sprinting to the location, the internationals arrived in time only to see the last of this family's house completely churned into the earth, as the mother of the family wept, looking on.

Internationals continue homestays in the Sha'ar area, immediately adjacent to the Israeli military's Salah el-Din sniper tower, from which two teenage boys were shot and injured today while playing in the street. The families in the area believe that they may be the target of house demolitions very soon, as collective punishment for their proximity to tunnels which run from Rafah into Egypt.

All of the homes which the internationals sleep in have bullet or shell holes in the walls. From the kitchen window of one apartment where a woman prepared tea for the group, the most immediate object in view is the eastern window of the sniper tower, about 100 meters away. The internationals observed several holes in the kitchen walls, apparently from shots fired into the kitchen window. The internationals have attached banners and stood on the roofs of some of the buildings with megaphones in order to make their continuing presence known to Israeli occupation forces in the sniper tower, as there is a recent history of houses demolished in Rafah by rockets fired from towers at a distance.

Sleeping in houses such as these on the front line, with the constant sound of machinery moving outside in the border strip and frequent gunfire from tanks, internationals report seeing small children get out of bed in the night in terror to come sit close to their parents, and report experiencing nightmares of their own homes being demolished. Internationals here, who can walk in front of tanks on Palestinian land without being killed, feel some degree of impotence in the face of this massive destruction of civilian homes. We can only imagine what it is like for Palestinians living here, most of them already once-or-twice refugees, for whom this is not a nightmare, but a continuous reality from which international privilege cannot protect them, and from which they have no economic means to escape.

The Palestinians and internationals in ISM-Rafah are still discussing strategy about how to use their members most effectively.

For information on the above report please contact Rachel.

March 1, 2003

Mayleeeeeee!

So good to hear from you. I keep thinking about you and your amazing Shelton group and wondering about ways to work with you from here, so I'm glad you beat me to it. The mothers-to-mothers idea is incredibly good for a number of reasons. First, it is the kind of humanizing work to portray the situation here (and in Iraq) that is effective for people who aren't initially sympathetic to anti-war activity. Secondly, many, many people I talk to here are yearning for contact with the outside world. The situation is extremely bad for people in Rafah, and they want to know that they are noticed. Many people have issued requests for help in developing pen-pal relationships. Also, I think it is a very good idea to work with women in both Iraq and Palestine. The two issues are so related. The impacts of an Iraq war will be felt acutely here. And Iraqi women may very soon be living under U.S. occupation in the same way Palestinian women are living under Israeli occupation, and of course Israel is flagrantly guilty of things Iraq is accused of. Finally, Rafah is probably the most religiously conservative place in Palestine, and we find that a lot of women are really invisible here, even more so because Rafah is such an invisible place. So I am super enthusiastic about doing any kind of work that affirms that women need to be heard, particularly in places of conflict. I will immediately talk to contacts here about writing letters. Very exciting. As far as finding out what other work has been done like this, I think Simona is probably the best person to ask that I know of. I'm sure Glen would also be enthusiastic, and he has connections to people who have done solidarity work in Iraq, so he might be able to help. I also have fairly regular access to e-mail now, so we can organize this way with some efficiency.

Thanks for all your continuing, inspiring, hard work. Say hi to Billy and Wednesday for me.

Love,
Rachel

March 8, 2003

Dear Fatima,

I came to see you today for International Women's Day, but I think that I came too late or was confused about where to find you. I would like to talk to you more about the products you want to sell and also about mothers in the United States who would like to write letters to mothers in Palestine. I'm really sorry I missed you. I am having trouble reaching you by phone. Please call me or I will stop by again soon.

Sincerely,
Rachel Corrie
(ISM)

March 2003

god

chex cereal

the prophet Mohammed

infiltrators

panama canal

play bus

weapons of mass destruction

corner grocery

tawdry affair

mel gibson

concrete bunker

sandstorm

venereal disease

malnutrition

proxy government

water contamination

Potential sources of money:

• IRS

• teach English

• ed scholarship

• loan/begging

• Visa

• borrow from Mom

Go back to Olympia/USA

- finish school
- work with Lincoln Options
- clean out Sarah's garage
- talk/presentations

Go to Egypt or Dubai: and earn $, learn Arabic. Come back to Palestine soon.

Go to Sweden: one month or more

- potentially horrible
- go broke
- easy, relaxing

Try to stay in Rafah

- money?
- productivity?
- I could help ISM, movement

Travel elsewhere

- money?
- travel cost

March 12, 2003

Hi Papa,

Thank you for your e-mail. I feel like sometimes I spend all my time propagandizing Mom, and assuming she'll pass stuff on to you, so you get neglected. Don't worry about me too much, right now I am most concerned that we are not being effective. I still don't feel particularly at risk. Rafah has seemed calmer lately, maybe because the military is preoccupied with incursions in the north. Still shooting and house demolitions, one death this week that I know of, but not any larger incursions. I can't say how this will change if and when war with Iraq comes.

Thanks also for stepping up your anti-war work. I know it is not easy to do, and probably much more difficult where you are than where I am. I am really interested in talking to the journalist in Charlotte. Let me know what I can do to speed the process along. I am trying to figure out what I'm going to do when I leave here, and when I'm going to leave. Right now I think I could stay until June, financially. I really don't want to move back to Olympia, but do need to go back there to clean my stuff out of the garage and talk about my experiences here. On the other hand, now that I've crossed the ocean I'm feeling a strong desire to try to stay across the ocean for some time. Considering trying to get English teaching jobs. Would like to really buckle down and learn Arabic. Also got an invitation to visit Sweden on my way back which I think I could do very cheaply.

I would like to leave Rafah with a viable plan to return. One of the core members of our group has to leave tomorrow, and watching her say goodbye to people is making me realize how difficult it will be. People here can't leave, so that complicates things. They are also pretty matter-of-fact that they don't know if they will be alive when we come back here.

I really don't want to live with a lot of guilt about this place, being able to come and go so easily, and not going back. I think it is valuable to make commitments to places, so I would like to be able to plan on coming back here within a year or so. Of all of these possibilities, I think it's most likely that I will at least go to Sweden for a few weeks on my way back. I can change tickets and get a plane from Paris to Sweden and back for a total of 150 bucks or so. I know I should try to link up with the family in France, but I think that I'm not going to do that. I would just be angry the whole time and not much fun to be around. It seems like a transition into too much opulence right now. I would feel a lot of class guilt the whole time.

Let me know if you have any ideas about what I should do with the rest of my life. I love you very much. If you want, you can write to me as if I was on vacation at a camp on the big island of Hawaii learning to weave. One thing I do to make things easier here is to utterly retreat into fantasies that I am in a Hollywood movie or a sitcom starring Michael J. Fox. So feel free to make something up and I'll be happy to play along. Much love, Poppy.

Rachel

Rachel Corrie was killed by the Israeli military
on March 16, 2003, in Rafah, Gaza.

Notes

page 5: The Options Program (also referred to as Options, Lincoln Options, and Lincoln School) is a public school alternative elementary education program emphasizing connections to the community and to the world, and is open to all students in the Olympia School District. Rachel attended Options from 1985 through 1990.

page 8: In the fifth grade, Rachel and her classmates studied world hunger. She wrote these remarks and delivered them in a press conference on the state of the world's children at the state capitol in Olympia, Washington.

page 9: Rachel listed these aspirations in her fifth-grade yearbook.

page 12: Rachel wrote this at the time of Operation Desert Storm, the January 1991 U.S. and coalition forces land and air invasion of Iraq.

page 21: Rachel wrote this about her grandfather when he was dying of lung cancer.

page 22: Rachel wrote this while driving with her family from her home in Olympia, Washington, to visit relatives in Iowa and Minnesota.

page 35: In 1995, Rachel participated in an American-Russian educational exchange program in conjunction with the Office of the Washington Secretary of State. Five students and their teacher from the Russian Far East spent three months attending Capital High School in Olympia. Then Rachel, four classmates, and their teacher traveled to Russia for six weeks and attended Yuzhno-Sakhalinsk School #2 on Sakhalin Island. Political changes resulting in the 1991 dissolution of the Soviet Union, the urge for economic change in Russia, and interest in trade between the Pacific Northwest and the Russian Far East paved the way for such exchanges. In Russia, Rachel witnessed the aftermath of recent political upheaval, extremely difficult living conditions, and economic hardship that many people suffered.

page 35: Magadan is a city on the Sea of Okhotsk in the Russian Far East.

page 37: Khabarovsk is a picturesque city in the Russian Far East, on the Amur River, near China. Rachel visited here before her return to the United States in 1995.

page 37: *Babushka* is the Russian term for an old woman or grandmother and, also, for the scarf that some wear which is folded triangularly and tied under the chin.

page 40: This incident occurred at the Crawford County Fair in Denison, Iowa.

page 42: Rachel traveled to Europe in the summer of 1995 with students from Capital High School's Foreign Language Department and visited Austria, Hungary, the Czech Republic, Germany, and England.

page 47: In Greek mythology, Narcissus is the son of a river god who fell in love with his own reflection.

page 50: Quentin Compson is a fictional character featured in William Faulkner's novels *The Sound and the Fury* and *Absalom, Absalom!*

page 50: The Crisis Clinic Resource Network is a twenty-four-hour-a-day, seven-day-a-week telephone service where trained volunteers provide confidential and anonymous crisis intervention. Rachel was a volunteer for both the teen and the adult crisis lines.

page 61: Rachel wrote this for a presentation at the Crisis Clinic Resource Network adult training session on talking with teenagers.

page 70: The Evergreen State College (TESC) is a progressive, public liberal arts and sciences college located in Olympia, Washington. Rachel attended Evergreen from 1997 until her death in 2003.

page 83: In summer 1998, Rachel traveled to Belize as part of a class at The Evergreen State College. She lived, studied, and worked at the Institute of Village Studies in southern Belize, ten acres of forest land with the Caribbean on one side and a wildlife sanctuary on the other. She was introduced to Belizean, Mayan, and Garifuna cultures and worked alongside local teachers and parents to teach study skills and build a school, using indigenous approaches to shelter, sewage, and electricity, and with sensitivity to the impact on traditional culture. Rachel studied Garifuna language (drawn from African, Caribbean, and English) and helped organize a Garifuna grammar.

page 85: The cays are small islands of coral reef in the Belize barrier reef system, the second largest barrier reef system in the world.

page 85: Dangriga is a port town in east-central Belize on the Caribbean and at the mouth of North Stann Creek.

page 105: The "shooting in Colorado" is a reference to the April 20, 1999, massacre at Columbine High School near Denver, Colorado, in which twelve students and a teacher were killed by two high school boys who then took their own lives.

page 105: "Gray whale hunts" is a reference to efforts by the Makah Nation of Neah Bay, in northwest Washington State, to assert treaty rights granted in 1855 to hunt gray whale. These rights had not been exercised since the 1920s. When the gray whale was removed from the endangered species list, the tribe successfully petitioned to resume hunting and killed a resident three-year-old female in May 1999, causing considerable outcry from environmentalists and animal rights activists. Lohn, Bob. "Makah Tribal Whale Hunt," 1 Oct. 2007. NOAA's National Marine Fisheries Service, Northwest Regional Office. http://www.nwr.noaa.gov/Marine-Mammals/Whales-Dolphins-Porpoise/Gray-Whales/Makah-Whale-Hunt.cfm.

page 108: Rachel worked for one year at Olympic and Mount Rainier National Parks and other locations with the Washington Conservation Corps (WCC), a state Department of Ecology program for men and women, ages eighteen to twenty-five years, who work in crews to protect and enhance natural resources. Crew members are paid minimum wage and, upon completion of the program, earn an AmeriCorps education award for college.

page 110: Cougar Rock is a campground in Mount Rainier National Park.

page 112: "Hoh" is a reference to the Hoh Rain Forest located in the Olympic National Park in western Washington.

page 116: A MacLeod is a hand tool used for trail clearing.

page 116: Rachel wrote this e-mail to her father after he departed from Olympia for a new job in the Cayman Islands. Rachel's mother remained behind to complete the move.

page 119: Smokey and Bart were the family dogs. Cara was Rachel's cat.

page 121: Rachel wrote this journal entry after visiting her parents in the Cayman Islands where they lived and rented a home for twenty months. Lion lizards, five to six inches long with curly tails, were frequent patio visitors.

page 123: Dadaism (Dada) was an artistic and cultural movement originating from antiwar proponents in Switzerland during World War I. One Dadaist technique was to use demonstrations and confrontations as performance art. Rachel studied Dadaism in an Evergreen program on Surrealism, an artistic outgrowth of Dadaism. Shipe, Timothy. "The International Dada Archive," June 2003. *The International Dada Archives at the University of Iowa Libraries.* http://sdrc.lib.uiowa.edu/dada/history.htm (13 Oct. 2007).

page 127: Rachel wrote this piece when she worked graveyard shifts at Hospital Diversion House (HDH), a program of Behavioral Health Resources (BHR), a large, multicounty provider of mental health services for low-income clients. At Hospital

Diversion House, the safety needs of some mental health clients were addressed outside of a hospital or emergency room setting, freeing up hospital space for those with more critical problems.

page 132: DNR, the Department of Natural Resources, is a Washington State agency charged with stewardship of state lands, resources, and the environment.

page 132: Carhartt is a brand of clothing often used by construction workers, farmers, and outdoorsmen.

page 132: A Pulaski is a combination ax and grub hoe tool for both firefighting and trail work.

page 138: John Rogers, former Washington State legislator and governor, is remembered with a statue in Sylvester Park in downtown Olympia, inscribed with his words, "I would make it impossible for the covetous and avaricious to utterly impoverish the poor. The rich can take care of themselves."

page 164: King Solomon's Reef is a restaurant and bar in downtown Olympia.

page 166: Centralia is a small community in Washington State, about twenty-five miles south of Olympia.

page 166: The Industrial Workers of the World (IWW), also known as the Wobblies, is a labor union that had a significant presence in western Washington in the early 1900s. They were unpopular with many locals because of their opposition to World War I, their aggressive efforts to organize to improve working conditions in the timber industry, and their appeal to the homeless and unemployed. On the first Armistice Day in 1919 in Centralia, Washington, conflict between the IWW and local American Legionnaires broke out during the Armistice Day parade when members of the Legionnaires halted along the parade route and raided the IWW hall. This resulted in the "Centralia Massacre," a gun battle in which members of both groups were killed. Wesley Everest, an IWW member, was arrested for killing two Legionnaires. That night, he was pulled from his jail cell and hung from a nearby bridge. A statue in a Centralia city park commemorates the four Legionnaires killed in the massacre. A mural, "The Resurrection of Wesley Everest," was created in Centralia in 1997, initiated by community members who believed the labor side of the history should be aired. Recalling Everest and the Wobblies, the mural was designed and created by labor muralist Mike Alewitz. Stough, Mary L. "Centralia's Union Mural 'The Resurrection of Wesley Everest' Depicts Labor's Side of the Centralia Massacre" *Columbia Magazine:* Fall 1999; vol. 13, no. 3.

page 166: Log Towns by Michael Fredson, Minuteman Press, 1993, provides a history of logging communities in the area, particularly in neighboring Mason County, which Rachel studied.

page 167: Rachel developed a weekly "Drop-ins Group" to support clients from Behavioral Health Resources (BHR) and Hospital Diversion House (HDH). The group worked on social skills while participating in field trips, art projects, and other group activities.

page 169: The Olympia Movement for Justice and Peace (OMJP) formed in September 2001, to advocate a nonmilitary response to the events of September 11. Rachel was a "participant observer" as part of her Local Knowledge program at Evergreen.

page 172: The "rhetoric of 1798" refers to the political climate as the United States prepared for war with France. This climate led to the passage of the Alien and Sedition Acts, which allowed for deportation of legal aliens who were considered "dangerous to the peace and safety of the United States" and restricted speech critical of the government. "Primary Documents in American History, Alien and Sedition Acts," 21 Sept. 2007. *The Library of Congress.* http://www.loc.gov/rr/program/bib/ourdocs/Alien.html (13 Oct. 2007).

page 172: Everett is a city north of Seattle, Washington, that, like Centralia, was the site of conflict between the IWW (Wobblies) and locals who opposed them. An "Everett Massacre" occurred in 1916. *Industrial Workers of the World.* http://www.iww.org (13 Oct, 2007).

page 173: "The working class and the employing class have nothing in common," is the opening line to the preamble of the IWW constitution. "Preamble to the IWW Constitution," *Industrial Workers of the World.* http://www.iww.org/culture/official/preamble.shtml (13 Oct, 2007).

page 174: LOTT (The LOTT Alliance) provides wastewater treatment for the area communities of Olympia, Lacey, Tumwater, and Thurston County.

page 186: Olympia Arts Walk is a community event that occurs every fourth weekend in April and the first Friday in October when downtown Olympia businesses invite hundreds of local artists to display their work and to perform. The spring Arts Walk includes the Procession of the Species, a parade that honors and celebrates nature and all life. After a month of costume-making, dance, and music workshops, thousands flock downtown to participate in the procession or to watch. Rachel helped to organize the first flock of doves for the 2002 procession. More than one hundred doves turned out for the 2003 procession, shortly after Rachel was killed.

page 189: The list of numbers in this journal entry are scores from a game of Scrabble that Rachel and Colin were playing.

page 192: Rachel wrote this for her Local Knowledge class at The Evergreen State College.

page 192: Local Knowledge (LK) was a year-long program at The Evergreen State College which took as its starting place the premise that the community base of knowledge must be acknowledged and supported. Through this program Rachel connected to hidden local histories and spent time applying those to her understanding of current events.

page 193: Larry Ogg was an employee of the U.S. Forest Service in the Olympic National Forest.

page 193: Shelton's Boom, the Classic Years, 1910–1933 was written in 1982 by Michael Fredson, a Mason County historian.

page 193: The "Islands" are the San Juans, part of the San Juan Archipelago located in San Juan County in northwest Washington State. They include more than 170 islands.

page 194: The Bonneville Power Administration (BPA), in Portland, Oregon, a federal agency under the U.S. Department of Energy, markets wholesale electrical power from federal dams and other sources. In 1941, the singer Woody Guthrie was hired by BPA to write songs for a documentary, *The Columbia,* a film to pacify those upset by the construction of the Grand Coulee Dam. Carriker, Robert. "Ten Dollars a Song—Woody Guthrie Sells His Talent to the Bonneville Power Administration"; *Columbia Magazine:* Spring 2001; vol. 15, no. 1; http://www.washingtonhistory .org/wshs/columbia/articles/0101-a2.htm (13 Oct. 2007).

page 196: HUAC, the House Un-American Affairs Committee, 1945 to 1975, was to investigate "the extent, character and objects of un-American propaganda activities in the United States." Investigations primarily focused on U.S. citizens' alleged connections to communism and are widely remembered for hearings targeting Hollywood elites. HUAC also investigated antiwar activities, civil rights activities, and the Ku Klux Klan. "Guide to the Records of the U.S. House of Representatives at the National Archives, 1789–1989 (Record Group 233)—Chapter 14 Records of the Judiciary Committee and Related Committees." *The National Archives—The Center for Legislative Archives.* http://www.archives.gov/legislative/guide/house/ chapter-14-judiciary.html (13 Oct. 2007).

page 196: The Canwell Committee was the Un-American Activities Committee of Washington State, chaired by Albert Canwell, a Republican from Spokane, who in 1946 campaigned on concerns about communists. The committee held hearings to investigate University of Washington professors, the Washington Pension Union, and the Seattle Repertory Theatre. Lange, Greg. "Washington State Legislature Passes the Un-American Activities Bill on March 8, 1947—Essay 1484." *HistoryLink.org, the Online Encyclopedia of Washington State History.* http://www.his torylink.org/essays/output.cfm?file_id=1484 (13 Oct. 2007).

page 196: COINTELPRO was the acronym used to describe a series of secret coun-terintelligence operations carried out by the FBI from the late 1950s to the early 1970s that were designed to suppress radical political expression and opposition within the United States. Wolf, Paul. Transcription of "Supplementary Detailed Staff Reports on Intelligence Activities and the Rights of Americans, Book III: COINTELPRO." 2002. *Paul Wolf's Homepage.* http://www.icdc.com/~paulwolf/cointelpro/churchfinalreportIIIa.htm (13 Oct. 2007).

page 197: Wild Man of the Wynoochie, John Tornow, was a recluse who roamed the Olympic National Peninsula from the age of ten, living mostly near the community of Satsop and along the Wynoochie River. After killing his two nephews (in circum-stances that are unclear) and later the bounty hunters who tried to hunt him down, Tornow was, himself, killed in 1913. Pierce, J. Kingston. "Wild Man of the Wynoo-chee, Essay 5079." 19 Jan. 2003. *HistoryLink.org.* http://www.historylink.org/essays/output.cfm?file_id=5079 (13 Oct. 2007).

page 198: FOVA stands for Foundations of Visual Arts, an Evergreen program that provides a basis for an art path at the college.

page 199: Larry Mosqueda is an Evergreen faculty member and founding member of the Olympia Movement for Justice and Peace (OMJP).

page 201: On May Day, 2001, Rachel joined more than three hundred Olympia resi-dents who festively demonstrated against the negative effects of globalization, cor-porate greed, and homelessness.

page 201: SPSCC stands for South Puget Sound Community College, located in Olympia.

page 202: Fry are young salmon or trout, usually less than one year old, that have absorbed their egg sacs and are growing in the stream where they were spawned.

page 202: A salmon redd is a nest of fish eggs prepared by the female salmon.

page 203: Watershed Park is a 153-acre area near the heart of Olympia, in the Moxlie Creek Springs Basin that branches out to create Moxlie Creek. Each fall, Chinook salmon fight their way from Budd Inlet through a storm pipe under Plum Street (a main thoroughfare in downtown Olympia) to spawn in the creek in which they were born.

page 205: Chris was a friend of Rachel's from Olympia who had traveled to the West Bank and Gaza in the summer of 2002 with the International Solidarity Movement's Freedom Summer program.

page 205: L&I stands for the Washington State Department of Labor and Industries, an agency that regulates safety and health standards in the workplace and also administers the state's workers' compensation program. Rachel was attending the meeting as part of her responsibilities with her local union.

page 205: PDX is the airport code for the Portland International Airport where, on August 22, 2002, President George W. Bush arrived and encountered significant numbers of antiwar protesters.

page 206: Rachel wrote this e-mail to coworkers at Hospital Diversion House (HDH). She was a member of the Washington State healthcare workers' union, SEIU District 1199NW, and had become active in her local chapter, following issues that might impact her workplace.

page 208: The International Solidarity Movement (ISM) is a Palestinian-led, nonviolent resistance movement with supporters from around the world. It was founded in 2001 after the United States and Israel rejected a UN resolution to send human rights observers to the region. The movement requires only that participants believe in the right to self-determination and freedom for the Palestinian people based on UN regulations and that they use only nonviolent forms of resistance.

page 209: In 1993 to 1994, Gustavo from Brazil lived with the Corrie family for one year as an exchange student.

page 209: Luiz Inácio Lula da Silva, known as Lula, was elected president of Brazil in 2003 from the Workers' Party, the leftist party that he cofounded in 1980.

page 209: FTAA stands for Free Trade Area of the Americas, a controversial proposal to eliminate or reduce trade barriers among countries throughout the Americas.

page 209: The Venezuelan coup refers to the attempt in 2002 to overthrow President Hugo Chavez and other parts of the Venezuelan government.

page 210: Beijos is Portuguese for kisses.

page 218: Sam Walton was the founder of Wal-Mart.

page 219: Ariel Sharon was Israeli prime minister from March 2001 until April 2006.

page 220: Christian Peacemaker Teams (CPT) organized in 1984 to devote the "same discipline and self sacrifice to nonviolent peacemaking that armies devote to war." CPT sends trained teams to conflict areas to reduce violence through "creative public witness, nonviolent direct action, and protection of human rights." CPT teams have served in Hebron in the West Bank since June 1995. "History/Mission of CPT." *Christian Peacemaker Teams.* http://www.cpt.org/publications/history.php (13 Oct. 2007).

page 220: The Ibdaa Dance Troupe is made up of boys and girls from Dheisheh refugee camp in the West Bank who since 1994 have traveled in the Middle East,

Europe, and the United States celebrating and sharing Palestinian culture through traditional Palestinian folkloric dance (debke) and theater. In Arabic, *Ibdaa* means "to make something out of nothing." Ibdaa Cultural Center. 2007. http://www.ibdaa194.org/index.html (13 Oct. 2007).

page 221: Burning Man is an experimental community that forms one week each year in the Black Rock Desert in Nevada. An annual art theme is manifested in large art installations, costumes, and theme camps.

page 221: KAOS is a progressive radio station on The Evergreen State College campus.

page 221: Glen Anderson is a longtime Olympia peace and justice activist and leader in the Olympia Fellowship of Reconciliation (FOR). Since 1915, FOR, nationally and internationally, has advocated for nonviolence in the quest for justice and peace.

page 222: Will traveled to Gaza in January 2003 and was an eyewitness to Rachel's killing.

page 222: One Land, Two Peoples: The Conflict over Palestine was written by Deborah J. Gerner, Westview Press, 1994.

page 222: Simona Sharoni, Steve Niva, and Jean Eberhardt were faculty and staff at The Evergreen State College whom Rachel consulted before her trip to Gaza. Simona, a visiting professor in peace and conflict resolution and women's studies, had grown up in Israel, served in the Israeli military, and was a cofounder of Women in Black. Steve, an Evergreen professor in Middle East studies and political science, was researching connections between the Israeli military's targeted assassinations and Palestinian suicide bombings. Jean had a twenty-year history with the Thurston–Santo Tomás Sister County Association (sistered with a town in Chontales, Nicaragua) and was a mentor as Rachel explored possibilities for an Olympia–Rafah sister city relationship.

page 222: SESAME (Sesame) is Students Educating Students About the Middle East, an Evergreen group founded by students returning from Palestine in 2002 to provide an on-campus resource to facilitate understanding of Middle East politics, culture, and society.

page 224: Michi and Barbara are teachers in the Lincoln Options Program in the Olympia School District. Before leaving for Gaza, Rachel visited the elementary school to explain her trip and to encourage students to write letters to children in Rafah.

page 224: Joe was Rachel's Arabic teacher at Evergreen. He urged Rachel not to go to Palestine, but to continue studying Arabic, for which she had an aptitude.

page 224: Adam Shapiro is one of the founding members of ISM.

page 224: AIC is the Alternative Information Center, a Palestinian-Israeli organization that gathers and disseminates information about Israel-Palestine.

page 225: Oslo refers to the Oslo Accords (the Declaration of Principles that resulted from secret meetings in Norway and were signed at the White House in 1993) and the Israeli-Palestinian peace process that was to follow. This called for addressing issues over a five-year period, leaving key issues of borders, status of Jerusalem, refugees, and Israeli settlements to later stages. Bennis, Phyllis, *Understanding the Palestinian-Israeli Conflict* (Lowell, Mass.: Trans-Arab Research Institute, Inc., 2003), pp. 45–46.

page 226: Occupied Territories refers to the West Bank, Gaza, and East Jerusalem, Palestinian lands occupied by Israel since the 1967 Six Day War. The Syrian Golan Heights have also been occupied since 1967.

page 227: This is the last journal entry Rachel wrote before leaving Olympia for Gaza.

page 229: Servis/sherut is a shared taxi.

page 229: Beit Sahour is a small West Bank town near Bethlehem with a history of nonviolent resistance to the Occupation. It gained international attention during the first intifada for community-wide refusal to pay Israeli taxes. ISM had an office in Beit Sahour during 2003. Gerner, Deborah J., *One Land, Two Peoples: The Conflict over Palestine* (Boulder, Colo.: Westview Press, Inc., 1994), p. 99.

page 229: Shawarma is a sandwich made with shredded meats, very popular in the Middle East.

page 229: Falafel is a popular Middle Eastern food made from soaked and ground fava beans or chickpeas, formed into balls or patties, and deep fried.

page 229: IOF (Israeli Occupation Forces) is a term sometimes used by activists and Palestinians to designate Israeli military operating within the Occupied Territories. The official name for the Israeli military is the Israel Defense Forces (IDF). IOF and IDF are used interchangeably throughout Rachel's writing to describe the Israeli military in Gaza and the West Bank.

page 230: Druze is a religious and ethnic group in Israel that is Arab but not Palestinian. Service in the Israeli military is compulsory for Druze men. Semyonov, Moshe, and Lewin-Epstein, Noah, *Stratification in Israel: Class, Ethnicity, and Gender* (Edison, N.J.: Transaction Publishers, 2004), p. 307.

page 230: APC stands for armored personnel carrier.

page 230: A drone is an unmanned aircraft.

page 231: Rachel wrote this e-mail to her mother. She hoped to share her experiences in Gaza through local media and was seeking contact information for these media outlets.

page 231: Nablus is a major West Bank city north of Jerusalem.

page 231: PFLP is the People's Front for the Liberation of Palestine.

page 231: The "green line" refers to the internationally recognized armistice line drawn in 1949 after the 1948 Arab-Israeli War.

page 232: Annexed Jerusalem refers to East Jerusalem, captured during the 1967 war and immediately declared a part of Israel. Occupied territory is subject to international law that prohibits unilateral annexation. The international community, including the United States, does not recognize the annexation of East Jerusalem by Israel. "East Jerusalem, Background." *B'tselem, the Israeli Information Center for Human Rights in the Occupied Territories.* http://www.btselem.org/english/Jerusalem/Index.asp (13 Oct. 2007).

page 232: The Old City is the walled, historic area of Jerusalem, divided into the Armenian, Christian, Jewish, and Muslim Quarters.

page 232: Reclamation refers to efforts to reclaim all of the Old City for the Jews of Israel.

page 233: This e-mail was written to Rachel's friends in Olympia. Anne Fischel was one of Rachel's Evergreen faculty in the Local Knowledge program.

page 233: Rafah has three parts—Rafah town, Rafah camp, and the housing areas of Brazil and Tel al-Sultan. Rafah town existed before 1948 with neighborhoods named for original residents and landowners. Rafah camp, divided into alphabetical blocks (Block J, Block O, etc.), was established after 1948 for forty-one thousand refugees who fled from what is now Israel. Brazil was built for those displaced by massive home demolitions in Gaza in 1971. After the 1979 Camp David Peace Accords returned the Sinai to Egypt and called for repatriation of Palestinians who were housed there after the Rafah demolitions of 1971, Tel al-Sultan was constructed on the Gaza side of Rafah for these returning refugees. Abrahams, Fred, Garlasco, Marc, and Li, Darryl, *Razing Rafah: Mass Home Demolitions in the Gaza Strip* (Human Rights Watch, Oct. 2004), pp. 26–27.

page 234: La, la is Arabic for *no, no.*

page 234: Khan Younis, like Rafah, is both a city and a refugee camp in southern Gaza near the Mediterranean Sea.

page 234: Shaheed is Arabic for *martyr*. For Palestinians, shaheed are people—militants or civilians, children or adults—killed by Israeli military or settlers. Posters with photos of shaheed are displayed throughout the West Bank and Gaza.

page 235: The Children's Parliament (Mini Parliament) in Rafah was founded in 1996 to encourage children to explore democracy.

page 237: Intifada means *shaking off* in Arabic and refers to the Palestinian uprisings against Israeli Occupation. The first intifada was from 1987 to 1993. The second intifada, also called the al-Aqsa intifada, began in September 2000.

page 237: DFLP stands for Democratic Front for the Liberation of Palestine.

page 242: Ashraf is an official with the Rafah water department.

page 242: "Transfer" refers to the expulsion of Palestinians from the Occupied Territiories and/or Israel proper.

page 242: "Bulldozer cowgirl" refers to work Rachel and other ISM activists did to provide an international presence and some protection for Rafah Municipal water workers from IDF fire. ISM activists rode on small Palestinian bulldozers used to rebuild Rafah's water wells, damaged or destroyed by the IDF.

page 248: Ha'aretz's Web site is www.haaretz.com.

page 249: CHF International has worked since 1994 in the West Bank and Gaza implementing community service, job creation, and lending programs to meet specific needs of the Palestinian people. "West Bank/Gaza." 12 Oct. 2007. CHF International. http://www.chfhq.org/section/gazawb (13 Oct. 2007).

page 250: Highlander (The Highlander Center) in Tennessee provides programs and training for social change, led by the people who suffer most from the injustices of society. Highlander Research and Education Center. 7 Oct. 2007. http://www.highlandercenter.org/index.html (13 Oct. 2007).

page 253: Eid al Adha is a Muslim festival commemorating the Prophet Abraham and occurring at the end of the annual pilgrimage to Mecca in Saudi Arabia (the Hajj).

page 253: Hamsa is Arabic for *five.*

page 255: "E-mail Phan and Michi about letters" refers to Rachel's efforts to have elementary school children from Lincoln Options in Olympia write pen-pal letters to children in Rafah. Phan was an Olympia ISM member who could read and write Arabic and assist with translation. Michi was an Options teacher.

page 255: PRC stands for Palestinian Red Crescent Society. The Red Crescent Society is the Arab equivalent of the American Red Cross. PRC is a member of the International Federation of the Red Cross and Red Crescent Societies.

page 257: Gush Katif was a group of settlements in the southern Gaza Strip along the Mediterranean Sea, dismantled in 2005 under the unilateral Gaza disengagement plan.

page 257: When Rachel's parents visited Rafah in September 2003, Naela, Rachel's high-school-age Palestinian friend, shared the notebook in which Rachel left this message.

page 258: Houda Nain Darwish was a twelve-year-old girl hit in the head by an Israeli bullet as she sat at her desk at an UNRWA school. She survived but was permanently blinded.

page 258: Nam Sowi (Al-Nimsawi) is a refugee neighborhood in the south of Khan Younis, supported by the Austrian government.

page 260: UNRWA is the United Nations Relief and Works Agency. It was established by UN General Assembly resolution 302 (IV) in 1949 to provide direct relief for Palestinian refugees from the 1948 Arab-Israeli War.

page 264: Brazil was built on a site used from 1956 to 1967 by UN peacekeepers from Brazil.

page 265: Sderot is a city in the south of Israel, located very close to the Gazan border.

page 268: Médecins Sans Frontières (Doctors Without Borders) is an international medical humanitarian organization.

page 272: The Geneva Conventions of 1949 are four treaties that established international law regarding treatment of people during war, primarily noncombatants.

page 273: Uncle Craig and Grandma are Iowa family who are farmers and landowners.

page 273: A Kalashnikov is a Russian AK-47 assault rifle widely used by Palestinian resistance groups in the Occupied Territories.

page 275: The term genocide continues to be debated but is articulated in the United Nations Convention on the Prevention and Punishment of the Crime of Genocide, approved by UN General Assembly resolution 260 A (III) in December 1948 and enacted in 1951. According to the UN, "In the present Convention, genocide means any of the following acts committed with intent to destroy, in whole or in part, a national, ethnical, racial or religious group, as such: (a) Killing members of the group; (b) Causing serious bodily or mental harm to members of the group; (c) Deliberately inflicting on the group conditions of life calculated to bring about its physical destruction in whole or in part; (d) Imposing measures intended to prevent births within the group; (e) Forcibly transferring children of the group to another group." Under the convention, genocide, conspiracy to commit genocide, direct and public incitement to commit genocide, an attempt to commit genocide, and complicity in genocide are all punishable, and rulers, public officials, and private individuals are all subject to the law.

page 277: Al-Haq and Al-Mezan Center for Human Rights are Palestinian non-governmental human rights organizations. Al-Haq is based in Ramallah in the West Bank, and Al-Mezan is in the Gaza Strip.

page 280: OPEC stands for Organization of the Petroleum Exporting Countries.

page 281: Matt Grant, Barbara Weaver, and Dale Knuth were three of Rachel's elementary and high school teachers.

page 290: Maylee was Rachel's friend from Evergreen's Local Knowledge Program.

page 291: Rachel gave this note to Fatima at the General Union of Palestinian Women (GUPW) in Rafah. Fatima shared the note with Rachel's parents during their visit in September 2003.

page 292: This was the last journal entry Rachel recorded. No date was attached.

page 294: This was the family's last correspondence from Rachel.

Acknowledgments

Numerous people have taken steps that ultimately led to the publication of *Let Me Stand Alone*. Many more supported Rachel in her journey as writer, artist, and human being. We thank all who contributed in any way to make this book possible.

We extend our love and gratitude to all our family who have generously and thoughtfully supported our efforts and who continue to provide respite when needed. Special thanks to Kelly Simpson for pretending that plastic tubs and boxes of paper make good chairs and tables when left for months in your living room—and for providing food, coffee, and forgiveness on long nights when the work would not end; to Cheryl Brodersen, for your proofreading help and for opening your heart and home when we ran out of steam on your doorstep; and to our accommodating readers—Gina Patnaik, Emily Robbins, and Linda Young, for offering your encouragement and valuable advice, whether or not we were wise enough to heed it.

Thank you to Jen Marlowe. We could not have made it through this project without you. You are our devoted friend, reader, editor, mediator, and source of comic relief. Thank you for your tireless energy and support and for your renditions of catchy show tunes as well!

Thank you to those who contributed directly to the book: to the friends and family who generously stepped forward with writing to share; to Denny Sternstein for allowing us to use your beautiful photograph of Rachel for the cover; to Ann Petter, for sensitively and creatively designing the cover; and to Bill Clegg, our agent, for believing passionately in the power of Rachel's writing and never faltering in your encouragement and empathy. Thank you to all at W. W. Norton & Company who believed in the importance of this book, especially our editor, Jill Bialosky, for your patient and steady guidance through a demanding and emotional process, and to Paul Whitlatch for your valiant, if often futile, efforts to keep us on track.

The Guardian in London first published Rachel's e-mails from Gaza in 2003. Rima Horton, Alan Rickman, Katharine Viner, Megan Dodds, and all at the Royal Court Theatre provided vision, talent, passion, and care in bringing the words to the stage in *My Name Is Rachel Corrie*. When others faltered, the remarkable group that became Rachel's Words, along with David Johnson, Virginia Buckley, Dena Hammerstein, Pam Pariseau, John O'Boyle, and others, had the courage and determination to bring the words and the play forward. To all of you, we are immensely grateful.

Thank you to the International Solidarity Movement (ISM) activists around the world who never forget and who continue to do nonviolent work so needed in the world. Loving thanks to Will, Joe, Greg, Alice, Tom, Richard, and Nick, who were with Rachel when she died and have remained in our lives and hearts since.

We extend love and support to Brian Avery, to the families of Tom Hurndall and James Miller, and to the Palestinian and Israeli families of the Parents' Circle—Family Forum. We are grateful for your friendship, comfort, inspiration, and strength.

Thank you to the Palestinian people who have embraced Rachel and our family as your own and to our Israeli friends who have done so as well. Thank you to all those around the world who look at Rachel and see a symbol of what the world can be—a place where the path to peace and resistance to oppression and injustice go hand in hand, and where for both individuals and nations, nonviolence becomes the mode for achieving them.

A special thank you to the family, teachers, friends, coworkers, clients, and community members who supported the author in her life journey and support us in ours.

And finally, thank you to Rachel, our daughter and sister—for the love, for the laughter, for the insight, for the experience and gift of having you in our lives. And for the words. We will always be grateful. We will always remember. We will always love you—with all our hearts.

The Corrie Family